Real-World Theatre Education

Real-World Theatre Education

A Teacher's Guide to Growing a Theatre Education Program

Chip Rome ❖ Zoë Dillard

EDUCATIONAL STAGES

The ideas and suggestions in this book are based on the experience of its authors, but do not constitute permission or authorization for any particular course of action, and the authors shall not be held liable for the consequences of actions taken based on its content. Actions that may run contrary to the policies or practice of a particular school or drama program, or of common sense in any specific situation, should first be cleared with school administrators or other appropriate authorities.

Published by Educational Stages

Project manager: Bill Linney
Copy editor: George Henschel
Editorial consultants: Patti Dezelick, Lori Knickerbocker

Photos: Henry Metcalf and Drew Lytle, Herndon High School production, photo by Sara Metcalf; Alex Alferov and Micah Chelen, Robinson Secondary School production, photo by Frank Ruth; Solomon Dixon, Herndon High School production, photo by Sara Metcalf; Jamie Green and Katie Rogers, Robinson Secondary School production, photo by Frank Ruth; Colby Dezelick, Herndon High School production, photo by Adrian Morgan.

Cover photo: Zoë Dillard and Laura Millon, Herndon High School production, photo by Sara Metcalf

Book design: Bill Linney

ISBN-13: 978-0-9863587-0-8

Library of Congress Control Number: 2015946824

*Dedicated to those who share their passion for theatre
with the next generation.*

Foreword

In our Theatre Education classes at George Mason University, I often ask students about their most formative experiences in the classroom—those they feel may shape them to be better educators. In these discussions, two names consistently come up as being at the top of their game and field: Douglas "Chip" Rome and Zoë Dillard.

I actually had the pleasure of working with Chip many years ago (we won't discuss how many), when he was just out of college himself and newly assigned to Wheaton High School in Maryland. He was as instrumental in my development as a young actor as he has been to his most recent students during his tenure at Robinson High School in Fairfax County, Virginia. Students who have worked with Zoë have noted that the creative, disciplined, yet nurturing environment she builds in her classroom is something they will strive to foster for themselves. Both continue to set the bar high, and are an inspiration to young artists and prospective teachers.

Chip and Zoë's *Real-World Theatre Education* is a goldmine for new and experienced teachers alike. This is a nuts-and-bolts handbook that will walk an educator through the academic year, preparing them for both curricular and extracurricular demands. It's more than just a checklist. It is a reality check in the best possible way: an honest, thorough guide to growing a successful theatre education program.

Through Educational Stages and the teaching tools Chip and Zoë are developing, a whole new generation of teachers will have a lasting gift from two of the most influential teachers in our region. I can't wait to use these tools and continue to learn from the best.

Mary Lechter
Performance Faculty/Head of Theater Education
George Mason University School of Theater
Fairfax, VA

Contents

Preface

Success as a theatre educator grows out of both training and experience, lessons well planned and lessons well learned. As a new teacher/director, whatever training you have will undoubtedly serve you in good stead—but how can you leapfrog over the years it takes to accumulate experience? We want to help.

We hope that this book will serve as an open gate through which you will find ways to reach beyond the lesson plans and classroom management *content* of most preparation. Here are ways to cope with all the rest of it—the *context* of a successful theatre program. From production planning to parent complaints, from managing musicals to dealing with the media, we guide new teachers season by season through their first year. Although this book was originally conceived as a methods text for college theatre education programs, we realized that it could prove valuable to any new or returning teacher charged with building a theatre education program. Many states do not require full licensure for theatre teachers; it is possible for any teacher to be thrown into the world of theatre education in order to fill out their teaching schedule or meet the needs of a school. We hope that our efforts will assist both the new teacher and the college theatre education professor in providing a lot of specific real-world, experience-based information in one place.

The constant professional judgment choices required of a theatre educator are job specific, and the job itself entails unique and multiple opportunities to implement that judgment. To address this challenge, we have included sets of questions entitled "For Reflection and Discussion"—items throughout the book that we hope will raise awareness and prove thought provoking. In addition, we have peppered the book throughout with anecdotes from our teaching experiences, which may prove both entertaining and enlightening. We have also included a robust appendix of templates and resources that can become the creation of lesson plans and other documents useful in a school theatre program. These templates may be downloaded in Microsoft Word format from our website, EducationalStages.com, so that they may be edited to suit your individual needs.

With over 60 years of theatre educator experience between us in a variety of educational environments and developmental levels, we hope that the next generation of theatre teachers will benefit from this volume of guidelines, information, triumphs, and lessons learned. Here's to passing the torch!

—Chip and Zoë

Achieving Balance

Chip Rome

The shift from theatre/education student—or theatre professional—to theatre educator is a critical one. In academia and onstage, succcss is measured by one's own performance, and that is the priority. But the moment a teacher steps into a classroom or in front of the school stage, the measure of success becomes the students and their performance. It's like going from bachelor to parent, and from working with peers to working with people whose actions *you* are responsible for. And therein lies "the rub."

As a theatre person, you know that there is a rhythm to the development of a production, and any one person's involvement in the production is probably limited to a single responsibility. By contrast, in educational theatre, there is likely to be just one person—you—overseeing every aspect of the production: direction, set, costumes, lighting, publicity, programs, tickets—you name it. Your balancing act is to oversee everything, but never to lose sight of the essential purpose of the project: to provide learning opportunities for the kids. In addition, you must remember that those kids may be experiencing theatre for the very first time. They will have little or no experience to share with the class or impart to the show; you are the one who will be nurturing them along, providing them with that experience. You will be flying solo in many ways, at least for a while.

As the instructor, you will be viewed as the expert on everything theatrical—whether you know it or not. However, now your goal is not to show how much you know; it is to devise ways for the students to increase their own skills and knowledge. What's more, the areas in which you are less well-versed (for many, technical theatre) can neither be avoided nor given less weight than the familiar, if you want to create well rounded students and productions. And there will certainly be areas of theatre arts in which you are less well-versed than others. You will find yourself having to address these areas, and you will often need to provide them with equal or greater attention than you give to the areas that you know well. You can learn along with your students, bring in guest artists, and otherwise just muddle along—but you always need to remember that every element, large or small, of the theatre program belongs to you, to teach, share and supervise.

It's worth remembering that as much as you are teaching theatre, you are teaching life skills: confidence, discipline, attention to detail, communication, collaboration, and a drive to excellence. The perseverance and ability to think outside the box that are so necessary to seeing through a production are of immense value to any student. This is especially true for adolescents wrapped up in searching for their own identities and values as people. You, too, are still developing, of course, but administrators, parents, and students alike will view you as a finished product, one who knows what your students are still eager (or reluctant) to learn.

What do you bring to the table, and at what risk? Your own education and experiences, as well as your own personality and passion for teaching and theatre. Leaning on the former can lead to treating a new high school position like a re-hash of your own college theatre journey. Many new teachers make the mistake of selecting the shows that they did in college, regardless of whether they are truly school-friendly. On the other hand, by focusing primarily on your love for teaching and theatre, you can be lured into the trap of treating your students as peers. That approach might seem to work well—at first—until a sensitive adolescent feels slighted, or someone gets hurt. Then the clarification of who is the adult and who is the child becomes painful to all, providing a whiplash from which you might never recover.

There is tremendous joy to be had by working with students in class and after school, watching your students pick up your best ideas, working habits, and catch-phrases, as well as sharing your love of theatre. But never, ever let that collaboration blind you to the contractual distinction which fixes you alone as the responsible party for everything that takes place during your watch. You work with the students, yes, but you also work for your department, principal, school, and school board…and the parents. Never lose sight of that.

You are the luckiest of teachers. Your work will be applauded regularly. You will get to see multiple years of growth in your students—such amazing growth. You get to see your students try their very hardest to succeed, and they will. You will be responsible for creating a community of friends that will last for many years. And you will have the opportunity to really get to know many of those kids who work with you, to be that trusted adult whose attention can literally change—sometimes even save—lives. You are that teacher the students will remember.

The Role of the Educator

Zoë Dillard

Teachers look at things differently. The moment you step into an educational setting, you become your teacher self—your best self—because you selflessly put the students first. Through the educator's lens, you see every situation integrated with its effect on students. You anticipate student reaction, interaction, and potential for growth or harm. As a theatre educator, in which you are often a one-person department, it is essential that you realize that although you are an artistic "theatre person," you are an educator first. You are responsible for the welfare and teaching of the students.

No matter how much you love theatre, you must love the role of educator more. That might be hard to hear coming right out of college, where you've just spent at least four years focusing on yourself as an artist. Why did you choose to become a teacher? There is a case to be made for loving an art form so much you want to share it with others. There is also the essential role that theatre plays in developing our humanity, both collectively and individually, as well as the importance of theatre in society. But without a love for reaching young minds, educators fall short; it's all about the kids.

Relationships

Although your relationship with the children you teach should be appropriately friendly, they are not your friends. They are your students—your relationship with them derives from the educational context and its goal to increase knowledge and create art together. Being in relationship with young people means that you are also in relationship with their parents. Parents naturally focus on their own offspring; you must remind parents that you must consider and attend to *all* of your students. Parents need you to communicate clearly to them how they can help support the theatre program as they respect your curricular and artistic leadership.

Respect and Responsibility

Respect your role in the educational process, and you will also respect the children. You are the teacher, the purveyor of knowledge, creator of opportunities. You are in charge, you are responsible—you are the adult role model—from the words you choose to the clothes you put on in the morning. Consistent honesty works. Don't inflict your head-trips on these impressionable young minds. Humor is great, and even sarcasm has its place in teenage relationships, but cruelty and manipulation should never be part of your game plan. Solicit feedback from students, collaborate and discuss with them—but they must always know who is in charge, because that is the same person who is ultimately responsible for everything that happens in the theatre department: *you*. Sometimes it helps to tell your favorite student, "If the curtains catch on fire because you hung the ellipsoidal too close to the teaser, I can't really say to the principal, 'Charlie thought it would be okay.' " While they may challenge your authority every other day, your consistent position as captain of the department actually makes your students feel secure.

Even as you require respect and assume the authority that comes with the proverbial territory, find a balance in kindness, compliments, and fun in the classroom. Although they need to keep you in the loop as they independently pursue tech or acting projects, students also need to own their educational and artistic choices. They need to investigate the consequences of their choices in a safe environment that promotes discovery.

Teacher Joy

Teacher joy is built on making a difference in the lives of young people, watching the bud open, petal by petal, until the flower is in full bloom. Sometimes we get to see the full blossom, but other times we must be satisfied merely with having planted and nurtured the seeds well—but it is all done out of love for humanity and for artistic growth. That is where your integrity as an educator must lie. Because you want to see them grow, you prepare the lessons, fill out the paperwork that provides opportunities, collect checks, sell tickets, and spend endless hours at school. It is almost constantly overwhelming and simultaneously exhilarating—because at the root of it all, you love the kids. Most of all, you love watching them grow. When love fails to inspire, you do it out of discipline, dedication, and professional integrity. Some kids are easier to love than others!

Growing Opportunities

While your students are hanging up posters, memorizing lines, reminding you to order show T-shirts, and counting up Thespian points, they are growing up. As an educator, you are in an advantageous position to influence them responsibly. You are not their parent—from whom they are trying to individuate—but you are often the adult representative of their favorite subject at school. You have the honor of providing positive educational growth experiences:

your lesson plans/activities, your play choices, field trips, guest artists, theatre conferences, and more. Every effort you put into these experiences is a chance for your students to grow. You know you're meant to be a teacher when watching students grow is an exciting prospect for you—the proverbial light bulb in a kid's mind that suddenly illuminates a classroom; the flower that springs into bloom before your very eyes. Like plants in a garden, not every student grows at the same rate or blossoms in the same way. The variety of tasks required to create theatre provides a wonderful variety of opportunities for students to discover their unique gifts—on or off the stage.

The honor of being present for the growth process in the life of a child requires an unbelievable amount of work and energy. They are looking to you for approval, even if they don't admit it or realize it. You don't have to be perfect—you just have to be honest, kind, strong, courageous, smart, and fair. If you are exhausted at the end of each school day (a full day of teaching, meetings, and rehearsals), then you are probably doing a good job. Of course, some days are better than others.

Perpetuating the Role of the Lifelong Learner

Balance is your lifeline to enduring as an educator. If you love the children and love teaching, it is easy to get obsessive and absorbed into the role of theatre director. If your shows are highly successful, cultivate humility—avoid the dangerous trap of falling in love with your own ego. Since educational theatre often requires some part of your weekend, it can leave you feeling burned out and can play havoc with your personal relationships. In order to be strong for your students, you must be strong for yourself and lead a balanced, healthy life. Give yourself permission to take a day off when you need it. You need some separation from the world of school—when you come back Monday morning, you'll appreciate both place and people more. Of course, production week, fondly referred to as "hell week," is just bound to be obsessive no matter what—but that's the nature of putting on a play. So grab your life away from school and hold it to your heart just as closely as you hold your teacher joy; it's all growth, and it's all important—for you and for them.

However, while you are focusing on the students' growth and giving this critically important profession all you've got, a wonderful thing happens. *You* become another flower in the educational garden. As they bloom, so will you.

Acknowledgments

Thanks are due to the many sources of support who made this book possible. Mary Lechter, professor of theater education at George Mason University, gave us our first real hope that future teachers would use our *Real-World Theatre Education* in the real world.

Our fellow Fairfax County Public Schools teachers and curriculum specialist, Judy Bowns, have been continuing sources of development and support in our journey. We greatly value their experience and encouragement as theatre educators employed in a creative and dynamic workplace.

The students, parents, and staff of our respective schools, Robinson Secondary School and Herndon High School, provided us with opportunities to reflect and appreciate what good theatre education programs can look like when a learning community comes together for the benefit of students.

Sincere thanks must go to John Dezelick, who created our first draft book cover, and to Patti Dezelick, a dear friend who used her expertise to serve as the editor for our first draft. For editing our final draft, many thanks to George Henschel who gave most generously of his time and talents. Extra special thanks to Bill Linney, publishing mentor, book designer, and typesetting guru extraordinaire; he has taught us so much and kept our eye on always working toward the highest quality product.

Last, but far from least, we thank our families: spouses who encourage and trust us, children who inspire us and parents who, long ago, planted the seeds of love for theatre and education that we are honored to pass down, forward, and around.

Part I

Autumn

1 Preparing for Employment

RELATED APPENDIX DOCUMENTS

- Ideal Job Worksheet (Appendix A, p. 250)

While you are in the process of preparing for a job as a theatre educator, the road is open and may lead you in many directions. This is your time to imagine the characteristics of your ideal situation. Where in the country, or in the world, would you like to work? Public school or private? What grade levels would you like to teach and direct? Are you drawn to students with special needs or circumstances? What artistic resources would you like nearby, to serve both you and your students? What will be different about teaching and directing from being a theatre student or participant? What issues must you consider and decide about that have nothing to do with theatre, but buttress your success now and far into the future? What organizations are there to support you as an employee, an educator, and a theatre person? Let's take a look.

Where and Whom to Teach

When jobs are scarce, any job may seem like the right job. If you are just out of college and have the option of relocating in order to begin teaching, there are a lot of choices in front of you. What would be the perfect place in which to teach and direct theatre?

Setting

Geography may be part of your decision. Would you like to be near water or mountains? In a city, a suburb, or a rural area? The more remote a location, the more significant your contribution can be to that community. The local high school may well be a center of activity for everyone, not just the students, and there might be wonderful support for your program. On the other hand, the larger the locale, the more opportunities for interaction with other like-minded people.

Do you want to be near a strong theatre community? There may be more competition for jobs there—but hey, you only need one, right? And there will be more folks to tap as resources for information as well as prop and costume loans—even chances to keep your own hand in the game. Working in or near a university town would afford those opportunities, as well as a chance to advance your own professional development with classes toward recertification points or toward an advanced degree (and its commensurate pay bump).

School Type and Size

School size has an impact like that of town size. Small schools tend to be places where it is easier to get to know everyone…have everyone know your business…and folks are used to pitching in for the good of the school. Also, if you need something, there aren't so many layers of bureaucracy to cut through. Large schools may have more facilities and equipment, multiple venues in which you can work, a black box theatre/classroom, a strong theatre program already established, and maybe even a theatre colleague with whom to commune and collaborate. On the other hand, they may be crowded with activity and folks jockeying for space and time, plus more red tape for everything you try to get done.

Working in an inner city school or high-poverty area brings its own challenges and rewards. Programs such as Teach for America (www.teachforamerica.org) pair teachers and schools and can provide "one of the toughest jobs you'll ever love." If theatre requires only "two planks and a passion," then you can still create theatre magic even without great facilities or money for equipment or supplies. "Devised Theatre" is perfect for this type of situation, and theatre can create the kind of outlet and hook that could keep some kids from dropping out of school.

Public versus private schools offer different experiences. Public schools tend to be larger, with more opportunities, and more bureaucracy—and after your first few years, more job security. Private schools often have smaller class sizes, more active parent involvement (a double-edged sword), and more financial resources available—although you may have less job security.

Schools with a Special Focus

More American schools are becoming aligned with the International Baccalaureate (I.B.) program (www.ibo.org) at the elementary, middle school (grades 6–10), and particularly high school level (grades 11–12). IB provides a framework for education according to strict standards established worldwide. These assessments not only measure skills and knowledge focused on connecting subjects and appreciating other cultures, but can also translate into significant college credit. IB includes theatre as an option and uses the following three tenets: Theatre in Context, Theatre Processes, and Presenting Theatre. No particular plays, skills or information are required. IB is a way of approaching education, so if you're heading to an IB school, read up about it, and do everything possible to get to one of the IB Theatre training sessions.

There are also schools out there that focus on students with special needs. If your training and temperament make you a good match for working with students with emotional, intellectual, or physical disabilities, you bring a lot of "value added" to the table with your theatre background.

Working overseas can be a wonderful first teaching experience. Several American teacher placement agencies help locate teaching positions, and some don't limit themselves to jobs in the U.S. Don't worry about cost because most of these agencies take their fees from the employer. Do a Google search for "international teaching jobs" and see for yourself. It's a great way to travel, to get your feet wet with other (often) young teachers, and to land in a place where culture in general, and theatre in particular, are highly valued. Another route to teaching overseas is through the Department of Defense (www.dodea.edu), which sponsors schools for military families in Europe and the Pacific, as well as in the States. Working in the arts within the military is its own kind of animal, so try to investigate thoroughly to understand how things would work for you there.

Elementary, Middle, or High School?

The choice of which level to teach is often determined less by preference and more by what job is available. While most theatre educators visualize themselves working on the high school level, middle school and elementary school both offer vital growth opportunities for all concerned. Keep an open mind as you consider the differences and similarities in teaching at these three different levels. You may discover an unanticipated love for teaching students at another grade level. Since most of this book is focused on middle and high school, what follows is an expanded section on elementary theatre education.

Job Interview Questions and Comments

The school is interviewing you—but you are also interviewing the school that you hope will offer you a job. Some things to find out:

- How many theatre classes will you expect me to teach? How many sections of each?
- Are any of the classes combined together? How does that work? How large are the classes? What is their minimum/maximum enrollment?
- What kind of classroom space is available? Is it shared with any other classes? Which ones? Are there desks or other obstructions? Is there carpet? Will there be any problem with our making lots of noise there?
- What kind of theatre/auditorium is available? Is it available for use during class? If so, with what exceptions? How busy is it with other events?
- If the auditorium *is* the classroom, where is the class expected to meet when others are using that facility?
- What support spaces do you have available (costume/prop storage, set construction area, script library, etc.)? Where can temporary loans (props/costumes from students) be stored?
- Who supervises the theatre program? What other areas are they responsible for (i.e., how divided is their attention)?
- What are your expectations for play productions? Competitions? Musicals? Other events? How much "lock-out" time do you make available prior to each production opening, when the set can be constructed and stay in place, props/costumes secured, lighting set, etc.?
- What start-up money is available for scripts, royalties, and play production costs? Do profits roll over into the following year? Is there an annual budget? Are classroom expenses separate from production costs?
- Must someone approve play production selections? Who? What is the process and timeline? Is there a parent drama booster group? What is its reputation? Helpful? Silent? Aggressive?
- What is the current reputation of your theatre program? Is it valued? Struggling? Ambitious? Bare bones? What change(s) do you hope to see in the coming years?

Elementary, My Dear Director

If you cringe at the very idea of teaching elementary school theatre, take a moment to think: what aspects of elementary school teaching make you uneasy? Do you have difficulty in relating to younger students? Are you concerned about your interest/ability/focus in working with theatre materials that are more age-specific and less "theatrical" than you are accustomed to handling?

Heightened Structure and Preparation

Everything in elementary school must be broken down to a step-by-step, clearly communicated process—take nothing for granted. Attention spans are shorter, so teach points in short chunks, while integrating activities that keep students engaged. Elementary age students are closest to the purity of imagination and want to create with all five senses. Take advantage of their love of play, and get them up and moving, creating and conveying the story at hand. The beauty of elementary theatre is that you really can play along with the kids without regard for how "cool" you may or may not appear. Little kids will love you for releasing your inner child and sharing your creative spirit. Beware, however: there is no down time when you teach elementary theatre. You may not have the long hours after school that a comprehensive high school theatre program demands, but you will go home exhausted every single day. Wash your hands and get plenty of sleep—little kid germs are even more infectious than their sweet laughter and spontaneous hugs.

In a nutshell, these are the most important points to remember:

- Elementary education = structure, structure, structure!
- Structure = preparation, preparation, preparation!
- Whatever big kids can accomplish, little kids can usually accomplish in smaller chunks, with more time.
- But you must make sure that the material is *developmentally appropriate*.
- Talk less—do more!
- Use a student-centered approach + a step by step structured process. Break it down!
- Don't take your eyes off of them for a single moment.
- Find your own moment in the day to catch your breath or go to the bathroom.

If you are not coming from an elementary education background, do some research and discuss developmental levels with your colleagues. K-2 students are creative and imaginative, but also concrete in their ability to understand processes. Abstract thinking skills start to kick in around third grade. Reading levels range greatly from kindergarten to fifth grade, of course, and so does suitable subject matter. While teaching is a sacred trust at any level, the innocence of younger children is especially vulnerable—even in the 21st century. The school media specialist should be a great resource for giving you that overall view of children's literature that will act as a guide for what is developmentally appropriate at different grade levels.

While you may have strong preferences as a college student concerning which grade levels appeal to you most, the bottom line is that you will be glad to be employed, regardless. When it comes to getting teaching experience and paying the bills, your mind may suddenly expand, and that elementary job becomes a golden opportunity.

Integrating with Core Curriculum

Become familiar with the basic curriculum for each grade level with an eye toward core subject matter that lends itself to dramatization. This is best achieved through conversation with classroom teachers: "What's the big project for third grade science or social studies?" or "Is there any particular story or project you'd like me to emphasize in theatre class?" Of course you have your own curriculum, but why not work on creative movement as functions of the solar system? Revolution vs. rotation is so much clearer when kids act it out! There are some short core material scripts out there, but you can also create your own or set up guidelines for the kids to create original masterpieces. Reading is always a vital co-curricular activity, whether it is the kids reading out loud or you reading them a story book, modeling vocal and facial expression. Elementary theatre is all about *process!*

Program Choices

If each class in your school has a class play, every parent will be happy, and every child will have the opportunity to shine. Create short ensemble pieces with parts for everyone and very few major roles; have ten narrators with two lines each, but give everyone a special moment. Collaborate with the school art teacher to create props and costumes—masks, painted paper ponchos, magic wands, and butterflies on a string. Add a little music—recorded or original—and parents will be thrilled.

More sophisticated performances may evolve if you have an after-school enrichment component to your program. Enlist the aid of the music teacher and do an MTI (Music Theatre International) Junior musical at the end of the year—cast it in October and perform it in May! Even edited Shakespeare can be successful if it is short enough (remember, small chunks!) and you keep it active.

Production Resources

In contrast to middle and high school performances, elementary school class plays are best performed during the school day without charging a ticket fee. You are allowed to use a limited amount of copyrighted music without permission or royalty fees (see our note about copyright on page 91). You may also use children's literature, especially if the play occurs during the day and is seen as part of the school reading program. Just make sure you buy the number of books needed—*never copy them*. Another resource for school plays or theatre activities is *Plays* magazine, which can be purchased by your school media specialist, or with any available textbook funds, since it is filled with a variety of developmentally appropriate and often historical short scripts. The right to reproduce the scripts, as well as amateur royalties, is included as long as the subscription is in force. There are also other children's plays and activities materials available, with minimal costs required. The best selection of these that we have seen is in The Drama Book Shop (dramabookshop.com) in NYC—go online to see what works for your particular situation. With the ever-expanding list of incredible children's literature available to you, it is best to check it out yourself.

When choosing material for classroom use and presentations, consider racial and cultural diversity. The materials you select may create a foundation and common ground for young minds, influencing their perspectives and attitudes. Make sure your selections are positive and compassionate.

Creative Dramatics, in which all class members are onstage for most or all of the play, creating an imaginative environment for the action, is an ensemble approach you may find very effective. You may also find it helpful to utilize some props, costumes, or stage scenery that the students can create and/or manipulate as part of the performance.

Puppets and Mask-Making: Creative Opportunities

If you have the money, you should definitely invest in a set of well-made puppets for your elementary theatre program. Granted, you may have to pass out hand sanitizer before each puppet session, but students come alive on an entirely different level when encouraged to express themselves through a puppet character. Sometimes the shy, quiet child in the back row will spring to life with "puppet permission." Stories such as *The Great Kapok Tree* lend themselves particularly well to animal puppet use. Puppets can also be wonderful facilitators of original student playwriting or improvised dialogue; somehow students experience less pressure and nervousness when their voices are masked by a puppet. Segue into mask-making—this is another means of subtle encouragement through which young people find their voices. Create a mask-making unit that coordinates with the story theatre presentation, and you add layers of artistic dimension to your students' experience without adding great expense. By using cardboard from cereal boxes and other recycled materials for their masks, you can also turn the mask-making process into a tool to teach your students about recycling and the environment.

Real-World Moments

The first theatre class I taught to kindergarteners was on a cafetorium stage—effectively a teaching space on a four foot "cliff." When they entered the space on our first day of class, I greeted them and told them to sit down. I didn't realize that I had to precisely communicate to them *how* they should sit down. As 20 five-year-olds exploded onto the space in every direction, I had terrible visions of children falling off the four foot elevation of the stage. Chasing chaotically after my herd of cats, I eventually got these little people back in a line, sitting in a circle. Every other class for the next ten years would be told to come onto the space in a line and follow me around the edge of a blue carpet that defined our safe, creative theatre space.

Financial Support

Elementary school programs, unlike many high school programs, are generally not able to support themselves through ticket sales and other related funding mechanisms. Fortunately for the elementary programs, their expenses and performance expectations are usually well below those at the secondary level. In limited cases, where more financial support may be needed, such as for "junior" musicals and other larger productions, you may need to seek funding from a variety of sources. These include grants, donations from parents, the PTSA, and other private sources, to supplement whatever school funds the principal makes available.

"Junior" musicals, available from Music Theatre International, are a wonderful resource. They are, basically, "Musicals in a Box." They provide the teacher with brilliantly organized production materials for a single flat fee, usually $500–$1000, which covers the materials, recordings of the production, and royalties. (It is too bad that high schools don't have a comparable product available for their full-sized shows.) Once you have one of these musicals in hand, you should immediately bring it to the attention of your PTSA and other potential sources of support. The PTSA, in particular, may love getting behind this project and can help you generate a list of parent volunteers to help out. This, in turn, gives you and your program the benefit of parent involvement and community connections. And while many elementary schools do not charge audience members for tickets to the performances, some do allow you to request donations to support the theatre program.

Collaborating with Colleagues

Collaboration with your teaching colleagues is an essential element of education—but when you have a great creative idea that inspires you, you first need to think it through and figure out which colleagues you will want/need to work with and what you will need from them. For example, if you'd like the art teacher to use some of her class time to have the first graders paint wild thing faces on paper ponchos for a creative dramatics reading of *Where The Wild Things Are*, be prepared to support your request. Order the craft paper (the art teacher will know these supplies better than you do); pay for it with theatre or PTSA funds; cut out every one of those ponchos and deliver them when the art teacher tells you s/he needs them. Once you demonstrate your work ethic and empathy, collaboration will increase and multiply. You must be a considerate collaborator regarding funding, materials, timeline and preparation; *everyone is busy*, and everyone has limited resources. In short, collaborate with your colleagues without creating more work for them.

Another way to cultivate collaboration on a larger scale within your school's community is to participate in your school's leadership team. This will provide you with opportunities to solidify colleague relationships and to share your "specialist" viewpoint and skills with both administrators and classroom teachers.

Monkey in the Middle

While some declare that middle school is the cruelest cut, don't knock it until you've tried it. This age group may awkwardly grope for "coolness," but there is still a good deal of childhood innocence within, as well as the gift of goofiness. Middle school students are often faster to plunge into improvisation or silly theatre games than their older counterparts. The level of middle school theatre material is understandably less complex than what you might explore in high school programs—you certainly won't be directing *A Streetcar Named Desire*. However, while a high school teacher may struggle to attract enough support for a full-time program (and position), there may be less competition for electives on the middle school level—at some schools, they are built right into the schedule.

Structure Variations

Different schools organize their middle school classes in different ways. Find out ahead of time which variation is typical at a school you're investigating. Here are some examples of how electives may be included in a middle school schedule.

THE WHEEL Some schools expose students to various electives by using a rotation during the year that places them in various arts (or other) classes for a short amount of time. It's a great way to let a lot of students get to meet you and get excited about theatre, but it is not a great way to get much accomplished or to build strong skills.

SEMESTER CLASSES At many schools, drama classes are available in a semester format, rather than as a full year class.

FULL YEAR CLASSES A full year class exposes fewer students to your subject, but it gives you a chance to really develop your students' skills.

ADVANCED MS THEATRE Ideally, students excited by theatre in seventh grade will be able to undertake more challenging work as eighth graders (and show up the following year ready to delight their high school theatre teachers!). A class restricted to successful graduates of the first-year course can really shine, and be a delight to teach, too. Over time, such a class should be your goal.

REPEAT CLASSES Whether a student can repeat the class (and whether you need to generate new material, or can repeat) can vary from place to place. Can a seventh grader take the class again as an eighth grader? Will both grade levels be mixed? Can they be separated?

Performance and Event Opportunities

Developing a strong theatre program at the middle school level involves more after-school activities than the elementary theatre program, but fewer hours than most high school production schedules require—as you might expect. In-school productions, scene sharing or production previews span the grades, depending on how arts-supportive your administration is and the availability of suitable facilities.

CLASS PERFORMANCES Your students will shine the brightest if they can perform for their peers and family. In order for students to do their best, additional preparation time outside of class always helps, if you can arrange it. Parent involvement is critical here, and it is amazing what can be accomplished with parent support, especially with tech help.

DRAMA CLUB There may be an additional stipend available for you if you sponsor an after-school drama club that is open to all comers. This is a great time for theatre games and improvisation. Meeting days and times may be restricted by after-school bus schedules, and attendance is likely to be haphazard.

THESPIANS Junior Thespian programs may delight you and your students. Find out more at www.SchoolTheatre.org.

THEATRE VISITS Whether by taking your students on a field trip, or by bringing a traveling troupe of players into your school, exposure to professional productions adds value to any drama program. It's also a great way to support and connect with your high school feeder school, by encouraging attendance at their shows (and vice versa).

PLAYS Everybody wants to see a "real" play come out of a drama program. Working with a cast that has auditioned gives you a more reliably committed group of kids with whom to enjoy working. You will have to facilitate parent support and transportation. Also, plenty of parent and colleague help with the technical aspects of production will be essential. When your students move on to high school, you can bring these alumni back in subsequent years to help your current students—with both onstage stuff and with tech stuff. Everyone wins.

MUSICALS Feeling ambitious? Musicals always generate more excitement (and audience, and income) than straight plays, and may require just a piano and perhaps a couple of other instruments. What talent hides among your fellow faculty or among the elementary school music teachers? As mentioned before, Music Theatre International offers junior versions of many of their musicals. The cost of each show covers scripts, royalties, and support materials—and at a *much* more affordable price than their big brother versions.

The Trade-Off

Perhaps the biggest difference between the levels of theatre education is the range of materials that are developmentally appropriate to the spectrum of students' ages. The sweetness of young children is the trade-off for the Tennessee Williams, Christopher Durang, and adolescent angst plays that you will not direct with them. The limited after-school hours of elementary and middle school students, however, may furnish you with an opportunity to not only run an excellent theatre program, but to work on higher education or professional development. If you have a young family, hobby, or part-time job that you enjoy, the elementary or middle-school theatre program is a common sense decision. And even if your goal is high school, a middle school program is an excellent way to get your feet wet both in the classroom and onstage, before diving into the deep water of expectations for a high school program.

Handling High School

Running a high school program is more demanding than an elementary or middle school program. Although elementary school requires preparation for multiple grade levels, neither the financial nor the extra-curricular obligations of a high school program are expected. Middle school covers a smaller number of grade levels for which to prepare, and the production responsibilities are important, but typically few and far between. At the high school level, you are basically running a small business with your production schedule. In addition, most high school theatre directors are solo acts—Theatre I-IV and Tech Theatre might be your five+

preps (unique classes to be prepared separately vs. multiple sections of individual class)—and you count yourself lucky to have them in a full-time position. Also, high school theatre directors must jump through the hoops of the electives enrollment competition every year to keep the student numbers strong. No matter how great the shows are, if your classes don't attract students each year, you will not have a full-time job.

Artistically, the more sophisticated material available for high school teachers to explore and direct with their students is an undeniable source of satisfaction for all concerned. After all, there is a big difference between MTI Junior musicals and, for example, *The Laramie Project*. High school students can share your love of the performing arts, creating meaningful teacher/student relationships. In four years, adolescents change from awkward to amazing—and you get to help them along the journey to discover themselves. Among the most fulfilling aspects of being a high school theatre director is the opportunity to assist students with college or conservatory auditions—talk about making a difference! In other words, high school teachers have the unique opportunity to see how their work has influenced the lives of their students, and how they have helped these students to grow into adulthood.

Consider not only the job, but other priorities in your life that will be impacted by the demands of doing your best professionally. It may be that an elementary mindset works well if you are raising a young family, or a middle school job makes sense if you want to simultaneously pursue your graduate degree. If you take on the high school theatre director position, be prepared to immerse yourself in your new educational home. Dive in and start swimming (and keep reading)!

School Theatre Programs Compared

Elementary School

Suggested	• 1 in-school class play each year • 1 after-school production at the end of the year (the culminating project of an after-school or magnet program)
Optional	• A talent show or "celebration of diversity" show, made up of individual short acts • A PTSA sponsored presentation

Middle School

Suggested	• 1 talent show or "celebration of diversity" show (fall semester) • 1 local theatre workshop or short play festival • 1 full-scale production (usually in the spring, so students have time to mature)
Optional	• A night of one-act plays or class scene work for friends and family • An overnight trip to NYC or to a college production

High School

Suggested	• 1 or 2 conferences sponsored by theatre education organizations • 1 full-length play or musical each semester (total of 2) • A night of one-act plays or class scene work for friends and family • 1 or 2 one-act play competition/festival events (these may or may not be part of a conference) • Improvisation events for your school improv team
Optional	• A third full-length production • A student-directed children's theatre production • A two or three-day overnight trip to NYC or college production • A talent show or cabaret-type event • Evening field trips to local theatre performances or workshops • Cappies training, mentoring, critique writing • Train and supervise student technicians

The Theatre Educator's Job Description

Teaching isn't, of course, just teaching—that's just your objective. Between the elements that are spelled out in your contract and the inevitable "other duties as assigned" clause, there are many tasks that will take up your teaching (and personal) time. In this section, we will provide you with a list—extensive but not necessarily comprehensive—of the things that you may be called upon to do as a theatre educator. If you are also asked to sign a coaching contract for doing shows after school, see if there exists an official definition of what duties are presumed to be included in that. Get yourself a copy, and file it away for future reference.

So what does a theatre teacher/director do? As much as you can! You'll see from the list below that the job—our focus here is on high school—goes far beyond the basics of teaching and directing, and may well include obligations that take you outside of your skill set and training. And then there are the zillion other little things that must be done—hey, they build character—and time management skills.

TEACH THEATRE CLASSES Teach Theatre Arts I, II, III and IV, as well as Technical Theatre. Also perhaps Speech or Film Studies—perhaps even IB Theatre.

PRODUCE PLAYS AND MUSICALS Choose; apply for licensure; cast; direct and produce the plays/musicals.

MANAGE THE MONEY Work with the school finance officer regarding show income and expenses.

MANAGE THE THEATER SPACE(S) Train student technicians to operate sound/light equipment for outside user groups, as well as every student services (a.k.a. guidance) and guest artist assembly, music department concerts, school fashion shows, international night, talent shows, etc.

DO EQUIPMENT MAINTENANCE Train the tech theatre class in how to avoid, spot and respond to problems. Check school rules for which manual and power tools are allowed for student use in your school system. Submit paperwork for repair or replacement of items as needed.

COLLABORATE WITH OTHER TEACHERS Offer students opportunities to interact with other teachers and departments in your school, such as:

- **ART DEPARTMENT** Work with art teachers and students to create props, do specialty painting on sets, and design computer graphics for show posters.
- **MUSIC DEPARTMENT** Collaborate with the vocal music director (probably the choral director), orchestra conductor, and student musicians to perform vocal music and serve as the pit orchestra. Note that your music colleagues may have huge preferences about when the annual school musical will work best for them. Listen to them and make everyone's life easier.

- **DANCE DEPARTMENT** If you are lucky enough to have a dance class at your school, that instructor may leap (so to speak) at the chance to choreograph your musical or may have a talented student who can do so.
- **ENGLISH DEPARTMENT** Creative Writing or Journalism teachers can become valuable allies if their students can write reviews—or even plays—or assist with dramaturgical tasks for your production season.

COLLABORATE WITH OTHER THEATRE DIRECTORS In your school system and in your school pyramid, find ways to connect with your feeder middle schools (a.k.a. junior highs) and elementary schools—you will sell more tickets and create a real sense of community.

PARTICIPATE IN LOCAL/REGIONAL THEATRE CONFERENCES One-act play competitions sponsored by various branches of the Educational Theatre Association and other organizations provide opportunities for you and your students to grow, including connections with local professional and community theatre groups.

PROVIDE COLLEGE RECOMMENDATIONS AND GUIDANCE It is important to cultivate professional relationships with college program professors, so that you can be familiar with the different theatre programs around your state, as well as others close by. An efficient way to do this is by attending the state conference for the Educational Theatre Association. Take your students to the conference, which provides opportunities for student workshops on various aspects of theatre, college auditions for seniors, and a one-act play festival.

BUILD YOUR PROGRAM Summer theatre camps for different age groups, usually sponsored by your theatre boosters, create connections throughout the community, build your audience, give your older students summer counselor and tech theatre jobs, and supplement your summer income. It's lots of work, but *everybody wins!*

Appendix 📄 Connection

Ready to try to envision your ideal job? Fill out the form in appendix A, *Ideal Job Worksheet*.

Wait! You also get…

- Attendance
- Tardiness
- Pre-arranged absences
- EpiPen training
- Internet security training
- Anti-sexual harassment training
- Anti-bullying training
- Field trip paperwork
- Cover letter to parents re: field trip
- Administrator approval
- Financial plan
- Sub request
- Sub payment
- Parent approval
- Emergency care forms
- Luggage search approval
- Bus logistics
- Hotel logistics
- Competition forms to host venue
- Contracts signed by principal
- Collect and track kid payments
- Deposit payments
- Parent phone calls
- Parent conferences
- IEP narratives
- 504 plan accommodations
- Fire drills
- Tornado drills
- Lockdown drills
- Shelter-in-place drills
- Earthquake drills
- Faculty meetings
- Department meetings
- Area/county meetings by subject
- Professional Learning Community meetings
- Book orders for next year
- Supply orders for next year
- Coaches meetings/training
- Repair requests for theater
- Train student technicians
- Schedule student technician jobs
- Serve on faculty/sunshine/advisory committees
- Sponsor ITS troupe and/or other festival/competition groups
- Cappies
- Improv competition team
- English-Speaking Union (ESU) speech competition
- Attend conferences
- IB training
- Computer repair requests
- Computer assistance
- Booster meetings
- Materials and supplies pickup
- Website upkeep
- Expense/income tracking
- Populate and update Blackboard for each class
- Second chance assessments
- Issue bus passes
- Send grade reports
- Prepare interim grade reports
- Prepare quarterly grade reports
- Provide club attendance data
- Create SMARTr goals
- Confiscate cell phones (if permitted)
- Deliver confiscated items to security (if required)
- Modify lesson plans to differentiate instruction, accommodate disabilities, etc.
- Schedule rehearsal and performance spaces

Changes from Student Teacher to Teacher/Director

Despite many years as a student, there are pieces of the educational institution that you never had to think about. Even as a student teacher, you may have only glimpsed the surface, probably focusing on lesson plans and classroom management. If you are coming from a professional theatre background, the world of education will greet you with different challenges. Here are some of the areas that change as you shift into the role of teacher/director.

Autonomy

For all the talk about support systems and Professional Learning Communities, you become your own boss (at least on a day-to-day basis) in the theatre classroom and king of your kingdom onstage and backstage. Despite the Program of Studies and other curricula mandates, it's really just you, now, who sets the agenda, the tone, the pace, the policies, and the priorities. You alone pick the units of study, the plays to be produced, and pretty much everything else that happens in your classroom and after school in rehearsal. You are swimming solo now.

Versatility

You may find some helpers, but you will be expected to be the expert on *all* aspects of theatre and production. If you trained in acting and directing, you are still the one called upon to help with lighting and sound for all theater users. You're the one to train students in your shows and classes how to do everything from media contacts to costume design, and to purchase and approve new equipment and supplies.

Culture

You will likely enter a school (and theatre department) with its own culture, and you will be instrumental in the evolution of that culture. The expectations of policy and practice that you embrace or adjust (or abandon) create that culture. What are different locations nicknamed? Do certain classes get to represent the school at particular competitions or festivals? What turns of phrase are (or become) your "shorthand" about getting things done that your students pass along to the newbies each year? Create that culture. It's a powerful and useful thing that lies beneath the surface, but it has a huge impact.

Safety

Your first priority (if you're single/childless) has been yourself. But in the classroom and backstage, your first priority is the safety of your charges. And since adolescents are notorious for bad judgment and not seeing the connection between action and consequence, you may

Real-World Moments

It was a weekend theatre convention, and the young teacher was checking on his students. In one room, several students were playing Truth or Dare, and they encouraged him to join one final round before calling it a night. His dare was to briefly wear a condom over his (bald) head. He did, figuring no harm was done...how did the story play at home? He was not rehired the next year.

need to spend a serious amount of time and energy ensuring that people and things stay safe all the time—*all the time.* Murphy (if things can go wrong, they will go wrong) lurks.

Liability

Someone else used to be responsible, but now it's you. If a student talks about being abused, the law requires that you not keep that confidence, but report it or be guilty of a crime. Your students may often be using multiple spaces simultaneously (stage, scene shop, dressing rooms), but if something bad happens, it will be seen as a lapse of your supervision. If students use bad judgment, you are the one whose response will be judged. The buck stops with you.

Politics

Parents feel intensely protective of their kids, and anything you do that brings pain to one (e.g., not being cast), brings pain to the other. But the parents aren't at all afraid of you. And they don't really care about your point of view, and they're not going away if there's an "issue." Intraschool politics are alive and well everywhere, too, so stay in the good graces of those with whom you will have a continuing relationship. As for the kids, keep the sharing of your personal life and beliefs to a minimum. Learning the art of diplomacy is critical in your role as theatre educator and director. And for goodness sakes, keep your critical remarks about students and staff off of social media!

Immersion

Theatre education is a calling, not a job. You can't decide you had a rough night, so you're going to blow off class and not show up. You can't paint the stage while rehearsing on it.

Real-World Moments

As a young teacher, money was always tight. Then I discovered a few ways to pick up some extra cash without a lot of effort. One was to volunteer to proctor the SAT or ACTs. Good money on a Saturday morning, and it is oh, so easy to do! Also, in many schools, there must be a building supervisor on duty if an outside user is there after hours. That just means you have the keys and can do crisis management if necessary—a wonderful time to grade papers and do other planning. Some of the larger events, like organizing graduation or being a class sponsor might come with a stipend, and any drama teacher/coach certainly has the skills to handle those jobs.

Grade reports are going to come due despite it being Hell Week. Your control over how you spend your time is largely gone. To handle all this, your only option may seem to be working days, nights and weekends, and the enthusiasm of your students only reinforces that. But it's essential that you drive the machine, and not let it drive you. Your own family and personal relationships will last a lot longer than any cadre of students passing through. Try hard to maintain a balance—including sleep.

Pay Yourself First

As a new teacher, one of the things you are likely to ignore in the crush of things to do now is the future—your own future. Teaching is a profession, a career, and you may be doing this for a very long time. And while there are lesson plans—and, frankly, all the other things in this textbook—to consider, here is one task to seize, deal with, and then ignore for the rest of the year: pay yourself first.

Many school systems offer a savings plan for retirement (*keep reading!*), where the savings comes out of your paycheck before your taxes do. So instead of having to earn $125 to have (after taxes) $100 left to spend, you can put away the full $125 now. If I put $2,000 into a retirement fund now (say it earns 8 percent per year) once only, and you waited ten years and then put in $2,000 every single year until retirement, you'd never catch up to me. Starting early is *huge*.

No matter how paltry your salary feels, put away something pulled out as a payroll deduction before you ever see that paycheck, and you will still make ends meet. An ideal amount is 10–15 percent, but even $50 a month is a start. The impact of interest earned compounding over time is simply amazing. Nothing beats starting immediately. Pension plans are getting weaker and weaker, so your discipline to plan ahead is critical to your future.

Don't know where to put that money? There are plenty of people and firms more than ready to advise you, and your school system may have vetted some already (and might restrict you to using only those companies). But any choice is better than waiting. If you can handle more details, keep reading. Otherwise, sock away some money *somewhere*, and then forget you've done it. Just keep paying yourself first, into that account, and do not touch it for anything!

Where to put that money? One easy option is a mutual fund (that's a collection of stocks and bonds) tagged to the year you might retire. Over time, the mix of stocks and bonds shifts without your doing anything, to give you the best likelihood (nothing is guaranteed with investments) of earning the best return while keeping your risk down as you get closer to needing that money. Many companies offer these plans as IRAs (individual retirement accounts) or 403(b)s (the non-profit equivalent of the corporate 401K retirement plans).

Certainly, if you find financial stuff interesting, there is a world of possibilities and options for investing. But if this all makes your head spin, do not ignore it: pay yourself first. Send some of every single paycheck to a retirement account. Start now. Let it compound. Be a teacher who has taught him/herself that we all must prepare for the future—and the sooner, the better.

Professional Organizations

Take time to investigate and join professional organizations. Teaching requires that you work with people; people are unpredictable. Having inexpensive access to legal representation could be vital, and it is certainly wise. Whether your state is a "right-to-work" state or well-embedded in the union tradition, a collective voice makes a difference in terms of negotiating for pay, working conditions, and benefits. The **National Education Association** (www.nea.org) and the **American Federation of Teachers** (www.aft.org) have state and local affiliates which provide ample coverage for your career needs. Both will represent you in case you get sued, and they will also provide liability insurance and legal defense.

Professional theatre organizations present a whole other level of resources for you, including the opportunity to network, attend professional development conferences, get recertification points for attending/presenting, and meet guest artists and vendors who may later provide equipment and services for your theatre program.

The **Educational Theatre Association** (www.SchoolTheatre.org) offers a broad range of resources, including general advice, a play lending library, networking daily emails, a magazine, a national convention, and International Thespian Society (ITS) student services and statewide conventions. State and regional affiliates such as the Southeastern Theatre Conference (www.setc.org), the North Carolina Theatre Conference (www.nctc.org), and the Virginia Theatre Association (www.vtasite.org) host annual events of great value to both teacher/directors and students.

The **American Alliance for Theatre and Education** (www.AATE.com) "connects...artists, educators, and scholars committed to transforming young people and communities through the theatre arts." They offer publications, networking, and an annual conference.

The **International Schools Theatre Association** (www.ISTA.co.uk) offers workshops for teachers and/or students around the world. They also train IB Theatre instructors.

The **International Drama/Theatre and Education Association** (www.IDEA-org.net) "lobbies regionally and internationally to raise the awareness of governments, key agencies and organizations, as to the importance of drama and theatre in the development and lives of children and young people."

For Reflection & Discussion

What values and priorities will you bring to your new job? How might those play out?

1. If you and the students are all fired up to do a particular show, does it matter if the administration or community might consider it inappropriate? Who draws that line? Where? When? Is it okay to cut objectionable material from a script, so the larger project can move forward?

2. Is it okay to lend your own car or truck to licensed students to run errands for your program? Can they go during class time if they are back before the class period ends?

3. What difference does it make if a cast list is posted at the beginning of the school day or the end? Or only online? How would you justify casting choices to an irate, protective parent? To the auditioner?

4. What is your best course of action if you attend a cast party and beer is available? Is it okay to imbibe if it's only offered to you by the host parents, but not available to the kids? Does it matter if you have a drink with dinner before returning to school for a rehearsal or show?

5. If you're directing, will there be tech work happening at the same time in another location? And if not, when will that work get done? What level of supervision is appropriate there? Will you be at school every night overseeing the tech work for the actors you were with every afternoon? If you are not supervising the work, who is? Does it matter?

6. Is it okay to drive a student home? Does their gender matter? Is it okay to wait with a single student until they are picked up by their parent? Is it okay to leave them alone in the building until picked up?

7. If you set a deadline for something in class, are you willing to let the student fail for not meeting that deadline? If you set a deadline for something in a show, are you willing to let that part of the show not happen if the student doesn't come through? What are your alternatives in either scenario? What is gained or lost either way?

2 Preparing for the First Day of School

RELATED APPENDIX DOCUMENTS

- Checklist for Newbies (Appendix B, p. 254)
- Tech Help Request Form (Appendix C, p. 265)
- Tech Booth Rules (Appendix D, p. 267)
- Cultural Catch-Phrases (Appendix E, p. 269)
- Theatre I Identity Assignment: Who Am I? (Appendix F, p. 271)

Once you have finally landed that big job, things can get very real, very fast. Hopefully, you will have time to think, plan, and set yourself and your program up as thoroughly as you can before the onslaught of the school year begins. That means getting to know the stakeholders—the administrators, secretaries, and custodians; the parents of any drama booster group; and the student leaders in the drama department. It means getting to know how everyone expects things to be done both in the drama department and in the school in general. It means deciding on your priorities and philosophy—the choices that will drive your other decisions all year long. It also means getting familiar with the physical spaces you will be teaching in and the equipment you will be using.

Driving into Your First Year

Remember when you first learned to drive? Remember the day you drove the car alone for the first time? You still had to think about where to put the key, which pedal was the gas and

27

which the brake, how the shifter worked, how to perfectly adjust all the mirrors, how to back out ever so slowly and carefully, brake, shift, gas, etc., etc., etc. Now, let's say that day is also your first day on a new job delivering pizzas—in the company car, not yours. Also, you are in new neighborhoods that are not familiar. And you're on a strict schedule, so you simply cannot run late. And there are other people in the car with you—who don't drive, but are happy to tell you how, or to criticize you—busy chattering away while you try to stay focused. And uh oh, the car is a stick shift, and you don't know how to shift gears smoothly yet. And did we mention that it was also your job to cook those pizzas before you got into the car?

That's pretty much the situation of the first-year teacher. If you look back over this scenario, you'll notice that nearly everything mentioned will become second nature eventually. You barely think about how to start and drive the car; you become familiar with the neighborhoods, even where the potholes and other distractions are located; you get to know how long it takes to reach each destination in time, even which shortcuts to take if you can see an obstacle ahead. You get adept at shifting gears when necessary without even thinking about it. And you get ever more efficient about preparing those pizzas ahead of time, so you can get rolling as needed, fully ready for your day.

Your Learner's Permit—Permit Yourself the Time to Learn

But you're not going to be there right away. You can't—no matter how great your outlook is, no matter how prepared you are, no matter how diligent your work ethic. And you can't really simplify anything while you're getting used to all this new stuff—you have to manage all of it all at once. It feels overwhelming, and you might feel like you're not doing a good job. Even though you're doing your best, you wind up stressed and exhausted nearly every day. It's just so much! Are you the type to beat yourself up over every pothole you fell into, and second-guess all night about how you might have avoided it? Would you relive the stress of trying to shift gears and move forward while on a hill with a huge truck right behind you?

In time, you can easily and safely join in the conversations of those going along for the ride with you, and still get the job done well. And spend much more of your mental energy planning how to make those pizzas better and better, and how to deliver them with optimal efficiency, instead of worrying about all the logistics, the route to take and the pacing along the way.

Be kind to yourself. If you're doing your best, give yourself credit for that. It just plain takes time to become familiar with the landscape, the routines, and timing of your classes, rehearsals and other obligations. Once you have survived that first year, 95 percent of what follows will be repetition and variations on experiences that now have a context. Year two is much easier than year one. And after that, so much is on automatic that you cannot only get it all done without collapsing, but have great fun with the very situations that drove you crazy at first. Hang in there!

Real-World Moments

Speaking as a first-year teacher... it's the hardest thing in the world. I found myself (and still find myself) going to bed at 8:30 p.m., not wanting to talk to anyone, and just coming home, putting on Netflix and doing the same thing over and over again. It gets easier as time goes by: knowing where bathrooms are, hallways, how to copy things, where to hang posters, specific grading plans, and all the other fun stuff they don't teach you in college. Everything for me was reactive rather than proactive; I couldn't guess what needed to be done because this was my first year and I had to remember what a third-year teacher and beloved friend of mine told me before I started teaching: "Phoebe, it's impossible. No matter how hard you try, pull all-nighters, burn yourself out, you're not going to get all of it done... and that's got to be okay." For a type-A personality who always has her stuff together this was not something I wanted to hear, but I have come to find out it is true. Though it may seem negative, this statement relaxes me; I take pressure off of myself with it.

Every day I have to remind myself that if I am having kids walk out of my room having grown, learned something, or feel better about themselves then I can go home and know that I have done my job. Every grade may not be entered on time or perfectly, I may get behind in typical school duties, every performance may not be to my standards but when my kids tell me that they learn something new in my class every day, or when I see a kid go from building walls against me to hugging me after her first performance? I know I'm doing something right... and that's good enough for now.

–Phoebe Dillard

The Culture of Your Learning Community

Every school—and theatre program—has its own, unique culture, and attention to that culture can go a long way toward helping you and your students feel comfortable in their environment. Culture consists of those beliefs, norms and expectations that connect its people and affect their relationships to each other and to their territory. Culture shows itself in language, dress, behavior, rituals and traditions.

In your new school, what are the priorities, the beliefs valued highly enough to show themselves in behavior among the faculty or administration? Safety? Control? Congeniality? Discipline? Honesty? Confidence? Diversity? Excellence? What is the mood in the school? Is it oppressive? Trusting? Do people feel safe? Do they smile and greet each other? Is there tension between students? Between faculty or departments? Are the support staff respected? Is there parent involvement at the school?

Do teachers greet students at the door as they come into class? Do administrators monitor the hallways between classes? Does the staff dress professionally or casually? Do they wear school colors on game days or special occasions? Do they go by their first names or last names or is there no standard? Are there bells between classes? What is the mood around the lockers between classes? Are students roaming the hallways during class time? Can students go outside or leave the campus during lunch? Are there senior class privileges? Pep rallies? Homecoming events? Junior or senior proms? Graduation rituals? Senior skip days? Are the administrators seen as enemies or as friends?

Within your theatre department, what traditions are current? Is there a common type of dress (black is awfully common)? Are there nicknames for places or objects around the theatre spaces? How are the new students greeted/treated by the more experienced ones? Is there any sort of rite of passage? A welcoming or "big brother/sister" teaming up? Is there tension between the actors and the techies? What type of audition process has been in use? What has been the balance between work and fun in rehearsal? Are there green room traditions among the cast before each performance? When is set strike held, and how is it structured? How much parent involvement is expected? Who controls the keys? The money? Is there a booster group? A Thespian troupe? How much authority do they have? What activities have they typically been responsible for?

As you see, there are many, many moments for which there is no right answer, but remember that the power of precedent is intense. Anything you try to change will meet with resistance however important or useful that change. "Once is a revolution; twice is a tradition." You may have to graduate away those seniors who cling to the old. But those turns of phrase you popularize, and those techniques and routines you set in place, will become part of the culture of *your* theatre program. And, before very long at all, that culture you create will be "the way we've always done it."

Appendix 📄 Connection

Some of the phrases we have found helpful are listed in appendix E, *Cultural Catch-Phrases*. Feel free to use or modify them as you see fit.

Getting to Know You

Information is power, but some of it may need to remain confidential. While it may be helpful to know how Sally and Sam were caught loving it up in the tech booth, you don't need to embarrass them or their families by telling the world about their indiscretion. You do, however, need to minimize opportunities for Sam, Sally, or any other students to be tempted in school spaces for which you are responsible. This may involve a firm, general announcement in class that asserts the need for all theatre students to be responsible and appropriate in their choices so that the theatre department can maintain a professional, respected reputation in the school. It may also involve the removal of specific pieces of furniture. You don't have to name names to get your message across. You also don't have to openly criticize the former teacher and his/her policies—you can just assert that this is the way things are going to work *now* ("Do I look like Mr. Formertheatreteacher?"). There's always room for improvement in any theatre department.

Cleaning Up

There are many different scenarios that a new theatre teacher/director may be walking into—which is why information is so helpful. Administrators, your department chairperson or administrative assistants will probably drop hints about how things were the previous year, whether or not your predecessor is forthcoming. If theft was a problem, you should look into security measures to lock up equipment or storage areas; ask for suggestions from your department chairperson or arts administrator. Pay close attention to student behavior: who is gone for twenty minutes to the bathroom or makes a habit of being late to class? Who expects to scan cell phone messages while you instruct or other students deliver presentations? Who assumes that theatre class is an easy A? It's amazing how consistently enforcing school rules and clearly communicating class expectations can create an entirely new vision for the department—one that now reflects the policies of Miss IlovetheatrebutImeanwhatIsay, or Mr. Havefunbutdontforgetwhosincharge (that's *you*!). You may have to write discipline referrals, call parents and get administrative support for the worst cases. You will have to be persistent, insistent, and consistent, as well as the most extreme role model for hard work

Appendix Connection

When you take over an existing program, it's a good idea to ask lots of questions and get the answers you need. See appendix B, *Checklist for Newbies*, a helpful list of questions you can use to prepare to hit the ground running in a new school.

ethic your students have ever seen—but that's nothing new in teaching. Be prepared to be hated by some, loved by others—but stand strong knowing you are earning their respect and sustaining your own in the process. It will get better as you build.

Measuring Up

If you come into a theatre director position following an epic legend who led the students to win every theatre award known to mankind—good luck! If you can elicit his/her support by way of an introduction to the students, go for it. In a hugely successful theatre department, the best advice may be: "Don't argue with success." You may learn a great deal by changing as little as possible the first year—as long as you are comfortable with the program. If what you've been handed is too much to handle, get feedback about what to cut (this competition or that special event), using your "But I'm new here" excuse for the short time it lasts.

Pick your battles very carefully and start with small adjustments that everyone can buy into. However, if there are any practices in the program that challenge your integrity or that you perceive as inappropriate, don't hesitate to make changes. Remind everyone that you are responsible for all aspects of the theatre department, and that your role as director requires you to use your best judgment. Assuming professional responsibility gives you the right to make decisions and lead.

Success still has to be ethical, and as the educational leader of your department and nurturer of young people, you may have to enlighten everyone concerning best practices. If you're not sure how to communicate your point diplomatically or effectively, talk to a colleague you trust and respect. One of the greatest teachers of teachers is collaboration; there is help and support all around you—seek it out.

Designing Your Own Path

"But Miss Teacherthatwelikedbetterthanyou always did it this way…" is the phrase you will hear for your entire first year following another beloved theatre teacher. While it's annoying, it's also how it should be, so accept it and deal with it. Theatre is a personal experience for students, and theatre teachers are privileged to nurture, challenge, and inspire students on their journey through artistic growth—of course they will resent the loss of someone who knows and cares about them! Change is a challenge, but those freshmen are your babies and the smart seniors will come around (or not … you may just have to wait until they graduate). As an educator, try to remember that *you are the adult*. You have a job to do whether the kids immediately bond with you or not; your relationship with them is based upon coming together to *learn*—and you are the *learning leader*. Forgive yourself (and them) on the days that you try really, really hard and still lose patience or leave school feeling unappreciated. Because part of being a good teacher is constant self-evaluation—"How can I do that better next time?"—educators tend to be self-critical. Give yourself time to get to know the school community and how you can creatively contribute to it. After a year or four, Miss Teacher-welikedbetterthanyou will become a distant memory, and someday the next theatre director will have to be annoyed by *your* departure.

Finding Your Personal Theatre Philosophy

Oh, so many ways to skin a cat! At some point, hopefully early on so it can guide your choices, or perhaps after you have survived the first wave of getting used to your new school, you will develop—intentionally or not—a philosophy of teaching theatre. Sure, you want to teach to your own strengths and interests, but you also want to explore new curricular objectives and round out your program. What do you want your classes and productions to do? Where should the emphasis be? What gets top billing in your lesson plans and what goes by the wayside? Will you assign homework routinely? Plays to read? To write about? To see and review? What kind of research will you require and will you provide only/any class time to do it? What are the essential questions to be answered by your choice of theatre productions? Let's consider some of the possibilities.

Future Fans

In middle and high school, theatre is not a training ground for professionals. It's about nurturing kids and their appreciation of an art form in which they can participate for the rest of their lives. Theatre without an audience is no theatre at all, and our students are the next generation of theatre-goers; the more they can enjoy its fun, richness, and energy, the more they are likely to continue to participate as they mature.

How: Take them to see plays whenever possible and watch the great movie versions (like those by Kenneth Branagh). Teach them to be discerning critics, perhaps even Cappies critics (www.cappies.com). The popular favorites are popular for a reason, but still largely unknown to your students—introduce them!

Take All Comers

The open atmosphere of theatre classes attracts all kinds of students—some with special needs or students unsure of an elective—in addition to those who already love the collaborative art. Welcome them all into Theatre I with open arms; students who find themselves in the margins of high school society often find a unique and comfortable place in the arts. The challenge is to meet the needs of a wide range of interest levels and learning styles.

How: Use theatre games, activities, ensemble productions and devised theatre to set everyone up for success and opportunities to contribute. Once they are hooked, students may audition for higher levels of theatre classes for the next year.

Meritocracy

Those kids who show real talent deserve to have it nurtured: they could become a step ahead of their competition in college and get the best opportunities there, too. Spending more time with those who hunger for theatre is time well spent. The others will still have plenty to do, and watching the work of those who truly love it can be an enriching experience of its own! Who knows…maybe as the person who first set those talented kids on their path, you will get a mention in their Academy Awards speech!

How: Do audition workshops; select challenging material; find small cast shows where they can truly shine and show off the quality of your work, bringing good press for your whole school.

Go Global

Theatre is a rich and varied thing. Across time and space, different theatre traditions have represented their cultures, challenged our mores and priorities, and moved people to social action and change. International Baccalaureate Theatre requires it, but all theatre programs can benefit from experiencing the diversity of styles, types, and forms of theatre across the globe. One need only look at the work of Julie Taymor to see how impressively those traditions can be fused to create dynamic, effective contemporary American art.

How: Incorporate units on Kabuki, Commedia dell'arte, Chinese Opera, African storytelling. Investigate the work of Augusto Boal, Bertolt Brecht, and others. Learn together!

Social Action

Theatre has the power to move the heart, and there are problems both out in the world and right in our back yards that can be illuminated through drama. Be it bullying, domestic violence, going green, teen suicide or the host of other issues affecting our students, there are plays that take on those challenges and help build coping skills and resilience. Studying and presenting material with socially-conscious content can truly affect lives.

How: Tour to classrooms and nearby schools—or administrative conferences—with issue-themed plays that reach far beyond the arts community. You'll still have all the character and ensemble building jobs to do, but leave behind things of lasting value to all.

Theatre Throughout the Curriculum

Theatre skills can be applied to any discipline, bringing its kinesthetic approach to core subject areas. Alliances with teachers of English, ESOL, special education, foreign language and even math, history and science can be forged, enriching both subjects. This can be a great way to make you essential to your whole school.

How: Go to other classrooms and perform scenes of plays being studied in English or other languages, or from plays from other academic disciplines, for example *Proof* for a math class. Modify theatre games to teach vocabulary or action sequences found in other disciplines (e.g., the math play *Proof* by David Auburn). Check out the interdisciplinary lesson plans on ArtsEdge from the Kennedy Center (artsedge.kennedy-center.org/educators/lessons.aspx) or Drama to the Core from Fairfax County Public Schools (fcps.blackboard.com) with username = artsvisitor and password = arts4u.

Back to Basics

More than anything else, the foundation of theatre is dramatic literature. It is the plays and playwrights, the study of what words mean and how they can come alive, that serves as the grist for the mill of theatre. The study of style, form, structure and language, as well as the creation of mood, and the sense of "voice" are all essential to the creation of great dramatic literature (and character development), and it's never too soon to give it a go, either!

How: Read plays aloud and alone; include "table work" that analyzes the language; teach dramatic criticism; playwriting can lead to incredibly rich results—even awards and productions. Use a student dramaturge as the research assistant on your productions.

The Whole Enchilada

Dramatic literature may be the foundation, but the walls, the carpeting, the framed pictures, and all the knick-knacks are what make the whole house, and that's technical theatre. Round out the experience of your students and build better productions by paying attention to the set, lighting, costumes—even stage management, budgeting, and publicity for a show, and not just one you are producing.

How: Trained or not, you are the expert and responsible for all technical aspects of your theatre program. So jump on in and learn both the art and the craft of stage lighting and sound, makeup and costumes, building sets and props, etc. Have students design costumes for any character they play. Teach basics of design. Make great show posters. Bring in local experts to teach what you can't—any nearby college is likely to be happy to provide someone.

Obviously, many of these approaches mix easily, and some don't. But you really won't have time to do everything, so make some conscious choices before you discover you've created an animal you don't really care for. Give some thought to your (and your school's) priorities and let them lead you to confident choices of how to move forward as you create your theatre program.

Real-World Moments

Mr. Rightoutofcollege came into a very successful theatre department that was selling video recordings of all of their productions to friends and family. Mr. Rightoutofcollege did not want to change his name to Mr. Gotfiredforillegalpractices, so he communicated to all concerned that video licensure from the play's publisher serves as a *legal* and appropriate model for the students to follow. Even though it was a transition for the drama boosters and students, Mr. Rightoutofcollege stood firm and transition quickly became tradition.

That Other Teaching You Do

The film *Mr. Holland's Opus* traces the life cycle of a high school music teacher from his wannabe composer aspirations while holding down a teaching job, to the realities of his life turning that job into his career, to the recognition that he has tremendously impacted hundreds of lives along the way—that *they* are his hugely successful opus. It includes a wonderful scene in which he is given a compass because, in addition to teaching music, he will be guiding the development of the moral compass of his students. And so will you.

Among the most valuable benefits of being a theatre educator is that the nature of the work lets you see the enormous arc of personal growth in your students over the years, and you can find the time (conventions can be great for this) to talk to them about their personal lives as they travel that arc. Of course one should never pry, but there will certainly be students who seek you out as a sounding board or a sympathetic ear about the drama in their lives. As an objective, trusted adult, you may be able to provide support they can find nowhere else in their lives. Just one warning: be clear that you are legally obligated *not* to keep secret any disclosure of abuse reported to you. Okay, two warnings: beware sharing details of your own personal life. Kids tend to be fascinated by that, but it sure can come back to bite you—their loyalties are intense but fickle.

Integrity

Integrity is doing what you say you're going to do and being honest about what happens. That readiness to take responsibility for one's actions, including the resulting consequences, is a quality not inherent in many students. You *will* come across students who damage things and keep it quiet rather than face you and the consequences. They behave as though any absence or lapse in judgment should have no consequence as long as their heart was pure and they can explain it. You will have kids who lie to your face about whether a homework assignment was done, how hard they worked on something, whether they followed your instructions, who said what to whom…the list goes on. What's more, their actions (even outside the classroom) reflect on your program and school, not just on them, despite their private intentions. Your response is what will help them build character or defend themselves even more intensely next time. Do hold kids accountable; stand by your standards; avoid public humiliation; recognize and praise integrity whenever you see it.

Resilience

In the era of helicopter parents, and the shift from teacher support to child defense, it can be difficult to stand by a decision that results in someone's baby being unhappy (that is, crushed, as in didn't get the role they had their heart set on or the grade they felt they deserved), especially when Mama Bear is sitting with you in the principal's office demanding you reverse your "unfair" decision that made her little cub miserable. But the ability to meet disappointment and roll with the punches—to learn to recover and move on from one's hopeful expectations—to fall down and get back up again—these are essential life skills. How much better to struggle through that development while still living at home with the parental support system, rather than to have mom and dad make everything always work out right every time, and delay those inevitable disappointments until that safety net is gone. Never reverse a casting decision—you will damage both the student who earned the role and your own authority. Instead, be thankful that the disappointed child has supportive parents who are there to help him/her develop that essential resilience that will be needed in the future.

Strength of Character

Strength of character can be quite the challenge as adolescents' primary influence transitions from parents to peers. As they strive for more independence, they can easily move away from lessons that keep them safe and making good choices. Friendships become all important, but that loyalty can be dangerous. Will students break their bond of loyalty to disclose that their friend is considering self-harm—even suicide—after being sworn to secrecy? Will they be able to speak out against bullying by one of their own in-crowd? Can they see that they are choosing friends who are leading them astray, out of fear of rejection and isolation? The character of your theatre department can get very cliquish, catty, even destructive if you let it. Or it can be that safe haven where relationships become the kind of family that everyone seeks—a family that that lasts a lifetime.

Industry and Excellence

In the arts, "good enough" is never good enough. You are lucky to be in a field where you will have many opportunities to bring together a diverse group of people and focus them toward a single goal which requires that every single one do their very best. And they will, if that's where you set the bar. A theatre program can be fun, or hard work, or the fun can come from the hard work. Help your students to recognize that the value of repetition with revision toward excellence—what we call rehearsal—can be applied to other subjects.

Would any real writer consider handing in a first draft the way so many students do? Would any actor consider putting their first rehearsal up in front of an audience? We are all about making our work better and better, working with incomplete information until we can fill in the pieces, and collaborating with others in pursuit of the best possible experience for our audience—and with no extensions on our due date. The show must go on, and you have great power to develop a sense of industry and excellence in your students.

One final note here: students are very keen at spotting hypocrisy. Practice what you preach and model the kind of behavior you hope to instill in your students.

Diversity in the Classroom and on Stage

American society is becoming increasingly diverse in every way possible: culture, race, socioeconomic level, and sexual orientation come to mind just to start the list. This is reflective of who we are: the great melting pot that collects the "huddled masses yearning to breathe free…" As a teacher, you must consider and respect all of these differences, regardless of your personal feelings. No one likes to feel judged—even in a humorous manner. Everyone likes to feel respected. Bottom line: don't assume—be sensitive and respectful. Your response to diversity will set the tone of everyone in the room.

It is important to establish an atmosphere of psychological safety and acceptance so that students are comfortable talking about their cultural heritage. In Theatre I, a lesson plan that requires students to explore and share their identity is helpful, since self-awareness is a great introduction to acting. Implement this lesson plan after the students have had some time to acclimate to each other and the openness of theatre, yielding more meaningful presentations. In subsequent levels of theatre study, discussion may be inspired by the text of different plays. Rather than assuming the common ground for discussion, ask questions that allow your students to create a respectful foundation for sharing ideas. Not everyone lives with two parents. Not everyone's childhood included those "standard" fairy tales. Not everyone is heterosexual. Not everyone's parents are heterosexual. Not everyone lives above the poverty line.

When discussing plays and casting, the time period may dictate certain choices if you wish to convey detailed period authenticity. On the other hand, Shakespeare, Moliere, Commedia, Kabuki and Bunraku offer opportunities for everyone to be everything—as long as they have the skills to create and convey character. Examining the text will give you academic, impersonal reasons to make choices that seem fair to your students, while simultaneously giving them the opportunity to explore conceptual choices and playwright intent.

As you choose materials to illustrate your class study of musical theatre history or famous American playwrights, make sure that you include a balanced list of resources for your students. Sure, we've all seen *Oklahoma!*—that iconic first fully-developed 1943 masterpiece—and certainly, we want all of our Theatre I students to finish the year knowing who Rodgers and Hammerstein are. But showing Hugh Jackman's filmed stage performance in England is probably a better choice than the oldie but goodie Shirley Jones version. They are both good films—but the more modern version, which has a more diverse cast and is actually a filmed stage performance—will resonate better with your students. It is also important to include African-American contributions to Broadway and Hollywood musical films such as *A Raisin in the Sun* and *Stormy Weather. In The Heights*, the Tony Award-winning musical set in a Dominican neighborhood, is another great show to offer your students for study. It presents the distinctly American immigrant dilemma of assimilation into a new society, combined with the struggle for preservation of familial culture. *Fiddler On The Roof* honors Jewish traditions and history. If you choose to produce any culturally dominated show, make sure that you research carefully with your students as part of the production process. Often, a student will offer to invite his/her grandmother from "the old country" who can come and enlighten your class or cast about the specifics of the culture in question. Again and again, the dominant word is *respect*—especially if you are not part of the culture in question.

Casting with Diversity in Mind

Since you are a theatre educator, not a Broadway director, you have the freedom and responsibility to be inclusive in your casting. Even on Broadway, "color-blind casting" has been in place ever since Pearl Bailey played the lead in *Hello, Dolly!* It is the ability to convey character and the talent to deliver the songs that matters in musical theatre. Gender choices, such as Julie Taymor's choice of Helen Mirren as Prospera, instead of the traditional male Prospero, are becoming increasingly flexible in the professional theatre and on film. As you explore these possibilities, make sure you discuss non-traditional choices with the publisher of your

Appendix 📄 Connection

In appendix F, we've included a lesson to help students define themselves and get to know each other, and in turn define a character—*Theatre I Identity Assignment: Who Am I?* Give it a try!

play; some playwrights are very particular about how their characters are portrayed, and if you mount a full production that requires royalties (as opposed to classroom study), you are bound by the terms of the contract.

Racial distinctions need not play into casting unless the play is about race and you choose to implement a concept that speaks to authenticity of time and place. This can be a slippery slope, however, depending on the demographics of your school. Our observation is that all students want to be respected, but most do not want the teacher to make statements that point them out as separate from others—after all, high school is all about finding your niche and belonging. If a student brings up race in a neutral, sensitive manner, that means that s/he has the maturity to handle the discussion. Make sure that your response is invitational and non-judgmental. Asking students what they think is usually a safe route for discussion; facilitate, don't dominate.

Casting Guidelines

Here are some educational theatre points to consider as you cast your high school production.

- Student gender may be flexible as long as there is no romantic interest—that's a different play.
- Student race/culture plays no part in casting unless the play is about race. Even then, theatre educators can choose color-blind casting.
- Talent, work ethic, focus and commitment win the role—as long as the student is right for it (e.g., a tenor can't sing a bass role.)
- If all things are *absolutely even*, a theatre student gets the role over someone who isn't officially enrolled in your program, and upperclassmen trump lowerclassmen. Look at your seniors carefully because they have grand expectations for their final year; hopefully, they have earned your consideration.
- As you make your choices, consider what will convey the playwright's intent. If you are true to that, you will make choices that do not distract the audience from the imagined journey of the play. What will assist the journey? What will distract the audience from the journey? These are great questions to use as guidelines in concept and casting consideration.

Building Use and You

Building use refers to whomever is allowed to use the school building and when. This term often refers to groups outside of school who wish to rent the auditorium for dance recitals,

Real-World Moments

Upon reading a play out loud in theatre class, some of my students expressed concern about a few terms used in the script, including "redskins." We had a spirited discussion about whether these terms would disrupt the audience's suspension of disbelief, and agreed that they probably would. One student declared, "We should not be concerned with whether it will distract the audience; we should be concerned with doing what is right." Another student asserted that changing a single word in a classic script would be offensive. I wrote the publisher and asked for three small adjustments to the language of the script; a few weeks later, we were granted the changes. The show was very well received by our community.

religious celebrations, or community functions. When run properly, building use can bring in a lot of revenue for the school, as well as provide custodians and student technicians with opportunities to make money. While building use may be more limited in elementary and middle school, on the high school level this is usually coordinated through the Director of Student Activities office. If building use is not coordinated through the DSA's office, find out who is responsible for it—in some cases the theatre director coordinates building use—it could be *you*!

Collaborating and Coordinating Building Use

If you are fortunate enough to collaborate with an administrative assistant to the Director of Student Activities in the high school in which you work, count yourself lucky. Ideally,

Appendix Connection

You can find a template for those who want your help with lighting or sound, etc. in appendix C, *Tech Help Request Form*. Distribute it early and widely, and require its use.

this person keeps the calendar for everything that is happening everywhere on your high school campus every day and night of the school year and beyond. Not only are they efficient, but they are experienced in making the school community a priority so that school events are not in conflict with outside community building use commitments. This person forwards the invoices to the theatre director that include how many student technicians will be needed for an event outside of school hours; this includes the date, hours, and equipment required for the job. You train the student technicians in class and help them with the employment process, then book your new techies for different building use jobs according to their availability.

If you don't have a technical theatre class, an after-school technical theatre "club" could work; give hours toward Thespian points and/or extra credit for theatre students to increase appeal. This is a win-win situation for all concerned—the students have an opportunity to assume additional real-world responsibility for which they are paid, and the user group gets a relatively inexpensive student technician who is familiar with the equipment needed for their event. Although it is certainly additional work, training student technicians and facilitating temporary employment opportunities for them is a great way to make your tech class relevant and demonstrate your valuable service to your school community. Often students who get paid to work as student technicians have a greater understanding of and commitment to maintaining the space. It also doesn't hurt your credibility as theatre director—students must have your approval to work. Maturity, dependability, expertise and the critical *trust* factor are all important criteria for those chosen to work building use gigs.

Protecting Your Students and Your Equipment

The typical building use job involves a trained high school technical theatre student who can run basic sound and lights for a school or community event that takes place outside the school day.

An equipment checklist includes:

- Hand-held microphone(s) and XLR cables
- CD player that works through your sound system
- Adapter for smartphone sound playback
- Basic house and stage lighting
- A projection screen (push the button that raises and lowers it)
- Follow spot(s)

Equipment you might choose *not* to include for outside users:

- Cyclorama (too expensive)
- Scrim (too easy to tear)

- Projectors (too difficult to secure)
- Wireless microphones (too fragile, finicky)
- Moving/intelligent lights (too complicated)

School events should be your priority and receive more of your time and resources than you might typically give to outside user groups. This is because with users from within your own school there is usually more time to prepare and better accountability with regard to facilities and equipment.

For school events outside of the school day hours, users should pay student technicians for both rehearsals and performances. While the band concert probably only needs basic stage lighting and one hand-held microphone to announce each number, the fashion show, step team or show choir events can be opportunities for your techs to design and work with other departments, using the full array of equipment available at your school. Make sure that your students keep you in the loop since they may not realize all the consequences of their technical plans—it's up to you to connect the big picture to the details of the current project. For example: refocusing the lights to use a scrim effectively for the show choir may not work with the time allotted for dry tech required for the musical the following week. On the other hand, keeping backstage litter picked up and fire exits clear works for everyone all the time.

Making Yourself a Valuable Guardian

The biggest argument for requiring that your students run building use equipment is to protect the investment your school has made (in the thousands) for sound and lighting. This is also the equipment necessary for teaching your tech theatre class and to do your shows, so there's a triple investment in terms of curriculum, fund-raising, and community expectations (equipment in good condition=better shows). When a circus of people who are inconsistently trained and unfamiliar with your equipment intrude upon your tech booth, there is little accountability for damage and/or abuse. If outside users want more complex sound and lights, then they can set up their own equipment in the house—no one should touch your school's equipment other than your trained techs and you.

The Tech Booth and its Protocol

The tech booth is also a teaching space which can become a social gathering space for untrained personnel, resulting in food, drinks and the plethora of issues that arise when a professional space becomes a social space. It's tough enough training your teenage students to see the tech booth as a work space, let alone adults who set a bad example or leave behind a mess for you and your students to clean up. *This is a battle worth fighting!* Try to be proactive with this subject and find out what current procedures are. Most principals will support your quest for making the tech booth a professional, *instructive space,* and training your students to see it that way. A consistently dependable method for coordinating building use is one less item for administrative concern.

Assuming that you've trained your students to treat the space and equipment with respect, the next expectation to communicate to all concerned is how these student technicians are to be treated when you are not around. A posted list of tech booth expectations is helpful (see figure 2.1), the first line in bold: **"ONLY AUTHORIZED THEATRE TECHNICIANS ARE ALLOWED IN THE BOOTH."** No one but the assigned student technician is allowed to touch the equipment. There should be no gathering of well-meaning parents or impromptu "assistants." The only people in the tech booth should be the assigned student technicians (no girlfriends, boyfriends, or last year's seniors) and the faculty adviser assigned for the event. User needs can be communicated outside of the booth, in an open space, such as the house. This is crucial to your students avoiding distractions and keeping them *safe* from uncomfortable situations in a relatively small, private space.

If a stranger comes into the tech booth during a show or building use job, the student technician should have the authority to ask the stranger to leave. This is a tough call for a lot of really nice, polite kids who want to do a good job, but it is essential. A walkie-talkie or cell phone call to the faculty adviser is a good communication choice so students have back-up in their resolve. Paid student technicians are usually between 16 and 18 years old, so a stranger in the booth with a minor is simply not acceptable, no matter how good their intentions might be: *don't allow it.* If an additional adult needs to take photos from the tech booth or clarify something about the event, the faculty adviser must introduce that person to the student technician who can then use his/her judgment to decide whether or not to stay in the booth. Use this same logic to keep student friends and former student techs out of the booth during rehearsals and performances. Be consistent with your assertion that the tech booth is a work space, not a social space.

Equipment

Theatre equipment will vary widely from school to school. Depending on your own level of knowledge and experience, you may need to ask for assistance—whether from students, colleagues, school system experts or outside professionals. Here's an annotated list of the equipment you might have available in a typical theatre program.

Computers

You may be required to use a computer for attendance, grading, or implementing programs approved by your school system. Medical flags and IEPs may also exist primarily online. Since more and more paper is being eliminated all the time, plan to spend a lot of time at

TECH BOOTH RULES

1. **ONLY AUTHORIZED THEATRE TECHNICIANS ARE ALLOWED IN THE BOOTH.**

2. No food or drink near electrical equipment.

3. The booth is not a lounge or a locker.

4. Check in with the user. Find out what they need. Be helpful. Check out with them when the event is finished.

5. Take great notes—use your cue sheets.

6. Stay focused on the task at hand.

7. Avoid distracting the audience or performers.

8. Report any equipment problems as soon as possible.

9. Shut down all equipment when finished, and store microphones or other portable items.

10. Assure the booth is left secured.

Figure 2.1: A typical list of rules for the tech booth

your computer screen—and hope it's connected to a printer that works. Get to know and love your IT folks!

Students who use computers must be monitored. One way to do this is by using a sign-in/out sheet to permit back-tracking of who might have abused their computer privileges. (Remember mouse balls? Kids were fond of removing those, for example, but even hard drives have gone missing!) Different schools filter out different online content, so you may find yourself unable to access various sites (Is YouTube a blessing or a curse?) Sometimes you can argue successfully to have a blocked site made available, such as a music site for access to sound effects for a show. Good luck! In any event, you will have to work actively to keep kids on task while using online resources. Work closely with your school librarians—they love helping out, and there is a wealth of legitimate resources that can be provided with some expert assistance.

If it's helpful in your situation, have the IT folks create an online folder for *DRAMA* that you can use for production related items outside of class requirements. Your non-student show participants may need access to this folder, and it's a great place to park documents such as cue sheets, finance, publicity, and program templates you can reuse from show to show.

Laptops provide better mobility, and more risk of damage from dropping and theft, so really read the riot act to kids before letting those loose. This is even more true for tablets.

Personal devices, whether laptops, tablets or smart phones, are likely to be subject to particular school policies of registration and use, but can also really expand the opportunities for quick access to research information. Be sure your policy is crystal clear as to when electronics may be used, and when they are subject to confiscation.

A portable hard drive—too large for easy pocketing—can be a terrific way to store sound effects, pre-show announcements, background music, etc. that was collected in one place for use in another.

Personnel Lift

If you have access to a powered personnel lift, you will easily be able to reach backdrop battens, lighting fixtures, overhead mic inputs and tall set pieces. With proper training, students can be "licensed" to use these safely, too, a tremendous benefit to all. The Powerlift corpo-

Appendix 📄 Connection

A copy of the sign you might want to post on your tech booth is also available in appendix D, *Tech Booth Rules*. You can also download a copy from EducationalStages.com.

ration makes the most popular brand, the Genie Lift, and can provide training materials. Sending kids up 15 or 20 feet can really scare administrators, so be viciously vigilant about using such equipment properly and according to the rules at all times!

Projectors

LCD PROJECTORS Once you figure out the right connections and adjustments, LCD projectors work great to display computer or other images, whether in class or as part of a production.

GOBO PROJECTORS If you just need to project one image in your show, this projector—Chauvet makes one—you can take a transparency printed from a computer image and use it like a slide. Cheap effects!

OVERHEAD PROJECTORS These may be on the way out, but are still very useful for creating road signs and banners. Print the design onto a transparency, project with one of these, and trace!

OPAQUE PROJECTORS These don't need a transparency or computer; they can project the image from a book, magazine or printout onto a screen. There are several lightweight versions made by Elmo (www.elmousa.com/education).

SMARTBOARD An interactive projection screen, this technological wonder projects a computer image that can be manipulated right at the screen by tapping and dragging. You can also write on it in a few colors with the special pens designed to do so. The uses are endless. Play on!

Lighting Console

You'll be expected to help the school with auditorium lighting and you'll have to teach others, too. So buck up, find the brand and model number on there somewhere, and hit the internet to find the support documentation, trying out each step as you read it. If that seems too overwhelming, solicit support and instruction from your school system tech specialist, another theatre teacher or the local sound and lighting company. It is worth some time at the beginning of your job to set up user-friendly lighting and sound systems in your auditorium; you must be able to provide simple sound and lights for a school assembly instantly. You are sure to have a couple of kids very eager to learn the intricacies of lighting, and they will put in the time to get really good at it for your productions. You and the students can learn together.

Sound System

Same as above: solicit assistance or instruction to create a user-friendly system. Read the instruction manual—it's online somewhere! Remember that sound works like a chain, or computer code: each step leads to the next, and even one piece missing or damaged will bring everything to a halt. The first thing to check with wireless microphones is user error—an actor who accidentally turned off a body mic pack—then battery life and signal reception on the individual receiver boxes, then connectors (hardware and cables), or something not plugged in properly. Nothing beats a thorough mic/sound check to strategically problem-solve *before* the show starts. You may also want to lock up the very portable, valuable wireless microphones upon which your school depends.

Other Theater Equipment

Your theater may have a movie screen, curtains, or electric battens (on which your lights hang) that are controlled electronically instead of manually. Find out! You may also be asked to project a laptop image or DVD onto the screen, and pipe the audio through the auditorium sound system. Oh, so much to learn!

Supplies

You will be purchasing a wide variety of supplies such as lumber, paint, batteries, masking tape, etc. Find out if your school system has preferred vendors whose prices are greatly discounted.

Your stage lights will eventually need new light bulbs (called lamps). You may order these online or buy them from a theatre supply house. When you are ready to make a purchase, make sure you have the three-letter code which identifies that particular bulb or lamp. If necessary, you can bring a lamp with you to the supply house to make sure you are getting the right lamp. Be sure not to touch the glass of a working lamp with your fingers lest you damage it.

If you've got a local vendor, go when you've got some time (LOL!) and learn tons from a nice, long chat and look-see around their shop. No time? Ask their sales rep to come out and assess your needs to create user-friendly tech systems in your auditorium. S/he can teach you plenty, even if you don't place an order then.

Ask other theaters or colleagues where they get their audio supplies. Online vendors are plentiful, of course. Shure and Audio-Technica make microphones and sound equipment that are durable, effective and within a reasonable budget. Crowne makes a sturdy floor mic for stage use.

Educational Software

So much, and changing so often, but here are some popular ones as of this writing.

BLACKBOARD compiles assignments, documents and audio-visual material for class use by a school or school system. It's very robust, and if available, you will probably be required to use it in a variety of ways. Competitors include Sakai, Canvas, Edmodo, Moodle and others.

GOOGLE has many apps of great use with your students, and for your productions. Create a form that becomes a database of students to track payments for field trips, books loaned out, etc. Use a spreadsheet to track your show expenses. Have your students write their cast biographies for the program. The list goes on!

GOOGLE APPS FOR EDUCATION is an enterprise version of several Google apps, but behind a fire wall that keeps the students' information within the school system, without access to the outside world. With this, students can share information with you or each other, fill out forms you create, and store documents from classes or productions. Everything auto-saves, so work will not get lost or forgotten, and you will hear no more excuses about printers running out of ink!

For a new show, if you can access a bunch of computers, each stage crew can fill in its column in a show spreadsheet you set up, noting each requirement as it comes up in the initial read-through. By the end of day one (or two), you can have starter cue sheets for the entire production! The email account can be used to report tardies or absences from rehearsals, too, and the calendar works great to post your rehearsal schedule. Then no one can claim they didn't know they had to be at rehearsal or that they didn't know a class assignment was due.

You can also create a form to fill out at the start of the year, to collect student (and parent) information, and use the spreadsheet that automatically creates to track book loans, payments received, forms returned, special needs, etc.

Theatre Software

There may be many hoops to jump through to purchase or even download free versions of software, but there are lots of applications out there that can be very helpful indeed. Here are a few suggestions to get you started, but there are many other resources.

HOW TO *YouTube.com* is stuffed with how-to clips. Why reinvent the wheel if you can find what you need to teach online—good for a "flipped classroom" approach, too.

SOUND *Audacity* is a useful sound recorder and editor, which can also layer sounds. For Mac users, *Garageband* should do the job nicely. And there are tons of sound effects sites out there, too, both free and paid.

LIGHTING *Virtual Light Lab* shows you a black box theatre on your screen, with an object in the center and grids all around on which one can hang lights. Use it to experiment with the impact of angle, distance, intensity and color (including all current gel colors from all major manufacturers).

SET DESIGN *Sketchup* is very user-friendly, and is much less complicated than the industry standard, *Vectorworks*. It's also a free download. Create and see your work in 3-D!

STAGE MANAGEMENT *StageWrite* is an iPad app for recording blocking. It's both expensive and clever.

PLAYWRITING *Celtx* charges a monthly fee for group use, but is excellent at formatting the writing of scripts for stage or screen.

For Reflection & Discussion

What traditions and expectations might there be for you to embrace or resist. . . or create at your new school?

1. You hear that each show's final rehearsal is done as a "fun run" with students swapping costumes, heckling, and throwing in new lines to try to make the others break character. You announce the end of that tradition, and two seniors—in significant roles—walk out of the rehearsal. What's your next move?

2. The cast and crew typically buy show shirts for publicity and as souvenirs of the production, but your pit musicians have had theirs paid for as a production expense. Is this divisive or supportive? Do you change this scenario? How?

3. Costumes have been rented in the past, and as a result of this huge expense, the shows never really turn a profit. But it is easier, and they do look good. Should you continue this tradition? Other options?

4. How might you "brand" your new theatre department to increase its visibility and the self esteem of the participants?

5. The pep rally is coming up and you'd like your improv team of "act-letes" to be included among all the other teams being presented to the school, but your students are afraid of being heckled. What do you do?

6. A huge Halloween haunted house has been sponsored annually by the theatre department but you don't know how that's supposed to work, and it seems likely to pull lots of energy from your fall show due to open shortly thereafter. What should you do?

7. When you arrive for your new job, you're informed that you're also going to teach IB Theatre, or some other elective choice outside your training and expertise. How can you get up to speed on that material, or at least stay ahead of the kids?

3 Preparing for the Classroom

RELATED APPENDIX DOCUMENTS

- Organizing Labels for Mailboxes (Appendix G, p. 274)
- Program Overview (Appendix H, p. 276)
- Sample Syllabi for Various Classes (Appendix I, p. 279)
- Suggested Materials (Appendix J, p. 292)

Now that you've got the lay of the land, so to speak, it's time to pin down the particulars of working with your students. Your teaching and daily schedule might include mixing different levels of students, or a mix of acting plus tech students. You might be assigned to more than one department, perhaps even more than one school. Where can you find ready-to-use lesson plans? What approaches to the material might you take? What if you have special-needs kids in your classes? How can you best handle disruptive students? How close can you get with your students? How can you keep all the lines of communication open?

Your Class Schedule

On the one hand, as the newbie, it would be rare indeed if you had any say about which classes you will teach and when. On the other hand, your class schedule has perhaps as much impact on how your day/year goes as anything else you can name. Your "preparations" are the different classes you have to prepare for, regardless of how many sections you teach of each. Many teachers teach five classes but have only two preparations. You may well have five

53

"preps," (perhaps even more, if you have a combined class such as acting and tech together), a true burden, but such is the life of an electives teacher. On the off chance that you get a say, here are some thoughts:

- The fewer the "preps" you have, the better for your sanity and time management.
- A planning period at the end of the class day gives you time to prepare for after-school rehearsals, and might permit a field trip to a matinee without needing a sub.
- A planning period in the middle of the day gives you a chance to catch your breath, make some calls, and think ahead some—or perhaps avoid rushing through lunch.
- A planning period at the beginning of the day tempts you to prepare at the last minute, but also provides the possibility of doing so. It also makes it harder to make business calls (how many theatre supply vendors are up as early as you?).
- Multiple sections of the same prep taught on the same day minimize the chance of getting out of sync. You will want to keep the same classes doing the same thing at the same time whenever possible.
- If you must teach other subjects, other electives may require fewer after-school hours grading papers, leaving more time for rehearsal.
- Think carefully about whether to overload enrollment in a class—although it may allow for under-enrollment in another class. This can cut both ways, depending on the kids who enroll.
- Think carefully about whether to combine class levels in order to boost enrollment to the minimum necessary for the class to be taught, and which classes to combine.
- Try to find out whether a particular class conflicts with a competing elective meeting at the same time, for example, what if Advanced Theatre and Advanced Chorus meet at the same time? Your musical theatre kids will want to take both, so try to get them scheduled during different periods.
- A split lunch (class/break for lunch/return to class) works best for younger theatre students. They benefit from shorter work times, and are less likely to have costume changes to deal with during class. Generally, it's a pain. It may, however, open the possibility of a working lunch in your classroom from time to time.
- In a school using block scheduling (longer classes held on alternating days), advanced classes will have time to prepare/perform/critique/clean up during that one long class. Shorter daily classes best fit the attention span of Theatre I/younger students. While it can be a treat to see your most enthusiastic and dedicated kids every day, each class is frustratingly short for the older students. Older and technical theatre students can easily use the whole long block for productive work.

As you gain seniority and get to know the guidance counselors and those who do the scheduling, you may be able to have input on these options. Choose wisely and reap the rewards.

Mixing Theatre Classes

A reality of many schools is that enrollment and staffing money may be limited, which results in multiple levels of theatre courses being combined into a single class—and those combinations can be quite daunting indeed. Theatre 1-2-3-4? Technical Theatre I with IB Theatre? Classes of 40 in one room? Trying to teach different courses at the same time is awfully tricky business. But since basic theatre skills are recursive (i.e., taught early and then improving over time with increasingly challenging material), it is possible to construct a mixed-level class that doesn't cause you to self-destruct.

Try to Talk Your Way Out of It

Nothing ventured, nothing gained—so it may be productive to approach your head of guidance (Student Services/Instructional Services) with the safety and educational concerns of combining classes that by all rights should be taught separately or in smaller groups. But do go in with your ducks in a row, and perhaps that one crazy class will morph into two smaller, more manageable ones. Stranger things have happened!

Construct One Basic Curriculum

Each mixed-level class can implement different levels or aspects of the same basic curriculum. This may not be ideal, but it is a survival tactic for you from which your students will benefit. There is no need to have part of the class working on improvisation while you try to teach Shakespeare to the others! The flip side of this is that you can tailor your assess-

---

Appendix 📄 Connection

Wherever you end up, keeping all your information organized is critical. If you can get or make some "pigeon-holes" (Staples calls these Classroom Keepers) for your handouts and items students hand in, you can make labels like those in appendix G, *Organizing Labels for Mailboxes*, by using the modifiable version online at EducationalStages.com.

ment/expectations to the skill level of the individual student. Freshmen may see a scene in terms of learning lines and not bumping into the furniture. Older students should be able to follow more complex directions, while advanced students should be able to initiate strong, fitting and creative choices on their own.

Share the Responsibility

Let your advanced students serve as student directors or stage managers. Taking on more responsibility for artistic decisions is a natural progression. Be sure to supervise them, of course (journals and plenty of spot-checks). They can research and prepare presentations on topics that you will be covering with the entire class—there's no better way to learn than to teach!

Scene Material Selection

The scripts that students explore for scene work present another opportunity for differentiation within a mixed-course class. If students select their own material (under your watchful eye), each student can work on an appropriate challenge. Or you can select material of various levels and offer a different collection to the different levels (but that may take up more of your time!).

Perks and Passes

It may be appropriate to give a pass to your younger students on some assignments that the upper level students are required to do. And it may be appropriate to offer some perks (e.g., attending the local state theatre convention or field trips) only to your upper class students. This won't change the day-to-day operation of your classroom, and it can reduce your workload without cutting down on opportunities for your students.

Balance Ensemble Work with Solo Work

Sometimes the whole group will benefit from working as one, and the young-uns will rise to the challenge. Sometimes the older students need to be unfettered and work to the best of their own ability—audition pieces work well for this. Younger students will often benefit just by watching the older ones at work.

Acting Mixed with Technical Theatre

Lighting, sound, makeup, costumes, publicity, props, painting, stage management, oh my! This is a big challenge because there is *so* much material to learn about technical theatre

> ## "Theatre" vs. "Theater"
> European vs. American? The art vs. the facility? As a theatre educator, take a stand and stick with it (and only accent the first syllable!). In this book we use the spelling "theatre" when referring to the art form and the spelling "theater" when referring to a venue or actual theater building.

alone, and supervision is so much more important when tools and electricity are involved. Train everyone in theatre and shop safety. Actors don't get to be "less safe!" If you can get a couple of upper-class students with theatre experience to take the class and accept leadership roles, these mentors can be of tremendous assistance to you. Recruit if needed!

Alternating Days

Switching out which days are "acting days" and which are "tech days" is likely to leave your supervision sorely lacking and everyone frustrated. Same problem with a half-the-period approach. Be consistent with your scheduling.

Production Teams

Divide the actors into pairs or small groups, each with one or more techies assigned to them. Let them find (or give them) a small scene to work on, and start each class with one group presenting their progress to the class. Whether it's a cold reading, a work in progress, or a finished product, there will be plenty on which to comment, both in terms of the acting and of the tech. Those notes can serve as the rubric for grading their next turn. Then send the actors off to rehearse while the techies learn new stuff from you or go off to their own supportive work sessions to enhance the scene. By the time each group has had a turn, that first group should have improved their scene as instructed, and so on, until each group has had enough turns to present a solid finished product—or they run out of time before the next unit.

Production Company

If you can find the right material, combining the classes into one production company working on a show for public presentation—you will *always* get better results when there's going to be a real audience—can unite a mixed class like this. Treat it like an after-school production, with technical crews, stage managers, student (assistant) directors, etc. All members of the company must be ready to assist each other, so direct all the basic technical training at the entire ensemble. Kids who are idle due to the scene work of the day can run lines, develop character biographies, design their character's costumes, help the techies, etc. Techies who are idle can do design work for some future show, help the actors run lines or do maintenance work in the shop. Slackers can always sort bolts by size or gels by color…*somebody* has to do that stuff! If you have access to computers, there is always work that can be done independently.

Teaching at Multiple Locations

It is not unusual for a teacher to be split between two (or even three) schools, especially upon initial entrance to a school system. You lack seniority to pick and choose, so you take what you can get. Like any other teaching situation, having your schedule split between two schools has its challenges and advantages.

The Challenges

Obviously, the top challenge of traveling between schools is having to keep careful track of where you are supposed to be and when. If you have any influence in how your schedule pans out, try to get the end of the day closer to home so that your commute doesn't include too much backtracking. Teaching at more than one school means that you must be ultra-organized. It also means that you must collaborate with two completely different sets of colleagues and administrations, so keep your eyes and ears open. If you are fortunate, you will be the second theatre educator at each of these locations, which means you need to be a proactive listener and observer, as well as an avid assimilator to a department culture that you did not create. Stand up for your professional ethics if there are conflicts, but in general, ask questions about how you can fit into the existing culture, and how you can assist the pri-

Appendix 📄 Connection

Constructing a syllabus is a very personal thing, and influenced by the requirements of your school system. But to get you started, we have included some samples in appendices H and I which include a *Theatre Program Overview* and *Sample Syllabi for Various Classes*, including IB Theatre.

mary theatre educator. If you remain at one or both of your schools, a natural collaboration should evolve; chances are, however, that you will move on to a one-school position at your earliest opportunity.

The Advantages

The position of assistant theatre director or "the other theatre educator" can be a critical growth experience, because it often allows you to put more of your focus on teaching rather than building a program. You also have the opportunity to learn from another theatre educator who may have more experience than you do.

If you are split between two schools, chances are that you will commit your time and energy more ardently to one of them, especially when it comes to after-school activities. The school where you finish the day is the logical choice for offering your after-school assistance—providing you also collaborate well with the primary theatre educator. It is completely appropriate to tell the theatre director at the other school that you are giving most of your after-school time to the program at which you finish the day; this makes your choice less personal and more logical—simply professional. You may still wish to offer your time and talents to the other school's department occasionally, as requested, or as it suits you.

Do remember to keep some time for yourself and your life! You are not the lead theatre director at either program, so less is expected of you; enjoy this learning opportunity for healthy shared responsibilities and don't get caught up in petty rivalry or ego games.

If your time is split between a high school program and its feeder middle school program and you are the only theatre educator between the two, rejoice! You can build the middle school program that will feed your high school program—the reciprocal advantages make every hour you spend at either school doubly worth the effort. If permitted, consider casting a few middle-schoolers in your large cast high school shows, and invite the middle school improv team to participate in a high school tournament or festival. Likewise, get your high school technicians over to the middle school to support the younger thespians; *everyone wins!*

Another advantage of working at more than one school is the legitimate excuse of trying to keep up with two schools—perhaps two different schools' schedules. Most administrators respect your dilemma and excuse you from faculty meetings and many other "time-sucks" that full-time-at-one-school teachers are expected to attend. You can achieve a liberated mindset when working at two schools—you can truly focus on teaching the students as some of the other building expectations fall away to someone else or schedule conflicts. During those weeks when you have to participate in two back-to-school nights, comfort yourself with this fact: you have a full-time job! *Yay!*

Career Choices and Trade-Offs

If your double school duty consists of chief theatre director at one school and overflow educator at another, grin and bear it for a year or two, with the plan of building enrollment so that your commute to another school becomes unnecessary. You may also wish to have a discussion with your administration about other singleton classes, in the school where most of your classes are, that might be available in the upcoming year. Perhaps there is a film or speech class that you could add to your class load to create a full schedule for you at that school.

If you are the assistant director at both schools, two basic choices—with infinite variations, of course—are clear: either get comfortable in that position or seek transfer. Before considering transfer, however, take stock of the advantages of your situation as assistant director: *shared* time on task in the after-school activities, a fellow professional with whom to constantly confer and vent, and the diminished degree of stress that results from daily partnership of theatre educators. While you may tire of playing second fiddle, being the lone wolf, large-and-in-charge theatre director is not always what it's cracked up to be. Much of this depends on how functional and fulfilling your ensemble teaching relationship is; make choices that fit your long-term career plan. What can you learn from your present situation? Do you still feel challenged and that you are growing as an educator? Are you ready for a change? Even if you choose to move on, you may find yourself longing for the days of less responsibility even though it means coordinating your multiple school schedule.

Technical Theatre

If you have a solid background in technical theatre, you are in the lucky minority. And whether you do or not, you will still be the local expert on every aspect of theatre from acting and playwriting to set and lighting design, from costumes and makeup to publicity and tickets. What's new is that your tech help is likely to be very inexperienced, your resources (money, tools, equipment, storage space, and work space) very limited, and your time unbelievably scarce. The more you can teach in class, the better your productions; the better your productions, the more students you can draw to your classes.

Don't know where to begin? Use *Teaching TECH* in the Book Appendix section of our website, EducationalStages.com. This 100-page document covers the basics of all aspects of tech theatre, with links to more detail, quizzes and safety information.

Thanks to Fairfax County Public Schools, Fairfax, Virginia for permitting us to share this document.

Survival Tactics

The Iron Triangle: good/fast/cheap. It's true that you can only get two of the three, and at the cost of the third. So do your best to give up *fast*—start early, schedule time for errors/absences/surprises, and set all deadlines *way* ahead of what you may have been used to in college or community theatre.

Delegation is a survival skill for the educational theatre instructor and coach. You get the final say on all matters artistic and financial, but that doesn't mean you have to do (or even know how to do) all the work. Giving students responsibility through leadership pays huge rewards. They are more likely to offer solutions to each others' problems, and their investment in the project will be contagious. Meet with these folks every single week, and your whole production will benefit. Think of the time you can put to other uses if students do these jobs instead of you. Treat them well!

Defining the Roles of the Production Team in Class

Details for each job are in chapter 4: Preparing for Production, but any training for these jobs that you provide during class time will be beneficial indeed. You could even modify these roles so students get practice doing production jobs by assisting you in the classroom, like this:

ASSISTANT DIRECTOR Your "right hand," able to use good artistic judgment even in your (brief) absence

PRODUCTION/BUSINESS MANAGER Helps track equipment and money coming in and out for supplies and field trips

DRAMATURGE First to jump online to answer any research question that comes up

TECHNICAL DIRECTOR Keeps an eye on all the equipment and supplies, and reports needed repairs or problems

STAGE MANAGER (and Assistant Stage Managers) Helps with crowd control and record keeping so you can stay on task. Can oversee the other crew chiefs

SET DESIGN Can select and assign furniture items to be used in class projects

SET CONSTRUCTION Assures tools and equipment are put back in place after any work session

SET DECORATION Bulletin boards, imagination boards, and props beyond the necessary

PAINTING Checks that all paint has been put away and brushes thoroughly washed out!

PUBLICITY Reaches out to other classes and/or parents when it's time to share class scenes

TICKETS Tracks paperwork and money for any class trips to see performances, etc.

HOUSE MANAGER Greets visitors, assures classroom is left clean

PROGRAM Helps put your daily class itinerary on the board

RUNNING CREW Assures set pieces, chairs, etc. are put away tidily before the next class arrives

LIGHTING Runs lights for class scenes

SOUND Runs sound for class scenes

PROPS Tracks loans and maintenance of prop items borrowed/used for class scenes

COSTUMES Checks out/in stock costume items

WARDROBE Helps the costumes person

MAKEUP Orders makeup kits/supplies for class workshop use

SPECIAL EFFECTS Whatever special events might come up (e.g., a Halloween classroom makeover)

Lesson Plans

What to teach? And when? That's not the focus of this text, but we do have some thoughts—and frankly, just Googling "theatre lesson plans" will lead you to some pretty interesting possibilities. You may be required to post your syllabus and/or distribute it on the first day of classes, and indeed, the more you can plan out your year, the easier it will be when the craziness of production is upon you. Even if you find out you're way off on the timing, you'll at least have a blueprint from which to make changes. A couple of sample syllabi are in appendix H and I.

Your school system may have a program of studies, or some such, which identifies what should be taught in each year of study, but it's not likely to pin down what plays to use or how to go about any of it. The IB Theatre program divides the discipline into Theatre in Context, Theatre Processes, and Presenting Theatre. Pretty broad, eh? So you have a lot of latitude in selecting your units of study.

Do investigate what scripts and texts have been left by your predecessor, so you can target specific choices to the materials you have at hand. Add to them as time and money allow. Jump in and include technical theatre right away to help build a program in which your students think in terms of the whole theatre experience, not just their own time onstage, and get over—or help you get over—the fear of "techie" things.

Online Resources for Lesson Plans

These links were live as of press time, but things change fast. No endorsement as to the quality or usefulness of individual lessons is implied:

ABOUT.COM CANADA K-8 theatre lesson plans for Canadian teachers; high school plans link to Brigham Young University Theatre Education database. (canadaonline.about.com/od/dramalessons)

ARTsEDGE LESSONS A variety of arts and cross-curricular lesson plans with high appeal graphics, media links and templates provided by the John F. Kennedy Center for the Performing Arts. (artsedge.kennedy-center.org/educators/lessons.aspx)

FCPS BLACKBOARD Go to Community/Theatre Arts/Lessons, Tchr Resources and/or Dra-ma to the Core, a set of lesson plans that use theatre skills to teach tricky areas of core subjects. Some lesson plan links not open to visitors. (fcps.blackboard.com sign in with username "artsvisitor" and password "arts4u")

IMPROV ENCYCLOPEDIA Improv made easy on this well-organized website of terms, games and activities. (improvencyclodpedia.org)

LESSONPLANET Broad range of lesson plans for many subjects and grade levels, including theatre; free log-in membership required to fully access lesson plans. (lessonplanet.com)

PUBLIC SCHOOLS OF NORTH CAROLINA North Carolina Theatre Arts Curriculum, containing links to lesson plans, complete with assessments, objectives and curricular connections. (dpi.state.nc.us/curriculum/artsed/resources/handbook/theatrearts)

SHAREMYLESSON A plethora of lesson plans, including study of Stanislavski, for various grade levels and Common Core information; AFT affiliation, but membership not apparently required for access. Requires a log in and password to access lesson plans. (sharemylesson.com/high-school-drama-teaching-resources)

TEACHER PLANET The Drama Teacher's Resource Room provides featured lessons and links to drama lesson plans. (lessonplans4teachers.com/drama.php)

TEACHNOLOGY Broad range of lesson plans for many subjects and grade levels, including theatre; no membership required. (teachnology.com)

THEATRETEACHERS.COM Theatre games, cast bonding and ensemble activities, many from Broadway workshop sessions.

You might start by asking what you want your Theatre II students to know and be able to do when they enter the class; these are the same skills and knowledge you need to provide to your Theatre I students, and so on. Admittedly, the start of the year is very hectic, but forcing yourself to have a long term game plan will pay off month after month after month.

Theatre: Art in Action is an excellent source of teaching materials, complete with alternate syllabi, a teacher's manual and a resource binder of handouts and projections for illustration. It covers both acting and tech, and could become all you need for four years of teaching. Expensive and worth it.

Methods of Teaching Theatre

Theatre is such a broad-ranging subject that there are many, many ways to "skin the cat." Each theatre educator brings his or her own style to the job, and you will undoubtedly develop your own. Even school districts with specific programs of study (or the International Baccalaureate program) to guide you provide plenty of room for choice and variety in both content and delivery style. There are many methods for delivery of material, development of skills, and both formative and summative assessment. Here are some:

Lecture

Woe to the theatre teacher who uses stand-and-deliver as his or her primary method of instruction—but there are indeed times when a good, old fashioned lecture or chalk-talk (or its whiteboard equivalent) while students take notes is the smartest course of action. This is what your administrator is often looking for when they need to watch your class to evaluate you and ask if you "are going to be teaching tomorrow?"

Theatre Games

Hundreds of theatre games are out there to meet every sort of need, from building ensemble to developing concentration. They are on-your-feet activities that kids tend to really enjoy, and they can be used to introduce other ideas, to reinforce skills, etc. They are your best bet for starting out the school year, to help everyone get to know each other (and you), for daily warm-ups, and to return to during spare moments throughout the year.

Improvisation

Another staple of theatre classwork, improvisation (improv) has many forms, from character development exercises to long form improvisation such as The Harold, to competitive improv à la *Whose Line is It Anyway?* or TheatreSports. Be sure to check out the "mother of all improvisation" (and theatre games), Viola Spolin's *Improvisation for the Theatre*, a marvelous compendium of theatre games to teach improvisation and a variety of theatre skills. Improvisation is a great way to help students develop both narrative and character, and to practice all the basic theatre skills.

Class Discussion

Do your students have the words to talk about what they do? How many times can you hear students evaluate a scene or play simply as "good" before you scream?! Just as you will continue developing your ability to articulate clearly the observations and critique you offer after a performance, so training your students to offer suggestions (not complaints) and compliments in specific terms puts everyone on the same page in a productive, constructive way. Also remember, class discussion is a legitimate form of assessment, especially formative assessment.

Workshops

Whether for improving audition techniques or learning how to build platforms, having small groups collaborate on very specific tasks can be a very productive use of your and their time. If you lack the specific skills, this is the time to bring in a guest artist.

Scene Study

Analyzing a script is essential to solid theatre work for both actors and techies. It is valuable training for students to learn how to mine a script for clues to character, time period, style, language, etc., and how to either score the script for performance or turn it into cue sheets for production. Table work is a great way to get started on new script material and gives everyone a chance to weigh in on the ideas—and to find the problems to solve—as the work begins.

Partner Work

Another staple of theatre classwork, partner scenes (perhaps as short as 3-5 minutes) are a manageable size for students to handle, and they enable you to be able to wade through an entire class in a reasonable number of class days. Early on they can focus on a particular acting problem and eventually can become a culminating activity, or even an evening of performances to share.

Small Group Work

Theatre is about collaboration, and working with actors, techies and a student director in a small group provides a microcosm of an entire production. For tech work such as making a set model or a costume, put together a team with an initiator, a decision-maker, a detail person, and a hands-on person (e.g. producer, designer, architect, engineer).

Full Classwork

Although it becomes hard to keep everyone active all the time, a whole class production during class time is possible. A Tech Rodeo competition can be set up for the class to move from station to station accomplishing a variety of tech tasks (focusing a light, striking a set, etc.), each trying to beat the clock or the other teams. You'll find lots of opportunities to keep everyone busy. Flash mobs are popular, though tricky to set up, and make sure to involve everyone.

Video

Videotaping scenes or exercises is a great way to provide feedback, especially to those who don't realize how they appear to others (like those who fidget with hair or buttons). And original work that can be posted to YouTube (subject to your school's rules about such things!) can provide a few minutes of fame and perhaps excellent publicity for an upcoming production. Posting choreography on Blackboard or some other private site is a great way to provide modeling or reminders for those who haven't mastered the steps, so they can rehearse at home. And of course, acting for the camera is its own specialized skill.

Research

Our creative types may prefer to rely solely on their imagination, but there is a ton of useful, valuable, and even fun information out there in the universe (and cyberspace) waiting to be discovered. Teaching research skills reinforces the efforts of your colleagues in other disciplines, and adds both knowledge and depth to the work your students are doing. Whether comparing directing styles, finding period costume items, or finding out how to build a lightweight mask, developing a love of searching a variety of sources for information is a most valuable skill. Are your students reluctant to approach a primary source for information? Have them start by searching on Twitter, and let that lead to someone who does (or knows) what they need.

Writing

Writing is a way of knowing. Most theatre starts with the written word, so put some playwriting in your lesson plans—and some journaling, for great feedback. Can your students distinguish what they did from how they felt about it, or from what they learned? A writing prompt can be a great warmup, and developing the skill to reflect on one's learning is well worth the effort. Character autobiographies are a great way to start finding one's way; rewriting Shakespearean lines into contemporary speech helps decipher the language; developing a directorial concept forces one to make decisions; and writing play reviews exercises the critical faculties in a most appropriate way.

Portfolio

Sketches, designs, cue sheets, inspiration collages, and process and production photographs are certainly also valuable tools for teaching, learning and assessment. Great for college applications, too!

Seeing Plays

If you can take your students to see others at work, and bounce it off their own efforts, there is much for them to learn. Watching professional actors model the behaviors you seek from your own students (e.g., focus, precision, depth of commitment, responsiveness) is tremendously helpful, even more so if you go to a show with a talk-back with the actors afterward. Many of your students may never have been to a live play. Take them! Other middle or high school shows offer a contrast from the same ballpark as their own. Compare notes: what's to be learned? Have *all* your students see your own school's shows; this provides a common ground for examples and talking points about most everything else you'll be doing in class. But make sure not to run afoul of a school policy about charging kids for their own education; provide complimentary opportunities for theatre students to see your shows, such as ushering or as dress rehearsal audience members.

Appendix 📄 Connection

Be it elementary, middle or high school, we have provided at least a short list in appendix J, *Suggested Materials*, of stories or plays you might teach. We also invite you to add to this list with your suggestions. Contact us anytime at our website, EducationalStages.com.

Setting the Scene

Use your classroom environment as a teaching tool. Post many kinds of materials around your classroom: theatre quotes, lesson objectives, rules of theatre etiquette, posters of famous actors, lists of vocabulary and theatre terms, creative inspiration pictures, and examples of written work, to name a few. Put labels all around your theatre space until your students learn the parts of the stage, etc. Rearrange the chairs from arena to thrust to proscenium setups.

Paperwork

Let's not forget the good old-fashioned stuff. Because, frankly, quizzes and tests are a pretty solid way of finding out if anything is sticking in those adolescent heads of theirs, especially tech terminology and history. No one is going to have the chance for multiple choice or matching or a word bank when they walk into a theater, so you need to be realistic about what kinds of assessment provide you with meaningful feedback, and provide students with an objective way of knowing what knowledge they have acquired.

Drill and Practice

Let's face it, some of the rehearsal process is sheer drilling of lines, or the development of muscle memory. You certainly want to help your students develop a rich toolbox of approaches to getting their jobs done, but the mundane are among those tools as well. So do allow time to just go over lines, but use that time to move the process forward, and not just as repetition for its own sake.

Productions

Of course, a full-on production is crammed with lessons to be learned. The proof is in the pudding! Want more detail? Keep reading—it's all in chapter 4.

Movies/Training DVDs

Films and DVDs can be a great way to put kids to sleep (or catch up on their texting), but if you select them judiciously (and they have been approved for use in your school system), you can use these materials to demonstrate, model, and teach ideas you are covering in class. Clips from multiple productions of the same show can be a terrific way to illustrate the concept of style, for example. There are short videos available which cover a broad range of very specific subjects, such as international forms of theatre, and DVDs can provide tech training on topics in which you have less personal experience to share with your students (www.theatrefolk.com/products/ptt).

Exceptional Students in the Theatre Classroom

As artistic individualists, it can be said that we are all special. We all bring exceptional qualities into the theatre classroom or to the theatrical process. Sometimes it seems as if talent and creativity are actually linked to high functioning students who struggle with disabilities, including ADHD, ADD, Asperger's syndrome or other learning challenges that may qualify a student for supportive services in school. These services may come in the form of an IEP (Individualized Education Program), a 504 Plan (accommodations) or another evaluation that qualifies the student for special education services. This system of support that is available to students may change as they mature and change in their need for higher or lower levels of support. One thing is certain: this support is vital to the development of these young people as they learn to advocate for themselves. It is important that you create an atmosphere of acceptance and encouragement in your classroom. Sometimes you will have the privilege of watching the anxious, awkward freshman with raw talent turn into the confident, award-winning, well-prepared, and ready for college senior who successfully majors in theatre arts.

Collaboration is Key

Special education students arrive with a variety of accommodations and/or specific challenges, so take the time needed to get information about the identified special education concern. Start by reading whatever files are made available to you by this department. Get to know the case workers involved with the special education students in your classes; they are usually eager to share their expertise on behalf of a student's welfare.

Just remember that this information is confidential; fear of being "labeled" is a controversial concern that leads many parents to reject the special education support available in public schools. Make sure that you are sensitive to confidentiality for both the student and parents involved. Some students are served by both ESOL and special education, so you will get double the assistance. It may be that the appropriate timing trajectory for these students is very different from most of the students in your class. Be prepared to create assessment tools, such as matching vocabulary with clip art that includes fewer words; retest as needed. Collaborate with your guidance/student services counselors to define your assessment expectations if a student is auditing your class. Depending upon the guidelines at your school, sometimes a highly motivated student who is auditing can receive credit at the end of the year.

Accommodations and the Law

In order to do their best, these students need more assistance, often more time and different, specific strategies that are unique to their needs. They may have accommodations which you must adhere to by law. Privately ask the student to advocate for themselves by reminding you of the accommodations they need so that you can assist them, or develop your own system of reminders that help you to meet each student's needs. You may find that your standard testing procedure of allowing everyone as much time as they need meets the extended testing time required for a special education student, or that your policy of allowing students to choose their own seats in the room allows an ADD student to sit near the front of the room. You may also find that students who have auditory or visual processing disabilities have already learned to compensate by developing an exceptional memory—making them the first cast member to get off book. A child with a reading disability may be able to show you more of his/her talent in auditions if you ask them to stop reading and simply repeat a short line using expression. Encouragement and patience are powerful teaching tools.

Special education students require the least restrictive environment possible in order to access the curriculum. Read your case files and recognize that every child's best is not the same. Encourage and hold students accountable by knowing what they need. Some schools offer a time-out room to which specified special education students receive a pass when they need to remove themselves from the classroom environment. In the interest of student achievement, find out from your special education colleagues if there are strategies or processes used by their department that can transfer to theatre class.

Keeping Them Safe

Tech theatre class can be a challenge for physically disabled students. In this case, safety rules the day. Communicate with the student's special education case worker to get a professional perspective on that student's physical ability. Communicate with parents so that they understand why you are concerned that Bobby's lack of balance and fine motor skills might make it dangerous for him to use a miter power saw with a ten-inch blade. Modify your lesson plan so that Bobby learns the information and maybe even emulates use of the saw—without power. Being the "wing man" for another student keeps Bobby from being singled out as different, which is what every teenager seeks to avoid. Even though it may be obvious that Bobby has a physical disability, as his teacher, you must try your best not to draw attention to it. Let your students be defined by what they can do, rather than their limitations.

Breaking it Down

Structure your lesson plans to meet the needs of the students in your classes; higher needs require more structure. Lower maturity means more structure. If you didn't start with a seating chart, let students know that the privilege of sitting next to a friend is not automatic. Spell out your expectations specifically and repeatedly—clarity and structure work for everyone, but especially for students with special needs. Implement a rewards system for students who are on time or who volunteer—whether it's a special pride card given throughout your school,

Real-World Moments

One of the many lessons that I learned from the wonderful director who gave me my first college role was to look beyond the obvious ability of an actor in casting. During a call-back reading, one of the student actors stumbled repeatedly over lines; as a teenager, my analysis was that he would never be cast. What a surprising and humbling privilege it was for me to play opposite this talented young man whose learning disability caused him to struggle with lines before they were memorized. Fortunately, our director's patience and intuitive perception led him to see the character beyond the reading, revealing a poignant performance that went all the way to the Kennedy Center for The American College Theatre Festival.

a pen, a piece of candy (no allergy causing nuts!) or extra points. Visual, concrete rewards will speak to all students.

Teaching all the students in your school is an awesome learning opportunity for you as a professional educator. If you hear moaning and groaning from other teachers, ignore it. Teaching really does require the cooperation and collaboration of all the stakeholders—the proverbial village. One of the advantages of teaching an elective is that you have more control over how you teach your class; use that freedom to benefit students. Learn from your special education experts who studied long and hard in their areas of expertise. Open your mind to a different pace for success, new strategies, and a different way of measuring achievement. The life of a child may depend upon it.

ESOL: A Distinct Opportunity

In American public education today, one of the most rapidly rising groups is students who are learning English, enrolled in English for Speakers of Other Languages (ESOL) classes. Diversity is the cornerstone of American tradition and social development; reaching *all* of your students requires knowledge, encouragement, patience, and most of all, an *open mind*. While considerable resources are being focused on how to best educate young people with very diverse educational backgrounds which exclude the English language, most of that work is in the core curriculum, not specifically in the arts. If your school administration offers you the opportunity to develop a theatre class exclusively for ESOL students, *take it*—in fact,

Ms. Brown's Story (Part I)

Ms. Brown has three ESOL students who speak no English. With administrator and ESOL teacher help, she learns that ESOL students need a completely different time schedule and illustrative drills to learn vocabulary, and is given special materials to use. She creates binders for them and index cards with definitions and vocabulary pictures. With English/Spanish dictionaries, she works with the ESOL students when the rest of the class is doing group work. Using her own high school Spanish, she makes her students smile, but she can tell they appreciate her efforts. By the second quarter, they are participating more in whole class ensemble work and have mastered close to a dozen theatre vocabulary words, making her very proud.

suggest it! Theatre arts is global and animated; everyone's story is important. If you believe that education is the great equalizer in American society, here's your chance to contribute to the journey of students who particularly need your very best creative teaching. Put your problem-solving skills to work and give your heart to the process.

Critical Communication

If you are multilingual, you will already have an advantage in teaching. ESOL students are looking to connect with the new culture and language in which they are immersed—they will welcome familiar words that help them understand English. However, if you aren't fluent in the native language of some of your non-English speaking students, learn a few words or phrases that will help you communicate and let your students know that you care enough to engage in the awkward process of speaking another language—it's what they have to do every day. As with any other group of students, communicating your expectations is crucial: reach out for resources, both human and material, that will help you connect with these students and serve their unique needs.

Colleague Collaboration

ESOL students present a particular opportunity for you to collaborate with your colleagues. ESOL teachers know more strategies to assist you with making your students successful than you studied in acting or directing class. *Collaborate!* Connect with your world (a.k.a. foreign) languages department; they may have suggestions for teaching strategies or resources. At the very least, ask specific questions that will help you help your students, so seek out these informed educators. Some other ideas to consider are:

- Be proactive in requesting that your ESOL theatre class be limited to twenty students, especially if this is your first year teaching an exclusively ESOL Theatre class.
- Make it clear from the beginning that you will teach the Theatre I curriculum using a modified pace and vocabulary emphasis.
- Success for beginning ESOL students is defined differently than for a native English speaker. Think of ESOL as a kind of IEP (Individualized Education Program), needing accommodations appropriate to their particular situation.
- Higher level ESOL students who have been mainstreamed into your regular theatre classes should be used sparingly as translators, unless they volunteer. They have hard-won assimilation in place and deserve to retain that more comfortable status. Be sensitive to their teenage needs for acceptance.
- Make sure that your students feel welcome and know that you are happy to have them in your classroom. Engage in group activities that will promote classroom community and connection.
- Check out online resources to help you with translations, such as Google Translate. Beware, however, that the accuracy of online resources may be inconsistent; ask a colleague to proofread anything that does not seem correct.
- Implement lots of visual vocabulary review, similar to foreign language teaching practices. Project vocabulary onto a screen with an LCD projector or SMART Board from your computer. Print off the same vocabulary in hard copy for students to take home, and put the same vocabulary on Blackboard. Use the same vocabulary visuals as cues for initial written assessments.
- Create experiential education activities for your students—theatre is full of this anyway! Use vocabulary in activities that include experiences. For example, eat grapes to remember Dionysus, or make masks for comedy and tragedy. Go to your school auditorium stage and have students walk to various stage locations while they identify the corresponding stage directions. For musical theatre, get them out of their seats to dance to, for example, *Oklahoma*'s "The Farmer and the Cowman Should be Friends!" This gives them a truly American experience in choreography.

Heightened Challenges and Complexity

ESOL students often arrive with a wide variety of skill levels and/or needs; get assistance in specifying the level of language acquisition and general education level for the students in

Ms. Brown's Story (Part II)

As the year goes on, the ESOL students become less interested in theatre class. One boy says that he is being teased. The students involved are warned to be more positive. Ms. Brown's class gets very busy and the ESOL students often refuse to participate. One student is transferred out, two more very silent students come in, and soon none of the ESOL students will participate. Ms. Brown finishes the year feeling that she has failed all of her ESOL students but doesn't know what else she should have done.

your classes, whether they are mainstreamed or in an exclusive Theatre I class learning community. Start by reading whatever files are made available to you by the ESOL teachers. Get to know any case workers involved with students who have been identified as both special education and ESOL—although often the time to test and identify students is not available at the beginning of the school year. Case workers are usually eager to share their expertise on behalf of a student's welfare.

Doing Your Best: An ESOL Educational Journey

With non-ESOL students, educators ask for the best the students can give to any learning opportunity; from experience, we know that the fullest commitment results in the greatest amount of growth for that child. However, a little bit of a paradigm shift is necessary for ESOL students. In order to do their best, these students need more individualized assistance, often requiring more of your time, and different, specific strategies that meet their unique needs.

Celebrate Baby Steps

Mastery of a dozen vocabulary words may not sound like much to most teachers, but it is important to remember that the schooling received by ESOL students in their own countries varies widely. Students who are not literate in their own language will find literacy in English overwhelming. A silent period, in which ESOL students say little, but observe constantly, can be a natural part of English language acquisition that theatre educators find particularly frustrating. After all, anyone can copy what the other kids are doing in warm-ups, right? Imagine yourself shy instead of outgoing; imagine yourself immersed in a learning culture

Ms. Brown's Story (Part III)

When Ms. Brown has two beginning ESOL students added to her tech theatre class, she is concerned that she cannot keep them safe when the class uses power tools. However, after a demonstration of how to change drill bits in power drills, one of these new students proves to be an expert. Ms. Brown asks another bilingual student to investigate, and he reports the answer, "Mi papá." After that, Ms. Brown works individually with her two ESOL students more, making sure they understand her. They seem happy to do what they are asked. One of them is exceptionally strong and helpful with set construction; the other student is great at organizing materials. Although neither pursue theatre further, they stop by to see Ms. Brown frequently.

based on achievement—and you don't understand how to even approach this process. On top of that, you are a teenager trying to fit into a foreign concept of what is not only acceptable, but "cool." Compassion, balanced with accountability, must be a huge part of your approach as an educator. If you are worried about how outsiders and administrators will perceive the integrity of your teaching methods, get over it. You are here to teach the students who walk into your classroom—all of them. You may have to work harder or differentiate instruction more to make success accessible to your ESOL students; get creative and do the best you can. You'll learn and grow as they do. Some students just need more time in a new environment—try to be patient.

Failure as Part of the Educational Journey

Despite our commitment to educating all the students, there are times when teachers' best efforts are not successful. The administrative decision to mainstream ESOL students may not always prove productive. Meeting the needs of students who are possibly traumatized from their journey to a new environment and whose confidence is shaken by an inability to communicate in a new culture is a huge challenge. You may well collaborate and communicate with your colleagues, you may implement appropriate teaching strategies and stay up all night worrying about your students. You are still obligated to keep trying to meet students' needs, whether you observe immediate results or not. Teaching is messy.

Ms. Brown's Story (Part IV)

The next year, Ms. Brown teaches a Theatre I class of exclusively ESOL I and II students. She is nervous but excited—she wants a second chance to grow beyond her previous efforts. Preparation for her new class requires a lot of work, but she enjoys creating new materials for her students, and the creativity of finding ways to modify theatre games and activities so her students are set up to succeed. Her natural friendliness is a valuable tool in establishing caring, appropriate relationships with these students; nurture is just as important as content. Instead of feeling alienated and inadequate in front of native English speakers, these ESOL-only students create a comfortable, unique learning community with Ms. Brown that promotes achievement and artistic development. At the end of the year, one of Ms. Brown's students thanks her for being the teacher who believed in him.

Resiliency for Both the Teacher and Student

As you know, teachers are not perfect or infallible. However, upon encountering an unsatisfactory situation, dedicated teachers owe it to themselves and their students to analyze the situation and endeavor to improve it. For example, if you ultimately decide to have a separate and exclusive theatre class just for ESOL I and II students, hopefully the collaborative culture of your school's administration will allow that idea to become a reality. Don't be afraid to make suggestions that will give students—and yourself—a better chance to succeed. ESOL students offer educators a vital opportunity to create new teaching strategies, materials and methods in theatre arts that support these students as they evolve and adjust.

Classroom Management

Theatre classrooms are typically far less structured than traditional classes, and the students often more extroverted than the norm. Accordingly, classroom management may require you to tailor your tactics to fit this unique environment and population. As always, you need to set standards, expectations and consequences as early as possible. The standards you set at the beginning will provide the essential framework for both you and your students throughout the year. Here are some tips on establishing effective communication with your students:

Keep it Personal

Kids are rarely rowdy on day one, so if some are, learn their names immediately! Try to give these kids responsibility as soon as possible; focus their energy into leadership. Name games are always worth the time. The kids must know each other, too, if you are going to have the kind of trust that makes your classroom a safe space for making mistakes. Try having the kids circle-up in alphabetical order, then call out their names as you mark attendance, and tell you who is missing if some student's slot is empty. After a while there is no need to circle-up first. (A variation is for you to call out the first name, then each person calls out the name of whomever should be next in the roster...the last kid calls out your name. This actually does a better job of catching any absentees.) This game is a quick and efficient—and engaging—way to cover this required administrivia.

Ways to Stop Talking or Distraction without Losing your Stride, or Your Temper

MAKE EYE CONTACT Relocate yourself in the room as needed to achieve this.

USE PROXIMITY You move close enough to a student...they'll get the message.

RELOCATE Separate the talkers so they are next to quiet helpful kids instead.

USE NAMES Just toss the name of the offender in the middle of your sentence with no change of tone or pace, and you'll usually catch their attention.

DON'T ENGAGE WITH KID ATTORNEYS Promise instead an after-class discussion, but refuse to break the class momentum. And never get into a public power struggle.

NIP IT IN THE BUD Bump up any real problem to parent and/or counselor and/or administrator, as appropriate, early enough to prevent misbehavior from becoming a pattern.

PRETEND TO BE ANGRY Do this well before you actually get angry.

PROMISE ONLY WHAT YOU CAN DELIVER For example, can you really kick a kid out of class? Better to keep your threats vague!

PRAISE PUBLICLY, BUT CHASTISE PRIVATELY But sometimes, you really do need to make the point to the entire class.

LET ONLY ONE PERSON LEAVE AT A TIME Restroom use is not a group activity.

KEEP A WHISTLE Have this in your desk and use it judiciously to shock your class to attention.

GO OLD SCHOOL Have students write on the board "If it's not mine, I won't touch it" or whatever the offense was 100 times. The experience may be memorable enough to prevent repeat offenses. If writing on paper, specify longhand and no ditto marks.

FOCUS If you call out "focus up!" everyone should respond by calling "focus up!" back at you. Don't let this get overused, and it can be very helpful.

KEEP THEM QUIET Saying "Quiet someone near you" works much better than "Be quiet" since the talkers don't hear you, but those who do become your instant proxies all over the room.

Make Life Imitate Art

Consider assigning kids theatre jobs for use in class, as described earlier in the section on technical theatre. Your stage manager can call attendance; the costume person can inventory—and rehang—costumes checked out for class scene use; your ASM, running crew or set decoration person can assure all furniture is back in place at the end of each class; the publicity person can post assignments for you, etc. Assign two students to each job to keep things running smoothly if someone is absent and to assure that everyone is included.

Teen Angst Crises

You may want to get yourself the bumper sticker or plaque that says "Save the drama for your Mama!" But there's no chance you'll avoid days when some student—or pack of students—are in the midst of one personal crisis or another. Remind students that if they are having a bad day, it's much better for them to tell you privately before class begins than to wait until you call on them to perform. It's a judgment call each time, but if one friend wants to comfort another, it might be wiser to send the crisis kid to their counselor than lose both kids from class.

Dealing with Interruptions

If interruptions during class are a concern, use them as performance opportunities. For example, teach the class a short, active speech (e.g., Juliet about to skewer herself with the dagger, from discovery through collapse) and train them to shout "VISITOR!" whenever someone enters the room, interrupting everything for a unison dramatic display. Then all remain totally still until the visitor applauds their work, at which point the class continues as if nothing happened.

The kids will really enjoy this, and any repeat visitors will realize how disruptive the interruptions are. A less disruptive plan might be to assign your classroom house manager to

Real-World Moments

There was a teacher whose classroom management tactic went sideways when he confiscated a cell phone, told the principal about it, and showed him how it worked. When it turned out there were "sexting" pictures on the phone, the teacher was arrested for possession of child pornography, removed from his position at the school, and ultimately went through months of litigation before the case was resolved.

welcome any visitors, thank them for staying quiet in the midst of the class, and inquire how they might be of assistance.

Subtext

It's worth remembering that a rough moment with a student may really be masking a very different problem with which they're struggling, from bullying that is practically under your nose to an illness, divorce, or other family situation of which you are totally unaware. Showing an interest in the underlying problem—without prying—can not only alleviate the classroom issue, but can also make you that trusted adult who can be a lifesaving anchor in very rough teenage seas. On the other hand, keep in mind that you must never promise to keep secret a disclosure about abuse—it is against the law not to report such a situation.

Texting

A simple, fair rule could be "Ask me first" before taking out—let alone using—any electronic device. If not done with your approval, follow your school's policy. Are phones to be handed in to administrators? Returned at the end of class? The end of the day? This is a great example of nipping distracting behavior in the bud. Be fair by being firm and consistent, and this won't become a problem.

Respect

Respect is an essential component of every classroom, theatre process, and production. In a perfect world, students will respect themselves, property, each other, and of course, you.

But since students' experiences, maturity and judgment vary widely, you may well need to take time both to clarify and model the kind of behavior which helps engender respect and promotes classwork which is appropriate and productive.

You will need to decide where to draw the line for how strict you want to be, but keep in mind the destructive power of disrespect. By contrast, respect generates an atmosphere of trust and productivity. What are some ways that your students can show proper respect for you, for each other, and for your community?

Language

Students should call you and each other by the name that each person prefers and expects, whether it's your first name, "sir," "ma'am," "coach," Mr./Miss/Mrs./Ms. So-and-So or an accepted nickname (Mr. S., for example). Especially if you have several students with the same name in the same class, you may find nicknames helpful…but don't let some poor kid get tagged with a disrespectful nickname the first day that could last throughout high school!

Cursing is disrespectful pretty much by design, an emotional emphasis that spits out one's dissatisfaction with whatever is going on…or sometimes, cursing has become a habit. Regardless, cursing is often upsetting to others and therefore distracts from, and degrades, the quality of the work at hand. Respecting the art of theatre requires language and actions that support the process, rather than distract or degrade.

Cursing in Dialogue

Whether in a script or improvisation, cursing can be an efficient way to vilify a character we only get moments to meet, and thus justifies the use of the language. But how much is too much? We suggest that when language or behavior distracts your audience from the story being told (do some kids turn to you, to see if you're going to object?), it has caused the *audience* to break character and therefore is counterproductive. If it enhances the moment and draws the audience further into the story, it is useful. Where this line is drawn changes over time, differs from one production or class to another, and varies with different communities, so get to know yours and avoid those angry letters of complaint.

Criticism

Critique is a basic part of every theatre class. Respectful critique means translating complaints into suggestions. For example, "I couldn't hear you" becomes "Please speak more clearly" or "Try using more volume" or "If you face the audience you'll be easier to hear," each calling for a different specific solution instead of just a criticism. Obviously, there is no place for "That sucked!" anywhere in a critique.

Attentiveness

If one is attending a play, it is respectful to actually watch the play and to note that others are also doing so. It's also worth remembering that if you can hear the actors, they can hear you. In class, the same points apply. As a result, here are some expectations for students' classroom and performance etiquette:

- If the teacher is talking, you're not. If someone else has the floor, you don't.
- Do one thing at a time. If there is classwork to do, focus on that.
- *Ask first* if you want to use anything electronic, whether it be a cell phone for a time-check or a classroom laptop. Ask *before* you take it out.
- Hold questions and comments until asked for them. Don't distract your classmates by asking them for clarification while someone else has the floor.

Action

If a picture is worth a thousand words, an action can be worth a thousand pictures. We are what we do. Encourage your students to do their best, and to help others to do theirs.

There is *no* place for bullying in theatre spaces. Teasing, mimicking, or harassment of any kind destroys the fabric of trust critical to successful creativity, and is just plain wrong. Any such actions should be brought to your attention immediately.

Raise a hand for attention. Train your kids to repeat "Focus up!" all together whenever you say it. Backstage, a shout-out of imminent change (e.g., "Work lights going out!" or "Batten coming down!" or "Five minutes to places!") should be responded to with a unison "Thank you!"

Teach the mantra: *If it's not yours, don't touch it.* This means backpacks, other people, props, costumes, and things around the room—all deserve respect by not being tampered with or disturbed. Students should also only keep at hand the things they need at the time.

Let the classwork be the focus of attention the whole time. For them—and for you. For example, you can't model respectful action if you answer texts mid-class when they are not allowed to.

Attitude

This is really the bottom line, isn't it? It is a delight to work with people who joyfully show up, who are eager to try new things, who show how well they have mastered what they have been working on, and who are happiest when everyone is working together. And it doesn't take many people with a bad attitude to poison the mood for everyone.

Theatre seems to draw those students who feel marginalized, and is truly a place where those with an enormous range of artistic/physical/mental abilities (and personalities) can join together in a common quest for the best possible show. Do your best to break up cliques, and find the right place for those seeking somewhere to belong. Spot and correct anyone who treats as different a class or ensemble member who is doing their best.

Seniors often have a sense of entitlement that is easily misplaced by lording their seniority over the underclassmen. In a theatre production, the jobs vary widely. It is extremely disrespectful to impede someone else from doing their job because one "outranks" the other. For example, a younger ASM trying to maintain quiet backstage is doing their job correctly. Anyone who disregards that call for quiet ("I don't have to listen to you. You're only a freshman.") is as out of line as one who yelled at the actor for delivering their dialogue correctly. Remind your seniors that they are teaching—like it or not—the others how to behave by modeling behavior while working together.

"Techies" are sometimes treated as second-class citizens by actors. But just try to run a show with no one opening the curtain, or turning on the lights, or providing the props or costumes, or finishing the painting, and see how the show turns out! It's also easy to forget that the actors typically get a head start of weeks, while some of those tech jobs are impossible to begin until the theatre becomes fully available or until others have finished their work. Encourage or require your students to become "bi-tech-tual" and all will be well. Thank and celebrate often and loudly the work of those who don't get to take that curtain call.

Your Students Should...

- Approach each class and rehearsal session with a positive attitude, ready to try new things and do their best.
- Encourage others. Be generous with praise and be specific, too. Trying is a way of discovering and is so very valuable.
- Promptly disapprove of disrespectful behavior in others to help set and maintain high standards of the theater and classroom as a place of creativity and support.
- Know that if they're having a bad day and just can't muster the right attitude, they should advise the teacher/coach privately *before* the class begins.
- Never get into a public power struggle with the teacher/director; this violates theatre protocol. They're wrong to do so, they're going to lose, and everyone around them will think less of them (and you) for doing so.

Disruptive Students

One of the most difficult parts of teaching is when students who are disruptive or disrespectful interrupt instruction, as in the old saying, "When you're up to your ass in alligators, it's easy to forget you came to drain the swamp." As much as you want to stay focused, they demand your attention. So you implement everything you've been taught: speak to them

Theatre Ethics

RESPECT THE THEATRE Show your respect at all times to its processes, parts and people.

BE PRESENT Arrive on time (early), and go over lines or help set up until the work begins. Participate in group warmups. Never miss an entrance! Stay active until you're done. Never choose to miss class or skip rehearsal.

BRING A POSITIVE ATTITUDE TO EVERYTHING YOU DO Leave your ego at the door, and try your best. Mistakes lead to discoveries, so learn from them and improve. Encourage and support others. Tell people you appreciate their efforts.

FOCUS ON THE WORK AT HAND Distractions never enhance the work, whether they come from texting or from the drama of your private lives. Use spare time to reflect and plan for future improvements or to help others. And when others are talking, be quiet!

PLAY IT SAFE Pranks and rough-housing have no place in class or backstage work. Stay away from tools, equipment and locations that require special training or permission. Learn to spot unsafe situations and what to do about them.

TREAT EACH OTHER AS PROFESSIONALS Support the chain of command. Question, but don't *challenge*. Stage managers really are in charge, so obey them promptly; they are trying to make the show its best. Bring up any concerns privately to those who can affect change, accept their decisions, and move on.

BE COURTEOUS Call people by the names they prefer. Use "please" and "thank you" liberally. Never tease, mimic, or harass. Offer to assist whenever you can. Avoid language and behavior others find upsetting. No swearing.

IF IT'S NOT YOURS, DON'T TOUCH IT Mind your own business. Leave props, costumes, tools, equipment, books, and backpacks alone. On the other hand, if you see something dangerous or out of place, either fix it or bring it to the attention of someone who can.

LOVE YOUR TECHIES Get to know those behind the scenes. Don't criticize their work in progress as if it's the final product. Help them whenever you can; there are always jobs to do that don't require special training, that you can do.

NURTURE ENSEMBLE Find ways to be inclusive. Join in. Welcome newbies and newcomers. Help others whenever you can. Treat others as you would like to be treated.

privately, ignore them, separate them—and later—call the parents at home, call the parents at work, call the parents again, assign detention, email the counselor, email the parents, talk to the administrator for their grade level, talk to your department chair, talk to the fine and performing arts administrator. In the meantime, your anxiety is building every time you think of that class and although you are determined to make things better, the situation is wearing you down.

Welcome to the world of teaching! "Mama said there'd be days like this..." "So you had a bad day..." "No one said life would be easy..." All of these platitudes are true. Enduring alligator attacks comes with the territory; you need some tools to tame the alligators.

Attention Mongers

Some of the most difficult students (initially) can ultimately make you a better teacher; they are usually freshmen (or younger) in Theatre I class. You'll have to become a better teacher to reach them and to survive. In high school, these students are likely to be immature attention mongers. They aren't bad kids, they just haven't developed the self-discipline to stop talking when you are teaching. They are so insecure about high school and how other people perceive them that they can't stop giggling during warm-ups; they laugh at other kids; they can't take their eyes off of each other because they haven't got the confidence, compassion, or maturity to understand what the word *ensemble* means. Teach them what it means to be part of an ensemble; teach them to be artistic risk-takers.

Preparation and Pacing

Be super prepared from the get-go for every minute of class, moving at a breakneck speed: pacing can be one of your most effective tools for classroom management. A quick video clip all ready to go, no techno glitches, no speeches, just a quick clip and quick comments afterward: "Why did we watch this?" Follow this with whole class, big circle warm-ups that *you lead* walking around the group, making eye contact with everyone. Then do some small-group work: In being super-prepared, you have, of course, already divided the class into small groups. You call out the group lists, time their work—maybe assign a quick scene or improv or activity that each small group will present to the class. Follow that with 15 minutes on the computers, researching topics such as musical theatre publishing sites (MTIshows.com, Tams-Witmark.com, rnh.com), or perhaps watch a YouTube video of Argentinian dancers who show the influence of vaudeville.

Contact the Parents

Young teachers may be hesitant to call home. Once you start doing it, however, you'll find out that teaching students with their parents' support is a wonderful thing. But sometimes

Real-World Moments

My first year teaching full-time elementary theatre, I had very challenging fifth grade classes. So challenging, in fact, that I cried almost every night when I got home after I tried to teach them. The other grades were sweet and eager, but the oldest grade in the school, as a group, was tough. They constantly interrupted my spoken instructions and made fun of me. One kid even ran away, and the police had to chase him down! I had to make it work; I had to have a paycheck, if nothing else! I analyzed the challenges (with the help of my supportive husband, who had to listen to my crying) and decided that listening was the biggest issue. So I stopped talking so much—which was a big achievement for me. I had materials organized and grouped for the students the moment they walked into my teaching space. I took attendance while I walked around and monitored their progress; I gave them just barely enough time to finish each activity before sharing with the class. I praised every tiny bit of progress and improvement. At the end of the year, they presented poems in groups, interpreted with movement, vocal expression, projection, and articulation. After one poem by Langston Hughes, a parent came up to me with tears in her eyes at the memory of that poem in her own school experience—when schools were still segregated. (As a teacher, you might find it inspiring: *Mother To Son*, by Langston Hughes.) Things got better the next year; the runner "graduated" and got assistance; the other kids got to know and respect me. I stayed for ten years.

you don't get support, and sometimes you just get excuses. When that happens, just tell the truth (diplomatically, of course): "Despite your daughter's focus on how other students are behaving, she is still responsible for her own behavior, wouldn't you agree? I'm sure we both want her to be successful in theatre class, and I need your help." One of two things will happen: either the student will come to the next class better, or worse. Either way, you keep calling, you keep contacting—parents, counselors, administrators—you can't give up on either the student or yourself—you have the unique ability to effect positive change in a child.

Call the Coach

This can be the coup de gras. The student may have a questionable home life, the home phone is disconnected, there is no email or work number available, but—the student is on the soccer team! Talk to the coach who probably already has a strong relationship with that student. After all, after-school sports/clubs are the true "electives." Sally may have been placed into your Theatre I by a counselor who couldn't come up with another choice, but it was Sally who decided to join the soccer team. If there is a real love of something in a student's life in another part of the school, find out what it is and use it to help that student to be accountable and successful in your class. Sally may come into theatre class with a whole new perspective and willingness to try harder.

Maintain Perspective

As the teacher, you will be called upon to maintain a healthy sense of perspective. Maintaining that perspective may be difficult, particularly on a subject that is so important to you. Like many theatre teachers, passion may be one of your strengths, which is awesome, amazing, and sometimes scary. Stay in control, stay professional—at least in front of the kids! If you have to vent (and you will), do it with people you trust, out of earshot of students or administrators—but learn to *let it go*. Prolonged venting can turn into whining and a negative attitude—as well as a reputation for negativity—so beware of that. What you need is an authentic perspective:

- You are the adult, therefore, model maturity.
- You are the teacher. Find a way to teach them!
- No one said this was easy. Teaching is hard work.
- Keep your mind open. The biggest constant about kids is *change*. Some of your most challenging kids may turn into some of your favorite kids (those favorites you aren't really supposed to have).
- Don't hold grudges. When any student shows improvement—but especially the immature attention-mongers—give them *praise*! This shows them that the right kind of attention is a wonderful thing and sets them up to learn and grow. It also shows them that you haven't written them off or labeled them in your mind.

Reach Out for Help and Guidance

Over the course of a long career in teaching, you will encounter some extremely difficult students whose needs are way beyond what you can or should handle alone. In addressing these students' needs, remember that collaboration is a wonderful thing. It's not a sign of weakness for you to contact the grade-level administrator and the student's counselor and set up a parent conference. Don't be afraid of this opportunity; if you aren't reaching the student, someone else needs to.

Unfortunately, sometimes a student has hidden needs that reveal themselves in time and aren't easy to categorize or diagnose. All kids are capable of success, but some need much more support than others. Programs such as ESOL, IEPs, 504 plans, and special education services can provide support systems for students. As an educator, it is your duty to call attention to a child in need—if you are in over your head because a student has substantial psychological issues, send out a confidential note or other contact and get help! The school psychologist, social worker, counselor, administrator can be part of an educational support team to work with parents to help kids who have larger challenges than you may be able to handle. A good administrator will appreciate your bringing this to the attention of a team that can really help a student with special needs.

Drawing the Line on Touching

It is important to authentically acknowledge that you may be surprised at, or even attracted to, the talent, beauty, and passion of your students. How you actively respond to that acknowledgment reflects upon you as a professional educator. Especially if you are within a decade of the age of your students, this can be a slippery slope. As they say in *Bye Bye Birdie,* "JAILBAIT!" If you find yourself in need of attention, students who may be enamored of you are not fair game. *They* may get to be playful or flirty, but you don't. There is no happy ending scenario out there if things get out of hand…according to you, them or some parent, administrator or other. Teaching is a sacred trust. Parents trust you to make appropriate choices in working with their children. Do no harm.

Especially in the informality of an after-school rehearsal, the exhilaration of a successful performance, or when dealing with a student who is upset, sharing a hug may seem okay. Can you initiate that "We won!" embrace? What if everyone is giving warm-up back rubs? Is it all right to participate? At a school social, can you dance with a student? Slow dance?

Do you play favorites? Do you favor those who are alert, respectful, prompt and industrious over the slackers who also crave your attention and support? Being more expressive with some students than others can cause real jealousy. Even greeting a student in the hall can bring about envy by those who were not greeted as you passed them by. Can you be lost in thought without being insulting? Can you treat everyone fairly all the time?

How Physical Can You Be with Students?

As you can imagine, the subject of teachers touching students is fraught with difficulty. For legal advice, consult a lawyer or your teachers' union legal counsel. However, your judgment in the moment will still come into play. Here's a litmus test: if the principal or the student's parent walked in at that moment, would you back off, or feel the need to defend or explain yourself?

During a weekend convention, can you do night hallway monitoring or a room-check in your nightwear? Can you speak privately to a student in your motel room with the door closed (it could be cold outside)? Should you let your classroom door be closed if speaking one on one with a student? Can you drive a student home from school? Can you wait alone with one student until their parent arrives? What types of situations put you at risk?

Some Reminders about Touching

- Never touch a student where a bathing suit would go
- Never initiate physical contact without a student's permission first
- Never be physically rough with a student
- Never sustain contact beyond the needs of the theatrical moment
- Never demonstrate a kiss by actually kissing a student
- Never persist with physical gestures that create discomfort in either the actors or those watching
- Never walk into a dressing room without announcing yourself first
- Never dress or behave in a manner that might be considered provocative by your community or school standards
- Never pay so much attention to one student that the gossip mongers have ammunition to accuse you of physical intimacy with that person
- Never nurture a fantasy about a student lest it lead you to inappropriate actions
- Never mistake love of dedication, talent and energy for actual romantic love

Sometimes it is more efficient to demonstrate than to describe. Say, for instance, you wanted to teach proper dance position for a waltz or foxtrot, or a fireman's carry. However, it is an irony of theatre work that we train students to communicate using physicality, but we are at great risk if we behave as they do, or even as we may direct them to, in a show. Be careful! Kids might engage in horseplay, but a friendly punch on the shoulder or swat to the backside could land you accused of battery or sexual harassment.

Communicating with Parents and Kids

We're all in the communication business, but everyone receives information in different ways, so developing a palette of communication tools is essential. "If you post it, they will read" is *not* sufficient. You have to reach out in several ways, as well as making your information readily and easily accessible. Parents expect—and rightly so—to be able to access all the information for which you are holding their children responsible, and in a timely manner. Your colleagues, administration—and your community—depend on you to clue them in about your events. Make your plans and expectations clear in all things.

Communication with parents and kids is a primary obligation and priority. Parents absolutely expect to know how their kids are doing, both academically and socially. The rest of the school and community need to know about the wonderful things you've got going on. Fortunately, there are lots of ways to tell them.

Handouts Home

When you were in school, did you *you* always remember to deliver handouts home to Mom or Dad? For example, the annual Federal Survey Form translates directly into federal dollars to schools. Oftentimes, parents not only need to read the handouts, they also need to fill out forms and send them back to you. Use whatever system—*every* system—of reminders you can think of, to get those forms back before they become a huge headache for you. A hard copy that can be posted on the refrigerator has its advantages, so choose carefully what to deliver and what to only post for printing out at home.

Email and Beyond

Stay on top of your email, reply with care (re-read before hitting the send button!), and recognize that some issues are better resolved in person, where tone of voice can be important and questions promptly answered. Sometimes a face-to-face conference is the best approach. Include a guidance counselor or principal as mediator if you suspect conflict with a parent may ensue. Always give an administrator a heads-up if an angry parent may be heading their way!

Callboard

Good old low tech! A large cork bulletin board in a prominent place near your theatre class or performance area is an essential place to post audition announcements, schedules, meeting details, reviews, show posters, and such. Assign this to some artsy kid to maintain and check regularly to see that it's attractive, informative, and un-vandalized. This may not be the best place for sign-ups if you discover that random or fictitious names get added to lists posted in public places; keep those sign-ups in your classroom.

School Resources

Your school may have a newsletter or an electronic message board indoors and/or outdoors, or a daily or weekly television news show that can be used to advertise your events. There might also be restrictions on where or how many show posters or banners can be hung for advertising. All-faculty emails can be very helpful (just don't spam your colleagues) not just for promoting shows—and inviting classes to in-class performances—but to track down prop or costume items, too!

Back-to-School Night and Touching Bases

Many schools use these events to enable parents to learn about their children's teachers and classes. Every school varies, but typically at back-to-school night, parents walk through their child's schedule early in the school year (yeah...in the evening...a long day for you...) and you get maybe ten minutes to make an impression, explain your classes, sneak in information about the drama program, and answer questions. Keep it general, and divert questions about a particular child to a request to schedule a conference; you won't have time to do otherwise.

By contrast, Touching Bases is a variant on the parent conference in which the entire faculty is gathered in the same location (main hallway, gym, whatever) so parents can circulate to their child's teachers without having to wander or get lost around the school. This provides individual parents the opportunity to discuss their child's progress or problems one on one—briefly—so be sure to know your students' names and have their grading sheets at hand. If issues arise that may need more than the allotted time, schedule a conference—and include the student's counselor as a witness and mediator, to keep things calm.

Boosters

A parent booster group is a tricky thing. It can be the very most valuable assistance you can ever get, to support your program and help make your artistic life manageable—or the most imposing, bossy group of "buttinskis" imaginable. During a transition from old to new teacher/director, this parent group can help maintain the routines that have kept the program going; but it can also be difficult for you to wrest the reins from them as you take charge of the program. In terms of communication, active drama boosters can represent your department at school events, create and distribute a newsletter to other drama parents, assist with publicity to the media, and provide a sounding board for class or production issues that arise. You cannot allow them to make any artistic decisions regarding play selection or casting, or give them access to school funds or keys. More about boosters is found elsewhere in this book.

Interim and Grading Reports

Your school is likely to have a system that requires you to send regular updates of student grades. Get used to it; that's not likely to change anytime soon. Some school systems use software that allows parents to view their child's grades online at any time.

Copyright Information

Federal law provides a "fair use" exception which allows limited use of copyrighted materials by educators. The factors to be considered include:

A. The purpose and character of the use, including whether such use is of a commercial nature or is for nonprofit educational purposes.

B. The nature of the copyrighted work.

C. The amount and substantiality of the portion used in relation to the copyrighted work as a whole.

D. The effect of the use upon the potential market for, or value of, the copyrighted work.

Getting caught with photocopied scripts, for example, can be cause for termination. For more information, see the section on copyright in appendix T, Online Resources.

Blackboard

If your school system uses Blackboard or similar software, you may be required to create an area for each of your classes to find your assignments and significant documents, and perhaps for them to use to send information. Blackboard also enables you to set up communities. You can create a drama club community into which kids can self-enroll. You can also enter individual names yourself, so that it's not limited to the students you have in class. A drama club community is a terrific place to post announcements, production contracts, rehearsal calendars, evaluations from crew chiefs to better inform their successors, how-to information particular to your facility, and a million other possibilities. It's limited to members, so even cast party information can be available without accidentally inviting the masses. You can also post videos of choreography for your dancers to practice or music clips for your singers (don't violate copyright in the process!). Your drama club community could have separate sections for each production, as well as for boosters, for Thespians, for student technicians, etc.

Website

Today, it seems that you hardly exist if you don't have a web presence. Does your theatre program have one? Who currently controls it—the school? The boosters? Other? Be sure that you can control it, even if you delegate someone else to do the grunt work (but beware letting loose the password to make edits!!). After all, you will inevitably be held responsible for anything posted there. Work hard to drive traffic to your website and you can minimize the need to post information elsewhere. Photos of rehearsals, tech work, class projects, etc. can be posted, as well as information about absolutely everything the world might want to know.

Caution: Never post full names, student ID's or other information that could lead back to an individual student on the web. Even if you post a picture, you need to have written, informed consent to do so (you can build that permission into your initial syllabus/grading sheet for your students).

A website usually involves two costs: (1) ownership of the website name and (2) a monthly fee to store your information there (if you exceed the amount of free storage space provided). You can avoid some of these costs by using a free Google website. However, you do have to deal with a more cumbersome website name, such as sites.google.com/yourschoolname, although Google and other hosts can provide easy and useful places for you to establish your website.

Thespians

If your school has a troupe for I.T.S., the International Thespian Society, you should know that their parent group is the Educational Theatre Association, EdTA.org and the website is schooltheatre.org. Lots of great information lives there, from troupe records to advice on theatre issues, to state and national/international conferences. How does/will your troupe communicate about its meetings and events to others? Whose job is it? How can you help?

Remind.com

This app provides a free (as of this writing) and easy service for communicating by group text with each of your classes, or production companies, or whatever groups you set up. Parents can join, too. You can send—or schedule to be sent at a later date/time—a text to the entire group or an email for non-texters, or chat with individuals about upcoming tests, rehearsals, etc. No personal information is shared and no replies are possible.

Facebook

Some schools forbid the use of software that can so easily link to inappropriate content, let alone the ease with which one can get lost in time and come up for air far too infrequently. On the other hand, if that's how kids are communicating, you need to get on board if they're going to hear you. If you do create a Facebook page for class or show use, keep it as professional as possible with no links to your own personal sites, and use school addresses and such for contact information. Alternatively, students may (even without your permission)

Real-World Moments

I was skeptical about Touching Bases that first year we did it. But then came the parent who was concerned about her daughter being bullied in my class. I was shocked—the kids had been very careful to assure that I never saw this happening. Once I knew about it, I was able to keep an eye out and handle a problem that might have escalated who knows how far, otherwise. I became a believer.

create sites for each show you do, or even class you teach, and should invite you so you can answer questions and post useful information. Keep in mind that information posted never ever goes away, and that you will be held responsible for anything that even vaguely seems to come out of your theatre program.

Twitter

Twitter provides two-way quick communication if students also use it and follow you or your program. Don't confuse your personal account with your professional one, as warned above. Twitter can also be a terrific way to reach out when researching, to find primary source material, and communicate with someone who actually does what they are trying to find out about.

Communicating with Colleagues

It's important to create professional relationships with the other adults around you; you need each other for perspective, for a sounding (and venting) board, for assistance and advice, and for some social time. And remember that they are also in their own little worlds, so much that they may not even know you've been slaving away at a show with kids they teach, coming soon to an auditorium very near them! So get to know those around you, to enhance your whole school experience.

Lunch Bunch

While working with students can be very energizing (as well as exhausting), it's important, useful and fun to spend some time with grownups each day, too—particularly those who can empathize with your situation and perhaps give you advice, or maybe just give you a break in the teaching day. The theatre classroom can be quite the cocoon, so make the effort to have lunch or spend some of your non-teaching time in a faculty lounge or place where other "old people" like you can gather and chat about things like rent, and car troubles, and other things that don't interest students…or shouldn't be shared with them.

New Kids on the Block

Pay attention during that first faculty meeting when all you new folks are introduced, then seek each other out. Misery may love company, but so does triumph, including those little victories that will one day become routine. You'll discover that your confusion, frustration and elation are all shared experiences.

Mentors

You may be assigned a mentor teacher in your building as your first line of defense when you have questions or concerns, and hopefully you will click with that person. But you might not. Don't feel reluctant to ask someone else to let you vent, or to ask those questions that might typically go to the official mentor. One way or the other, befriend the older (hopefully wiser) colleague who can help you learn the ropes. Go out for a drink after school on Fridays, or lunch together if your schedules align, or swing by during a non-teaching period. Everyone likes to feel valuable and helpful, so don't be reluctant to connect with this person whenever you feel they could help make your life a little easier.

Artsy Types

Theatre was for many years—and sometimes still is—grouped in with English, but more often these days is considered a fine and performing arts class. You will find you share much with the music department, such as rehearsal toward excellence, auditorium use, daily collaboration as an essential for success, as well as bringing in an audience. You also share much with the art department: allocating and maintaining supplies and equipment, thinking in terms of color/texture/mass/pattern, etc., and moving an idea from a vision to an observable reality that is shared with others. As a practical matter, you may do a musical with assistance from the music department staff, or collaborate on set or publicity design work with your art department. So get to know these folks; you may really like them!

Administrators

Administrators' stories are as varied as ours as to why they are doing the job they do. But not only do they have the authority to require you to do something, they also share your genuine desire to help kids reach their potential. They usually have plenty of experience on which to base their opinions and advice. And sometimes they are faced with mandates and rules that they don't understand either—things they can't change but must enforce. Although you don't want to become that needy new teacher, you also want to use the resources that will assist you in constructing the best possible educational situation, and the resources that you need may well be your administrators. Hey, administrators are people, too, so why not get to know yours? It can only help you both to know each other better.

Peers Near or Far

If there are other high schools (or colleges) near your new school, try to connect with their theatre staff as soon as possible. If you're lucky enough to have a formal way to do this (county-wide in-service meetings or some such), be sure to do the paperwork in a timely fashion and attend those meetings! These are the people who share your war stories and know the most about your situation and how to best handle everything from finding reliable vendors to knowing which plays work in your community to dealing with unruly kids in rehearsal. Certainly, form a bond with the theatre folks who feed your school (e.g., the middle school, whose kids will come to your high school). Their success affects your future, so work together as much as you can!

Remember: you are never alone. If your school is in the middle of nowhere, check in with former classmates, or contact a nearby (or distant) community or professional theatre. Remember that www.SchoolTheatre.org is always available to assist.

Communicating with the Community

Hopefully, the shows you produce will be of value not just to the parents and friends of the participants, but as entertainment and education in their own right. Certainly children's theatre is a draw for families with youngsters, but you will likely be doing shows of general interest, too, and of quality that brings folks back for more. But how will they know about your work?

Newspapers

Your events are genuine news in your community, so make sure that you keep your local newspapers and online sources like Patch.com informed about what's going on and how to find more information. Note also that many housing developments publish a local newsletter. Be sure to get included! On the other hand, if there is an incident at your school, let your administration communicate with the press, not you.

Radio and Television

Find out which stations are popular with your target audience(s), and send in public service announcements for them to read out as your show dates approach. If there is a local cable station that publicizes community events, hit them up, too.

Road Signs

Take one sheet of plywood, cut it in half, add a couple of hinges, and you've got a sandwich board sign to place near the key intersections to advertise your productions/camps, etc. Be aware of and comply with state and local requirements and limitations on types of signs and acceptable locations. Keep the words large, clear and to a minimum, but be sure to include your website for more information.

Gimmicks

Your students may be able to come up with all sorts of creative ideas for publicizing shows— inserts in the boxes of the local pizza joint or school lunch trays, parades around the shopping mall, a flashmob, etc. Pull out all the stops, but keep it all safe and supervised. You're responsible, so know the limits and stay within them.

For Reflection & Discussion

There will be battles to pick and choices to be made. It's in your hands whether a situation escalates or gets resolved.

1. What's the worst way you can think of to quiet a class?

2. Suzy always seems to need to go to the restroom at the same time each day. Does she happen to have a boyfriend in a nearby class?

3. You catch a child cutting himself/herself, who swears it's the first time, promises it will never happen again, and says that disclosure would bring their family to the brink of collapse. How do you respond?

4. A student discloses fear that another is suicidal. What do you do?

5. What buttons of yours are most easily pushed? How do you respond?

6. Your students after school...and then in class...begin to call you by your first name. Does that matter? Will you deal differently with the treasured stage manager than the slackers who use a sarcastic edge in their voices as they call your name?

7. Some students are adamant that the cursing in their scene will only help it, not detract. You're not so sure. What do you do?

8. You've got a student with Asperger's Syndrome who is clearly getting on everyone's nerves, but you can tell that they're doing the best they can. How do you handle it?

9. Items are reported missing from a garment bag in a dressing room. What do you do?

10. Mr. Mischief continues to play with the props stored around the classroom and on the backstage prop table despite numerous reminders and warnings. What's your next step?

11. Some actors are trashing the show on social media while you're in the middle of the rehearsal process. Suggestions?

12. One of your drama queens is in crisis again, and her friends all want to comfort her during class instead of participating since she is *so* upset. What do you do?

4 Preparing for Production

The public face of your theatre department is the productions you put on. If your productions go well, most everyone will presume your teaching is going great. These shows bring honor to your school and support to your program. They are also what separates you from most other teachers—yours is a double job, part in class and part after school. Where can you find help along the way? What shows will you do? How will you decide and follow up? How can you best prepare your students for the production process? How should you deal with the drama in the drama department? What *is* a successful production?

Theatre Booster Support: the Good, the Great, and the Ugly

If your new school already has a parent drama booster group, make the effort to meet these folks as soon as possible. Before the school year starts is best by far. They are a wealth of information, and having them on your side from the get-go can be hugely helpful.

If your new school does not have such a group, find out if one is permitted. If so, you can easily create one. Pick an evening date/time, send an invitation home with your students (and/or cast/crew), and whoever turns up hopefully will turn into your first booster board. www.ParentBooster.org can provide a ton of information on how to make it all legal and tax deductible, including documents such as a constitution and by-laws. Eventually, you can expect the group to meet with you regularly to discuss how things are going and how they can help your program go even more smoothly as the season moves forward.

The first thing to remember and appreciate about a parent support group is that their intentions are positive. They are volunteers who give of their time, talents, and often their money, to support the theatre program at your school. You can avoid a lot of misunderstandings if you clearly define both your role and your expectations for their roles. In a nutshell, your role is artistic and educational leadership; their role is support for production, field trips and logistics. Your training and expertise drive the program. While parent support should by no means go unappreciated, the theatre program can exist without the boosters. It cannot exist without a teacher/director.

Booster support can ultimately make the production experience less stressful for you and enhanced for the students. At its best, the parent booster/theatre director relationship is a meaningful, fulfilling model of ensemble work that can extend into your learning community, creating a positive reputation for both you and your department. With parents who are dedicated to the overall good of the department—not just the experience of their own children—you and the boosters can share the best of educational theatre.

The Good

Theatre boosters provide an organized volunteer base for your program. Among the tasks that theatre boosters might perform are the following:

- rehearsal and tech day dinners/snacks
- parent expertise in tech tools that students may not be allowed or comfortable using
- assistance with procuring and transporting set-building materials
- procuring, building, and organizing costumes and props
- handling ticket sales, front of house
- publicity in your learning community

- chaperoning and/or organizing transportation for field trips
- decorating for awards night or senior recognition events
- cooking/decorating for guest critics' receptions
- creating display cases
- fundraising for field trip scholarships and senior scholarships
- purchasing commercial tickets and setting up online ticket sales
- coordinating program, T-shirt and poster printing
- photography
- fundraising for additional equipment (i.e., microphones, scrim, backdrops, tools, anything your school won't/can't buy)
- hosting cast parties
- setting up and maintaining your department website
- hanging posters on the cinder block walls of your room that need a special drill bit that no one in your school building was ever able to accomplish.

How much of a role the boosters play in production and publicity support is often dependent upon the size and maturity of your department. Whenever possible, students should take advantage of the opportunity to engage in production and publicity roles that you deem necessary and appropriate for them to handle. However, adult supervision is often helpful to ensure student success. All of this can be wonderful and positive for the students, the school, the community, your work load, and your sanity—as long as your role as theatre director is clearly defined, maintained and respected by all concerned.

The Great

Great booster parents are active and supportive regardless of the role in which their child is cast; these are often the officers in the booster organization, who "get it." This means they understand that educational theatre is all about the group experience, not the individual prestige of any one student. It also means that they understand that being part of a school theatre department is its own reward and provides a positive example for all of the students involved. It's about supporting your child's interest in an organic way instead of a specifically self-centered way. This works against the whole "what's in it for me" concept that is so prevalent in society and human experience and that translates to "what's in it for my kid?" How do you combat this? How do you respond when your booster parents have a weeping child at home who didn't get the part he or she wanted? Be sure to express your appreciation for parent support of teamwork for the good of the department.

For your devoted booster parents who "get it," it's not about "my kid is the star"—it's about "my kid is growing" or "my kid is acquiring skills that they can use in the job market." It's about everyone in the department, the department's function in the school, the school's function in the community; it's about creating goodness and growth together. Find the common ground on which you and your parent boosters can agree: we all want all the kids to have positive growth experiences in theatre. When dedicated parents buy into this philosophy, wonderful things happen: everyone feels supported, united, less stressed, and more fulfilled.

The Ugly: Resistance

What if, alas, you have theatre booster parents who are simply hostile? What if you have theatre booster parents who feel entitled to be part of casting? Who want to tell you what shows to pick or how to run your department? Who smile in your face, tell you how wonderful you are, then influence other booster parents to try to reverse decisions you have made? Sounds scary, doesn't it? It is, but you may very well have to deal with these issues—but do your best to keep the drama on the stage.

You should expect to encounter the full range of emotions, psychological conditions, and knee-jerk reactions that humanity has to offer. There are many ways to deal with difficult parents, but they all center on your control of the situation as theatre director. For the openly hostile parent, for example, make your point, assert yourself as calmly as possible, then recognize the situation. Use a phrase that asserts your authority but diffuses the hostility: "We'll just have to agree to disagree." Circumvent that issue by going through the school account/procedures; what would you do if there were no theatre boosters? Get advice from your department chairperson or administrator or other theatre directors in your school system. *Pick your battles*; remember: "Once is a revolution. Twice is a tradition." That preexisting $30 cast fee you really want to get rid of can be reduced to $20 this year, and then joyfully eradicated two years later. Especially your first year in a new job, it is wise to get the lay of the land before dictating multiple changes. Choose the most important issues that speak to professional integrity first; those are your most important battles. Time and consistency will be your greatest friends. Eventually, the difficult parent will graduate with their child, the controlling parent will either learn to respect your parameters or drift away, but you will still be the theatre director.

Welcome, Drama Boosters!!

Welcome, everyone. First let me congratulate and thank you a million times over for agreeing to help build and keep our theatre department strong through your participation and support.

I know it's the very beginning of the school year, so we haven't had time yet for anything to go wrong. To get us off on the right foot, and keep it that way, there are a few potential issues that I would like to address with you. Of course, they would never apply to *this* wonderful group, but I have heard of other booster groups running into conflicts which I'm sure we can avoid.

So…first of all, please know that your primary job is to "boost" the program into the places I want it to go. Not to decide where it should go, but to help support me in my decisions. Mine is the artistic responsibility.

You will *never* decide what shows we do here. You will *never* have any involvement in casting decisions—ever. That is a difficult, lonely responsibility that I carry out to the best of my ability and I trust that, to the best of your ability, you will respect and support my decisions in our theatre community. I love and appreciate your help, but your participation will not give your own child a leg up come audition time. Casting just doesn't work that way, any more than the seniors deserve a role over someone better suited to it simply because they are seniors. You must trust me on this, and I thank you for doing so.

You will never get the keys to the theatre areas, unless I specifically loan mine to you—which I'm probably not supposed to do, even to other adults (I'll check on that). They don't belong to me, either, so I cannot be handing them out or permitting non-school personnel to have them.

You will never decide how to spend school drama department money. You may raise funds to help our drama department, but school accounts are separate from booster accounts and are bound by different rules. One of your most important jobs may be to run errands for fabric, lumber, props, food, etc., but if those are paid for by school money, the items must be approved by the school prior to purchase, and even reimbursements must be done according to our school's finance procedures.

Your most important job is to help fill the seats for our shows. So, whatever you can do to promote our productions and give our kids the huge audiences all their hard work will deserve, is to the good. As a practical matter, we will also need chaperones, drivers, and upon request, help with the backstage work like construction of the set and costumes. It's not a chaperone's job to pitch in, but only to supervise and keep kids safe…unless we call upon you to be our safety net when time runs short, or we lack expertise you can help provide.

And, of course, food. I don't have to tell you that teenagers are constantly hungry. So, from water to keep our singers hydrated, to snacks during rehearsal, to coming up with last-minute pizza so a work session can run longer, to catering meals for our few really long rehearsals, keeping the troops fed is an important job that will get you great popularity among the kids.

So, I'm the one up front, making the decisions. And you've got my back. We all want the kids to be the stars they can be and to make our shows the best they've ever been. I really look forward to working together with you.

Direct and Lead

As the employed theatre educator hired to teach, direct and lead your school's theatre department, you are in charge, because you are responsible. You have to make decisions about how things are done in your theatre department, and that may mean changes from what has become established tradition. Everything comes back to you; you will have to provide an explanation to any administrator who brings issues to your attention. No matter how dedicated your school theatre booster parents are, they were not hired to do the job, you were. This means that you must be solidly integrated into the communication and decision-making processes of the theatre boosters—you should be copied on all email communication.

Your leadership responsibilities pertain to all aspects of the theatre program, including safety rules and school policies. This means that parents who think it is okay to hand a circular saw over to a student need to be corrected before anyone gets hurt. So you have to take the initiative to communicate your tech safety rules and procedures, not only to the students, but to the parents. This means that the "tradition" of charging $40 for students to attend the end of the year awards ceremony might need to change. This means that unless you can be with every student who is with a parent volunteer, all the time, each parent volunteer should adhere to the policies of your school district (i.e., don't leave a student alone with a parent, especially not a parent of the opposite sex). This means that the cast party will be on school grounds, instead of the booster home where alcohol was served to well-meaning parents last year, while the kids ate pizza in the basement. This means that the videos the boosters were selling for the musical last year (without video licensure) won't be sold this year, because you are promoting professional ethics with which you are comfortable.

If it's an official theatre department activity, then school rules apply, on or off campus. You may meet some resistance—some of the hardest working, most dedicated booster parents get used to being in charge and will challenge your authority because they may have been working to keep the theatre department from falling apart longer than you have been teaching. Thank them and validate their hard work. Emphasize the things the boosters do that you appreciate and don't intend to change. Then communicate your vision for the theatre department and do what you were hired to do: teach and lead responsibly.

Your Department Production Schedule

First things first: has your production season already been scheduled on a school calendar somewhere? Who creates and updates such things? Have the shows been announced? Where? Can you live with those decisions? Do you want to? What can and can't you change?

There are a lot of pieces to the production schedule puzzle. Who else uses your performance venue, be it theatre, auditorium, black box, cafetorium, or gymnatorium (eeeew!)? When have other users already blocked the space out? Is the city symphony scheduled to perform the night before your musical is to open? How is *that* going to work? Does the music department have a series of pre-competition concerts locked in the same parts of the calendar every year? Has the student government planned an event at some arbitrary point in the year? Will the space be used for SAT testing on the day you'd like to tech your show? Might your show conflict with another school event? Find out what's going on when and where and by whom!

In a perfect world, what would you want, and when? Fall straight play, winter one-acts, spring musical? Are there competitions and/or festivals at which you'd like your students to perform or participate? Are they worthy of the extra after-school time you'd need in lieu of a less demanding production for your hometown crowd? Or perhaps there is something more challenging for your students that would suit a theatre kid audience but not draw much of a crowd from your local/school demographics?

Does a musical in the fall avoid conflict with spring testing—but conflict with marching band for the football season, making musicians hard to get? Do you need/want live musicians? Is the music department expecting to help with a musical? Avoiding it? Do your students need more experience before tackling a show with the scope of a musical? Do you? What about the winter? Are you in an area at risk for being snowed out on a show weekend? Now *there* is an expensive headache!

When do vacations fall? Can you rehearse during the weekend that starts or concludes one? What about teacher workdays or long weekend holidays? Can you get in the building then? How do you personally view these breaks in the schedule? Are they an opportunity for great extra rehearsal time, or do they give you a chance to catch up on the rest of your life? What about the test-heavy last week of a grading quarter? Can you take that into consideration? If so, how?

Do you want your classes to perform publicly during the year—in what format? A collection of class scenes? A set of one-acts? A full length show? Do you want to do a children's theatre piece in anticipation of potential students signing up for classes next year? When does that happen? Do you want to tour a show? Use student directors? Do multiple shows at once (think carefully about that one!)?

What about storage space and construction space? Are choral risers or a sound shell taking up all the wing space? If so, can they be relocated, even if only temporarily? How much time can you have—or negotiate—to build a show and light it and rehearse it with more or less exclusive use of the performance space?

So many questions to answer! Take your best shot at a reasonable rehearsal schedule, and always plan to learn from your experience the next time around.

The Next Step: The Production Process

Try to develop a production concept that is shared and available to all. As time permits, meet early with your production staff to take their ideas and input, and to clarify to all how you want to approach the production. You can post an "inspiration board" to which anyone can

Real-World Moments

After ten weeks of rehearsal, the show was about to open. Elsewhere at the school, the football team was having a terrific season. The regional finals were to be hosted at our school—on opening night. Parking would be a nightmare. The Director of Student Activities approached and asked if we were going to cancel the show to support the team and ease the logistics. I knew it was only because of my solid history at the school that I had the nerve to reply, "Has the football coach been asked to reschedule or relocate the game, to support the theatre program and ease the logistics?" That was met with silence and a "What, are you stupid?" glare. "No, I'm not going to cancel a performance for an event that could be rained out. This is a really big night for us, too." "What about the parking?" "I guess that's the price of having such a successful school!" Both events took place, parking was a nightmare, and both were sold out triumphs. (A nearby school had been in this situation and the director was ordered by the principal to cancel the show.)

add a picture, sketch, swatch of fabric, or whatever might help get the creative juices flowing. Can you distill the essence of the show down to one sentence? Can you decide on a color palette for it? What images predominate that might lead to design or acting (or casting) choices?

If your initial concept is no more complicated than "learn the lines, get the blocking, and make the plot reasonably clear to the audience," that's OK. More nuance comes with time and experience.

Get scripts for each of your staff people—they are just as important as your actors. At a read-through and/or during table work, when the whole cast discusses the script, provide each crew with a chart to track each page, cue, item, and detail as it comes up, that pertains to their job ("it's so dark" = lighting cue; "Nice hat" = costume note, etc.). If you have access to computers, let all work together on a shared Google spreadsheet, and you'll end up with a master plan of the entire production before regular rehearsals even begin! (Doing this for a short class scene from the production would be a relatively quick process but would create the expectation and familiarity for the full production version.)

Set your technical rehearsal date as early as you can, after you can get into your performance space and set up your set and lighting. Make this—and *not* opening night—your absolute drop-deadline for all aspects of the production and you will buy your techies the chance to both play catch-up with all those actors and find their own comfort level for running the show smoothly. You will thus enable your techies to have fun running the show, not having to rely on a wing and a prayer to make things go right. Let your actors know that you're done with them by then, too, and that you will now shift your focus to coordinating their efforts with those of the lighting/sound/running crew. So, no more calling for lines. It's also time to troubleshoot: to practice what to do if someone goes up on (i.e., forgets) their lines or something goes wrong.

Getting Organized

Now is the time to:

- Teach basic safety, leadership skills and run what-if scenarios.
- Get production contracts and emergency care cards from your staff so you know that they have permission to do the show, and also what to do and whom to contact in case of emergency.
- Have *parents* come in and do a walk-through of your stage, backstage, storage and classroom areas if their kids will be doing tech. Once they sign off that all is okay— *or not*—regarding use of tools, ladders, etc., then you are ready to proceed. Be sure to respect their restrictions for their kids.
- Set up mailboxes in the theatre classroom for each crew, and post attractive sign-up sheets to solicit crew members.
- Talk about budgets and purchase orders and receipts and reimbursements and other finance office procedures with your crew chiefs.
- Sketch out a calendar or fill columns on a white board of each and every thing that needs to be done, by whom, and by when.
- Read or reread the evaluations of those who have done their jobs before so that you—and they—don't have to reinvent the wheel (or advise that you're going to begin such a tradition).
- Poke around and inventory the supplies already hiding, but available for use. Identify those items in need of repair or replacement, and schedule that work.
- Begin the design work in earnest. And while you're at it, why not draft the show program, too, rather than waiting until it's time to print and having the whole works in panic mode?

Selecting a Show

What to produce?! And where to find it? When searching for a show to produce, there are myriad considerations:

What Shows Have Been Produced There Recently?

You don't want to repeat a show the school still remembers. Also, for example, if recent shows have included *Grease, Bye Bye Birdie, Hairspray,* or *High School Musical,* what do you do next? Do you just go with another peppy show about high school, or do you look for a change of pace, perhaps a drama?

What Type of Play are You Looking for?

Comedy? Drama? Musicals sell the best and are the hardest and most expensive to do. Comedies sell next best; everybody loves a good comedy, as long as you can keep it moving along crisply. Dramas are the hardest to sell, especially if the title is unknown, but can present the best challenges for your actors, and be the most memorable productions you can do both for your actors and the audience.

What Genre Do You Want to Do?

Classical? Musical? Children's theatre? Mystery? etc.? Mix it up—you will all enjoy the variety. It's a good idea to vary what you offer your students as their theatre education journey continues.

What Does Your Available Talent Pool Look Like?

Think in terms of talent, yes, but also in terms of numbers, gender breakdown and other intangibles. Ethnicity mostly doesn't matter, but for some shows it might (it's tough to do *Hairspray* will an all-white or all-black cast). It's just plain depressing to choose a show for a cast of thousands and have only ten kids come to auditions. At the same time, it's also a problem to have a hundred kids show up when you only need a cast of ten. Now you've crushed the dreams of ninety kids who will be in school the next day (and the next…) feeling disappointed, bitter and angry. Then again, you don't want to cast so many girls vs. boys that your onstage town looks as if its male population had been wiped out by a plague or something. A ratio of three girls to one boy is the most you can get away with before that happens.

Real-World Moments

We needed a prop gun for a very silly skit we were doing at school, but I was told by our school administration that I had to send a letter home for parent signature to everyone in the cast (even the kids who weren't in that skit) with a description of the gun.

I asked my administrator to find out if I could just use a small, brightly fluorescent squirt gun. He said that would still necessitate the parental permission notes. Then I asked the administrator to inquire if I could use a balloon animal. When told the balloon would be in the shape of a gun, he administrator said yes, but that it would still require parental permission for using a balloon!

I opted for a golf club with the word "BANG" attached to the end. Needless to say, the effect was somewhat diminished.

What Technical Resources are at Hand?

What skills and experience are available to you (students, colleagues, parents)? What materials do you already have? Consider your available stock flats, platforms, lumber, costumes, accessories, set pieces, furniture, lamps, and various prop items.

Do you know if you've got kids who can run the lighting and sound equipment? Design for it? What about set design? Can you do it? Can the kids? If not, what then?

Can you rent set construction plans from ScenoGraphics.com? Do you want parents to build, help build, or supervise—or just stay away from—the process of set construction? Will you have to be on site day and night for weeks in order to ensure that the set is properly constructed?

Do you know where you can borrow costumes? Can you afford rentals? Do you have kids available, or can you solicit outside assistants who can make costumes as needed…and on time?

What Financial Resources do You Have?

Whatever is needed for your show, there is the basic question: can you afford it?

Your expenses will include royalties (don't even think of not paying them!), scripts, music rental, publicity materials, lumber, paint, fabric, props to be built or bought, even the tickets themselves. Costs do add up. Do you start with enough money to cover your costs? Does the school have to "loan" you your up front money, hoping to recoup from ticket receipts? Must you stay within a tiny budget? And what *is* your budget, anyway?

It's often true that it takes money to make money, and a lavishly teched show can look more professional and draw more of a crowd than something minimal and cheaper. But you've got to learn to estimate your audience so you don't risk losing money on a show (try pegging ticket prices to movie ticket prices if you know your kids go to the movies). Publicity is *huge*. Make it a major priority. Do not just let everyone hide in the dark walls of the rehearsal rooms. This takes time, planning, and some money—and plenty of good word of mouth by absolutely everyone!

What is Going to Attract Your Prime Audience: the Students in Your School?

Obscure theatrical choices may challenge your actors and techies, but everyone loves a full house. Also, some material really is not appropriate in a school setting.

Remember, you are not in college anymore. Resist the temptation to re-mount every show you were in then.

What is Going to Work Well for Your Larger Community?

You want to draw a repeat audience from far beyond those coming to support their friends or family. What will appeal to them? What's the nature of the community? Can you find out what shows have played successfully nearby in the past?

How sensitive is your community to cursing or other language that could be considered sacrilegious? In some places you can say "God" and you can say "damn" but you'd better not put them together without expecting howls of complaint.

Are there many young families in your community? Is children's theatre popular? Consider it!

What Do You Like?

What would you find exciting and fun to direct and produce? You are simply going to be spending much too much time on a show to be working on something you personally don't much like. A show that speaks to you is one you can rally the "troupes" around and attack with real enthusiasm.

Acquiring a Show

So...where do shows actually come from? In your own acting experience, scripts were probably simply handed out. But now, you'll need to get yourself a cast and crew's worth...and not by photocopying (always illegal, and no one will stick up for you)!

Publishers

Playwrights contract with publishers to market their work. Publishers advertise and print scripts (or make e-scripts available) and charge you for each copy, and also charge you royalties for each performance of that show, whether or not admission is charged. All publishers have websites on which you can read synopses of the plot, see character breakdowns, instrumentation, etc. (how much info varies from place to place), and you can order online or by fax, email, or snail mail.

Musicals

Musical companies will send you perusal copies of up to three shows (you have to pay postage) for three weeks. Other companies will require you to purchase a copy of the show (under $10), and some straight play (non-musical) companies will let you read most of the show online. Looking for the publisher of a particular show? Try www.FindaPlay.com. While not comprehensive, it's pretty good.

Plan to pay for shipping, too, and to wait for those scripts to arrive unless you pay extra for faster shipping. For musicals, the scripts and music are typically rented, not sold, and will arrive two months prior to your show dates unless you pay extra to get them earlier. Music for the orchestra also presumes that you have talented players who are also versatile. So if your clarinet player can't also play saxophone, for example, you may need to rent additional musical parts. The orchestra music may also be offered in more than one version: the full orchestra, the combo, the expanded orchestra, and sometimes even the option of vocal parts (and accompanying instrumentalists) transposed to fit the range of the vocalist or errata (listed corrections of errors in the score). You will need to pay attention to these types of details before you commit to doing a particular musical. Work closely with your music director because much of this information is requested along with the contract.

Contracts

You should never sign a contract for a production. Only the principal, as the official representative of the school, is authorized to do so. In some school systems, it must be approved first

Appendix Connection

Who are these great and powerful play publishers? Find a list in appendix K, *Publishers of Musicals and Plays.*

Save the Drama for Your Mama

Wait to announce your show until you have both the publisher's and your school's permission to do it! Otherwise, great ugliness may ensue!

by even higher up the food chain. This means that even after you've decided on a production, it could take days or even longer before you can send for your material.

From time to time, a show will be "restricted"—usually meaning that a professional touring production is scheduled to be in your area around the same time as your show dates—so the publisher will not grant you the rights during that time. In that situation, sadly, you are out of luck—find something else. Some authors (like Neil Simon and the estate of Thornton Wilder) refuse permission for their work to be done partially, or excerpted. For example, you can't do one act of *Plaza Suite* even though it totally holds up on its own without the other two acts. Sigh, and move on.

Never announce a show until you have permission from the publisher (and your school) to do it. Backtracking on an announcement is an ugly situation, indeed. If you talk about what you are considering before you have the go-ahead, keep those "asterisks" looming large; it ain't over till the i's are dotted and t's are crossed.

Among publishers, there are big fish (those that handle the rights for most of the shows that have been on Broadway) and little fish (everyone else). For straight plays (and a few musicals), the big fish are Samuel French, Inc. (samuelfrench.com) and Dramatists Play Service (dramatists.com). There are plenty of other companies out there, however, and their work may be just what you're looking for. Dramatic Publishing Company (dramaticpublishing.com) and Playscripts (playscripts.com) are among the best for the educational market. For musicals, the big fish include Tams-Witmark (tamswitmark.com), Music Theatre International (MTIshows.com) and the Rodgers and Hammerstein Music Theatre Library (rnh.com). The newest kid on the block is Theatrical Rights Worldwide (TRWmusicals.com).

Each of these publishers has its own idiosyncrasies that you will need to deal with. For example, Tams-Witmark only sends "sides" (slim scripts containing only the pages needed by each individual character, instead of full scripts. Not great for building company unity) and has few rehearsal resources available, but they own many of the standard, reliable classics among musicals. MTI offers "RehearScore," a computer program that will play the accompaniment for all the songs, with adjustable tempos and the ability to pull out certain parts, but not for performance use. TRW has something similar and offers electronic versions of both script and music for perusal (same day! yea!). Expect to pay a $400 deposit along with your

Contracting a Show

Here's the whole process:

1. Go online and read blurbs from the play or musical publishers' websites, and look over the plays you've already got access to.
2. Order perusal copies to read (and ask everyone you know if they already have a copy you can borrow).
3. Read, read, read. Find a show that you love and that fits your needs.
4. Go back online with the publisher, fill out their form to request the rights, and receive an email reply with your contract attached.
5. Give your administration a heads-up that this is the show you hope to produce, and get their approval.
6. Get the contract filled out, approved as needed, signed by the principal, and sent/faxed/emailed back along with any required deposit.
7. Be sure you have ordered all the items you need, including scripts for your techies as well as your full cast, available publicity materials that you might want, additional rental time if needed, and the like.
8. Get confirmation that the contract has been approved and your materials are en route.
9. Announce your show, publicize auditions and any pertinent audition workshops you will offer. Send back the perusal copies.
10. Watch for arrival of the boxes with scripts and other material. Save the packaging to return musical materials that you've rented (they are very expensive if lost!).

signed contract before anyone will rent you anything other than perusal scripts, except for TRW, with whom you can elect to pay more for the show—but you get to keep the scripts, so no deposit is required. Expect to pay thousands of dollars in rental/royalties for several performances of a musical, and hundreds of dollars for several performances of a straight play.

AUDITION CARD   Fill out this card now, and hand it to the stage manager as soon as possible. Write neatly.

NAME	GRADE	STUDENT ID #	HEIGHT	WEIGHT
EMAIL		PHONE		
PREVIOUS EXPERIENCE				
SPECIAL SKILLS (MUSICAL INSTRUMENTS, JUGGLING, ETC.)				

CHECK ALL THAT APPLY:

☐ I WANT A CERTAIN ROLE _____

☐ I CLOSELY MATCH A CERTAIN ROLE _____

☐ I DON'T REALLY KNOW THIS PLAY YET

☐ I WILL ☐ WILL NOT UNDERSTUDY

☐ I WILL ☐ WILL NOT BE IN THE ENSEMBLE

SKILL LEVEL SELF-EVALUATION

	Can solo	Good in a group	Not my strength
ACTING	☐	☐	☐
DANCING	☐	☐	☐
SINGING	☐	☐	☐

CONFLICTS   On the back of this card, list any time day or night you're unavailable for rehearsal. Include what the conflict is, when it is, how long it lasts, and whether or not it is flexible.

Figure 4.1: A sample audition card

Pre-Audition Workshop: Communicate the Process

It can be very helpful for you to include a unit on auditioning for your classes, and perhaps also have an after-school workshop for those not in your classes who can audition—especially for your musical. As you know, auditions are pretty stressful, but as unpredictable as they can be, there *are* things one should do to make the best impression. Invite the brave to come prepared with some audition material to use as examples to all. This will give you a chance to show some of the things to aim for, or to avoid, at the official auditions.

Decide and announce how you plan to conduct your auditions. For example, decide whether or not you will permit people to watch each other audition, audition one group at a time, or audition each student privately, etc. You may find it helpful (especially in case of a parental challenge) to invite some colleagues—even if they're not theatre teachers—to participate in the audition process. That way the decisions are made by a panel of auditioners, rather than relying solely on your professional judgment. Imagine that!

Tell students that when they arrive, they should first find your stage manager to get an audition card to fill out (see figure 4.1). The card identifies them, provides contact information, and whatever other specific information you feel would be helpful, as well as pointing out any conflicts they may have with rehearsal times or show dates. On the subject of conflicts, it's not unusual to have someone audition who also does sports or music five days a week... when were they figuring to be available for your show? Or what if they aren't available on a show night? After they complete the card, they should hand it back to the stage manager and sit quietly until their name is called. You also may want to use your production contract (see appendix N) as a "ticket" to callbacks, to make sure that everyone you cast does in fact have their parent's permission to do the show.

Remind your auditioning students that breathing slowly and deeply will force one's body to be more calm, and that the best way to use nervous tension is to channel it into the character, not to bottle it up. They should approach the audition as a chance to perform—which is exactly why they're auditioning in the first place.

You are going to see all sorts of flaws in your students' sample auditions. Suggest how these can be avoided. And if you don't see such flaws in the workshop, it can be fun for all if you demonstrate a series of flawed auditions yourself.

Speaking of flaws, you are likely to see kids do any or all of the following in their auditions:

- Fail to answer all the questions on the audition card.
- Dress like advertisements for bands or various products, or in work or cheerleader uniforms, or in shorts or clothing very unlikely to be like what the play calls for.
- "Slate" their name so fast that you cannot catch it.
- Back up as far as the space allows instead of playing forward, to the audience.
- Side-step slowly and unintentionally across the stage as they speak.
- Recite words as if the audition was about whether they could memorize.
- Stick to the script, reading, usually looking down, cutting off their air/projection, lacking focus on their objective.
- Select material designed to shock, to get a rise out of their peers, without considering a possible negative reaction from you, the auditioner.
- Be unfamiliar with the play their monologue is from and its purpose in the moment.
- Play with their necklace or hair, tug at pockets or pick at invisible navel lint.
- Display active faces but conflicting or absent appropriate body language.
- Express themselves with active voices but placid faces.
- Use arbitrary blocking and gestures.

Appendix Connection

See appendix M, *Audition Card*, for a copy of this audition card (two to a page) that you can photocopy as needed. Feel free to use or modify it as you see fit.

- Drop final consonants and trail off at ends of sentences.

In your auditioning unit/workshop, you may want to demonstrate several "bad" auditions: the nearly silent one, the totally fidgety one, the outstanding vocal but stiff as a board one, the hysterical because they lost their place one, the giggly one, the utterly bland one, the overly melodramatic one, the monotone, etc. Also demonstrate positive things you're looking for, such as taking one's time; clear articulation; using the space well; including levels; delineating beats; incorporating variety both vocally and physically and building to a climax, etc.

In addition to casting for specific roles, you will obviously be looking for some of your students to take on the less glamorous role of understudy. Explain and stress the value of the understudy. Create a culture that values the role of the understudy. Show your students that it is a great way to support and be part of the production, to demonstrate work ethic and talent, and to develop a character and practice a role, even if there is no guarantee that an audience will see it. On the other hand, the understudy may literally save the day if misfortune befalls their counterpart. Working with that counterpart is also the best way for both of them to learn lines and have extra time to discuss character choices. There will always be rehearsals when someone is missing, and having an understudy ready from the get-go to simply step in lets your entire rehearsal process keep going smoothly. You sure don't want to hit disaster and *wish* you had cast an understudy.

Make sure all of your students know where you will be posting your callback list. At callbacks, students should expect to read from the script itself to help you match couples and make final decisions about who fits where the best, who will understudy, etc. Let them know that it's possible that you don't need a callback reading from someone whom you are already certain you want to use. They should check the cast list even if they didn't feel good about (or get called for) the callbacks. Finally, direct students to watch that cast list for instructions about what comes next.

Working with your volunteers throughout this workshop, stop your brave guinea pigs (your "hams"?!) and tell them whenever they do something worth pointing out to the watchful masses, be it for a compliment or a suggestion. Then let them continue until the next point of interest. There will be those who shine and those whose unpreparedness makes a strong impression on those whose real audition is yet to come. Both are of great value. It should be

Appendix 📄 Connection

What you *want* to see at an audition is identified in the handout in appendix L, *Auditioning using the ADDIE system*. (This system also applies to many other types of projects.)

pretty instructive, and most kids really appreciate the one-on-one feedback. Be sensitive to a range of student confidence and ability to accept constructive feedback in front of a crowd.

Developing Leadership

A chief hallmark of progress in any field is the transition from participant to leader. As the teacher/director, you are now in a position of leadership but also of one who develops leadership in others. Giving students responsibility and holding them to high standards offers them what may be the most valuable experiences they can get from high school. Your production staff and crew chiefs become the backbone of your program. Leadership training is always worth the time. They will be training others in turn, hopefully resulting in a smooth running machine that is constantly reinforcing the values and best practices you have established.

Training students for leadership roles means being willing to let go of some control—the control of doing everything yourself. Delegating to students means everything may not get done exactly the way you would do it. But if you train them, they will complete their tasks one way or another, and they will learn more in the process. Consider giving students opportunities to direct scenes, one-acts, even a main-stage children's theatre or play event. Directing all or part of a musical is probably too much to ask of any student.

Another potential source of leadership can be found in your Thespian troupe officers. Encourage them to make the troupe their own by creating departmental bonding events, big brother/sister (upperclassman/lowerclassman) connections, taking charge of the callboard, Thespian state activities, and a plethora of other opportunities. Your Thespian officers can be in charge of organizing your end of year awards celebration and work with your booster group to create a special evening for your whole department—and you may even get to relax a little by delegating.

Materials for Developing Leadership

On the next couple of pages, you'll find some notes useful for putting together a workshop (or several) on leadership, to help train your crew chiefs. Meet weekly without fail to help stay on top of show-related challenges, logistical, personal, and artistic. Each crew chief meeting could begin with some leadership training as your students increase their interpersonal skills. Have some discussion of these ideas before getting into the particulars of that week's show issues and status reports.

THE OBLIGATIONS OF LEADERSHIP

The leader has special obligations. As a leader, you/your crew chiefs

* Set the agenda -- Break down work into tasks; work within the calendar; coordinate with other crews
* Set the priorities -- What's going to get done first? Next? How much of your budget gets spent on what?
* Set the tone and standards
* Determine the division of labor (incl. ACC)
* Set the pace
* Supervise the work and the crew (and safety)
* Handle the problems and resolve the conflicts; share at staff meetings
* Dictate the mid-course corrections
* Assure timely completion of the tasks
* Evaluate the success of the task/crew

PLANNING

Take time now or waste time (and money) later: Read previous crew chief evaluations; glean good advice, plan to add your own advice. Divide work into tasks. List tasks. Allocate # people & estimate time per task. Match tasks to calendar. Add leeway "fudge factor" sessions. Assign tasks to the right people. Provisioning---Where can you get the things you're going to need? Where to store them?

LEARNING STYLE

What's your (your crew's) learning style (4 colors or Meyers Briggs)? So what? What's Leadership? Structure vs. Content

BUDGETING MONEY AND TIME

* GOOD vs. FAST vs. CHEAP (one can only ever achieve 2 out of the 3!)
* How much do things cost?
* Purchase Orders and Finance Office rules and procedures, etc.
* Shopping (and receipts)
* Transportation (list of parents with time and trucks)

<u>PICK TWO:</u>

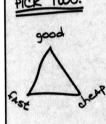

good

fast

cheap

THE QUALITIES OF A LEADER

Priorities: Rank order for you-- Rank order for a leader

* Being encouraging
* Being punctual
* Being organized
* Being patient
* Being safety-conscious
* Being popular
* Being talented
* Being capable
* Being clear
* Being experienced
* Being industrious
* Being a "big picture" person
* Being thrifty
* Being detail-oriented
* Having high standards
* Being relaxed, fun to work with
* Being:
* Being:

TROUBLESHOOTING---Discuss what to do in each of these scenarios (and others):

What if...you're sick? No supplies? Doors locked? No chaperone? Left alone to clean up? Someone hurt? Item stolen? Rowdiness? Bad-mouthing? Bad attitude? Running out of time? Insufficient expertise? Crew errors? No-shows? Slackers? Divas?

TEAMWORK

-Jigsaw puzzle vs. dominoes (what's gotta be done before others start)
-Tech Day deadlines and what's next
-Integration of ideas (lights vs. costumes vs. makeup, etc.)
-Actor support and patience
-Staff meetings
-Sharing people on multiple crews; ITS pts; scheduling

CREW TRAINING DOSSIER

Resources where crew chiefs can find
answers to questions:
* Catalogues at school from vendors of
    theatre supplies and equipment
* *The Backstage Handbook* by Paul Carter
    and George Chiang
* *Backstage Forms* by Paul Carter
* *Stage Production Handbook* by Kathryn
    Michelle Busti
* The show's dramaturge
* The show's production manager
* The director or the assistant/student
    director
* Boosters
* Vendors
* Internet/forums
* Your crew
* Their parents (and yours)
* Other theatre teachers
* Other school staff, kids
* Textbooks and theatre magazines
* Blackboard

LIES

- If it's important to you, it will be impor-
    tant to others.
- Nothing will go wrong.
- If you cancel a session, everyone (in-
    cluding the chaperone) will know.
- If you schedule it, they will come.
- The equipment will work now because
    it did the last time you used it.
- Things will be where they were.

Student leaders may not:

- Hire/fire without approval from higher up
- Spend money without prior approval
- Modify the design/specifications without
    approval
- Permit sabotage (including bad-mouthing) of
    others' work

Leadership Training should
include discussion of various
issues:

* Timely and clear
    notification
    (scheduling)
* Budget and work load
    elements (breaking the
    job into pieces)
* Crew mentoring (learning
    names; train v do;
    encouragement;
    discipline)
* Troubleshooting/
    Anticipating (content
    and people)
* Resources for more
    info/help (books,
    people, vendors, etc.)
* Teamwork (working
    collaboratively, as an
    ensemble)

You're going to live or die by the strength of
your communication, but there are lots of judgment
calls to be made:

* How much? How soon? What kind(s)?
* Redundancy: Waste? Or worth the effort?
* Personalizing communication
* Follow-through and its impact
* Work sessions vs. chaperones, space available,
    coordination w other crews, etc.
* Where to post work sessions: Who gets your
    crew list?

PEOPLE SKILLS
Names -- learn them soon and use them often. Background info -- the more you
know about a person, the better you can tailor your leadership to their
learning style. Train with clarity and encouragement. Eye contact, glazing
over, avoidance, shining eyes are all signals about how successfully you are
reaching the other person. Accountability. Know when to cut your losses.
Friend vs. crew member -- how to balance the two? Safety. Discipline. Getting
help with people: Contact the production manager, director, AD, boosters,
other. Conflicts within the group or conflicts with you. Social time -- its
value and its weight.

Cleanup of Support Space

Having your equipment, tools and supplies well organized makes it possible to get right down to work. In the course of that work, things get moved, go missing, get broken, get used up, etc. So periodically, you need to get the slate back to as clean as possible, to be ready to write on it all over again. If you are fortunate enough to have a scene shop and/or costume shop, this problem is frighteningly easy to observe and trickier to fix.

If you have a technical theatre class, assign a pair of kids to each separate theatre area so that everyone has a job. At the beginning of each month, send them off for a very few minutes to check their area for things out of place, in need of repair, things gone missing, clutter, safety concerns, etc. Then have them report back to you the action they took or that you need to take (like submitting a work order request) to bring that area back to its optimal condition. You may have to reassign some groups when you find out who can actually see an empty soda bottle and four candy wrappers as trash, and who can rearrange furniture to take up half the space and not look like a bonfire waiting for a torch. But you will also be amazed at how efficiently a large group can tidy an even larger area. Be sure to follow up on those safety and maintenance requests, including purchase orders to replenish supplies that have run low.

When you begin a production, each crew chief becomes responsible for "their" theater area. For example, anything made of fabric becomes a costume item to be stored by that crew chief. Any object is a prop, except things that belong to other departments (if it plugs in, it goes to lighting; if it's wood, it goes to set construction; tape goes to running crew; paint stuff to paint, and so on). Start each show with a massive cleanup (should be easy if your tech class is doing its monthly check) and you will save time and money, particularly on tools that used to be underneath furniture and things like that. Be ruthless about throwing away enough to enable you to keep your inventory under control. But don't let kids throw things away just because they don't know what they are. You are responsible, after all. Check on what they plan to trash; explain what needs to stay and what can go.

Also use this time for each crew to inventory its supplies. How many platforms are ready to be repurposed? How many flats are there, and of what size? How many working sewing machines? How much lighting gel and spare lamps? And so forth. Now is the time to replenish supplies you know you are likely to need—like more gaff tape!

Establishing a Production Team/Crew Chiefs

The sooner you put a leadership team in place, the sooner the kids start learning leadership and taking responsibility for their piece of the puzzle. Putting heads together at a weekly staff meeting yields huge benefits, keeping everyone on the same page and letting all discover that we are each others' solutions—like when the actor's projection problem is solved by the cos-

Real-World Moments

"OK, sir, here's my purchase order for you to sign, to get the wood we need."

"$1,200? Why?"

"To build platforms."

"Don't we already have a bunch of platforms?"

"Well...I dunno."

"Why not?"

"They're behind other stuff."

"But you think we should spend money to build all new ones?"

"Yeah."

"Why?"

"I just love the smell of fresh wood!"

"Go dig out the old platforms and use all of those first."

"Well, it was worth a try."

The moral of the story: beware accepting anything at face value. Taking the easy way out (good and fast) has a cost (cheap). If something smells suspicious, check it out!

tume person adding a pocket to the garment so it can hold a wireless microphone transmitter. It saves you time and energy and keeps you in touch with all aspects of production, so you can troubleshoot as needed instead of always trying to be everywhere at once.

Who do you need on this production team? Kids who can take on responsibility, be reasonably organized, and work well with others. In fact, those traits may be more important than experience. Be generous about giving out titles—it makes people feel important and makes clear who to go to for status updates. Division of labor makes the whole production job more manageable for you and fun for them. Some kids will glom onto a job and keep it for several years, while others will try a job and next time try something different. Prefer the former, as long as the seniors are training an underclassman to take over the following year. If you can put your entire production staff of crew chiefs in place even before auditions, you can get tons of design work done, and these kids will know they are valued as much as the actors.

Production Staff

ASSISTANT DIRECTOR (AD) The AD can lead warm-ups, take your rehearsal notes, rehearse one set of actors while you work with another, minimize your distractions by screening questions while you are busy, act as your sounding board, etc. Be clear that you may overrule their artistic decisions. This student may also be seen as more approachable if there's a problem that others are reluctant to bring directly to you.

PRODUCTION/BUSINESS MANAGER Your business manager can track all income and expenses, receipts, reimbursements and related paperwork. Be sure they understand and make friends with the school finance office folks, who may not want to deal with students, and follow all of their standard operating procedures.

DRAMATURGE Use your dramaturge to watch for and translate unfamiliar language or cultural references for your students who may not do their due diligence without help (that might be nearly all of them...). This research assistant can also provide your tech staff with pictures and information to assist with the authenticity of your production.

TECHNICAL DIRECTOR (TD) The TD can coordinate scheduling among the various tech departments to track and maintain work sessions, consolidate purchases for different departments but from the same stores, advise regarding safety standards, mediate between you and the crew chiefs if needed, generally keep an eye on which departments are progressing and which are falling behind or running into problems, and keep you informed.

STAGE MANAGER (SM) The glue of any production, the SM can handle the "administrivia" of auditions, set up and strike the stage area for rehearsal prior to bringing in your running crew, record blocking, take down your rehearsal notes, and ultimately, call the cues and handle anything expected (or unexpected) that occurs during performances.

Appendix Connection

An appendix bonanza awaits you with several items: appendix P, *Crew Chief Explanations and Expectations*, appendix R, *Crew Chief Sign-Up Instructions and List*, and appendix S, *Crew Chief Task Calendar*. Feel free to use or modify them as you see fit.

ASSISTANT STAGE MANAGER (ASM) These students can be vital to backstage success during a performance. One can be posted on each side of the backstage area with Telex communication to the booth and stage manager, who calls the show. Two or three trusty assistants can help the SM run errands, keep actors quiet backstage, fetch actors, and whatever else might be needed. This can be a great way for students to apprentice towards SM and to get to know the whole production process.

CREW CHIEFS These positions consist of one person in charge of each technical department with the leadership skills necessary to attract, organize, and assist their crews in getting the work done in a safe, timely, and cost-effective manner. The crew chiefs' leadership skills may be more important than the technical skills they are overseeing. Division of labor reduces the pressure for everyone, and lessens the risk to the show, if someone doesn't pan out. Encourage each crew chief to have an assistant crew chief, and impress upon them the necessity of attending or sending a representative to every single production staff meeting, without fail.

SET DESIGN You may have a student whose passion is set design or whose ideas are best communicated to the production team by the use of artistic renderings or models. Students usually need assistance with set design; depending upon your comfort level with this aspect of technical theatre, you can develop original student set designs individually or in tech theatre class. You can also rent blueprints for sets that students can build from ScenoGraphics.com. Sketchup is a very user-friendly set design program, especially after you (i.e., get a student to) make a template of your performance space, and save it online for next time. PowerPoint can also be used to easily create a clean ground plan or other set drawings.

SET CONSTRUCTION Your stage crew construction team may come mostly from your tech theatre class, but schedule tech or build days in which all theatre students may lend a hand. Call in the parents if you must, but be sure there's lots of teaching going on, of safety, building basics, and age-appropriate skills for students to develop— including cleanup!

SET DECORATION Many of those nonessential items that create a realistic sense of place may come from homes, antique stores, etc. Assign an artistic student to be in charge of details that can make a huge difference in the finished feel of a set.

PAINTING It is up to you to decide whether the set designer or your crew chief in charge of painting will develop a painting color palette for your set that will coordinate with lighting and costumes. Assign your paint crew to publicity until the set is ready for them, unless they can paint some stage props or mobile pieces that come out of your storage area ready to use if painted a different color. Home Depot may be able to donate paint that was returned for being the wrong color, but turns out to be fine for your purposes. Just stay away from oil based paint, as it is not worth the trouble in terms of safety or cleanup and is often prohibited for student use by school systems. Spray paint is also a disaster waiting to happen as graffiti or overspray, and is nearly impossible to paint over, so use it only with great care! Store paint out of sight to avoid tempting vandals. Latex paint is safe and cheap, as well as inherently fire retardant, but you may choose to order the more expensive, specifically theatrical-use paint from Rosco, through a local theatrical supplies vendor. These pricey paints are supersaturated for scenic use and may prove instructive in a class scene painting unit, as well as for especially brilliant backdrops and colorful scenery for a show.

PUBLICITY Be sure to create a team of students for this vital job. When you are in the throes of production it is deceptively easy to ignore this critical aspect. And after all, don't you want as many seats filled as that hard work deserves? Make publicity a priority! Befriend your local newspaper reporter who is, after all, seeking truly newsworthy events in your community—such as your show. Use bulletin boards, display cases, road signs, posters in stores, T-shirts, banners around school, public service announcements, press releases to local neighborhood newsletters—heck, anything and everything you can think of! And do share your successes with your administration! Be sure to have a website (Google Sites is free and very easy to use), and drive your traffic there to get people used to checking it out for the latest in theatre news. Coordinate with your school's marketing class and/or art department. Indicate on posters what ages are appropriate for your shows (perhaps use movie ratings?). And if you're doing family-friendly material, be sure to involve your feeder elementary and middle schools in all publicity efforts. Coordinate with your tickets crew for special deals for feeder school patrons, faculty, groups or senior citizens, and the like.

TICKETS Online vendors like BrownPaperTickets.com, Ticketleap.com, TicketTurtle.com, Vendini.com, SeatYourself.com and others can greatly improve the accuracy of your record keeping, your bottom line (you'll soon sell the majority of your tickets online), and your customer satisfaction. You may have to work with both your school finance office and your booster group to set this up, but it's worth the hassle! Arrange for an adult to supervise the student ticket chief and follow school finance procedures.

HOUSE MANAGER Ushers, lobby displays, concessions, ticket collection and program distribution add up to a significant role for this person. National Honor Society (or other) service hours may be an incentive to attract ushers, but give your own students first shot at this. If you require students to attend your productions, ushering offers the opportunity to see the show for free. Find out how to contact a custodian and administrator in case of unexpected trouble or problems.

PROGRAM This job requires an industrious and dedicated student. Rule of thumb: when your student reaches what they call their final draft, you will have at least three more drafts to go. Watch out for ads for products/places your school may not want to promote (e.g., the local college pub), misspelled names, and omitted crews. Give easy thanks to any adult or business who volunteers time, funds or materials, or barter program space for discounts or donations. Try to stay in-house for printing if you can and, if not, at least make those program ads pay for the cost of printing. From printing to posters, Kinko/Fedex can be very expensive. Call around! Get the name/date/time of each call; the printing industry is very competitive.

RUNNING CREW Running crew is a great way for students to get involved with your program. Train students to use spike tape and glow tape (well-charged), and pride themselves on their ninja-like qualities. Practice moving heavy things first in pantomime. Try "red-light-green-light" shifts to catch potential collisions or inefficient traffic patterns. Hot glue small objects onto false table tops to avoid spilling items all over the stage in the heat of the moment. No one wants to see a bunch of scene changes interrupted periodically by a play. Careful organization (*make* the time for it!!!) and consistency are the keys to swift, safe, and silent set changes. A quick, dimly lit scenery shift may be a huge improvement over a dark, tedious one.

LIGHTING A student who masters your lighting console (and associated lighting instruments) is a beautiful thing! Make sure to give this student—and their apprentices for the future—time to plan and record cues, focus lighting instruments and even play with moving lights if you have them. A cyclorama with silk color gels on your cyc lights and a few gobos in your ETC Source Fours can create a plethora of artistic lighting choices. Gobos are stencils put inside stage lights to project their shape onto the stage. Paint with light! Windows, jail bars, leafy patterns, skylines, words, hundreds of choices are available from Rosco, Gam, Apollo, and other vendors. Stage lighting vendors are always happy to come demonstrate their wares—a great way to show your students the differences even if you don't know them yourself. Resist buying stage lighting lamps until the PE department funds their own bulb replacements in the gym! Find out if your school system has a contract with a particular company to purchase equipment at a bulk discount price, even if you need only a few items; perhaps your school's building use account will prove to be a funding resource for lamp replacement.

SOUND Students who run sound for your shows need your patience—especially if it's their first time running 20 body microphones for the musical! Bring your head sound technician and designer into rehearsals as early as possible so that they get to know the actors' vocal variety and cues. Assign an apprentice/assistant for your lead sound technician, to help change batteries in body mic packs and to monitor receiver signals, as well as to run the critical errand backstage to adjust actors' microphones. Advise your sound technician to remind actors that they must *never turn off the mic pack*— unless instructed to do so by the sound technician. Be sure to make time for thorough sound checks prior to all rehearsals and performances, changing all batteries before the run of the show. Demand careful, organized treatment of all equipment from both cast and crew, and require your sound tech to communicate their procedure for returning mics at the end of the show. Sound effects and music for your shows are available online and can be run through your analogue sound board with an auxiliary cable to a computer or smartphone. Be sure to respect copyright laws in making these selections. Buy a couple of wireless microphone systems and over-the-ear mics each year, and the supply will really add up over time! An example—as of this writing—of a good quality, reasonably priced body mic that withstands arduous student use would be the Audio-Technica 3000 series. Shoe trees (the hanging pocket kind) can make good temporary mic pack holders. Floor mics can be very useful: a Pressure Zone Microphone (PZM) is used on rostra or floor. Better yet are PCC's. PCC's are like PZM's but pick up sound mostly in one direction (the stage, not also the audience…but there is a front side, so place with care!). Crowne makes sturdy floor mics but the cable is non-standard where it plugs in to the mic, so treat them with care!

PROPS Providing your actors with rehearsal props the instant your initial blocking is done will inspire stage business that enhances both your characters and your show. And then, of course, your actors will lose their props and your props crew will get all mad at them and threaten to quit. So plan plenty of prop-related reminders to minimize your losses. And by all means, make sure you have an easy-to-follow plan to track and organize your props and arrange for their construction or purchase, as needed. Remember that your props crew will consist of students with different skill sets and personalities. One kid may be a whiz at prop construction, while another may excel at locating pre-made props in stores or online. Yet another student may demonstrate an ability to maintain props and keep them organized. Next thing you know, you've got a whole crew!

COSTUMES Finding and making costumes is a whole art form in and of itself: measurements, research, sketches, experiments, patterns, sewing, organizing …so glorify your costume crew, for they shall deserve it. Let newbies make something easy and showy first—that will get them hooked. Other middle or high schools, community theaters, and colleges should be included in your crew's search for available garments. Renting is unbelievably expensive but may be necessary sometimes. Places like TheCostumer.com will send you a free full plot of most shows, showing exactly what they'd recommend for each character—what a helpful start!

WARDROBE Someone has to help with quick changes, maintenance (ironing, maybe even washing), and the quick repairs essential in many shows. The wardrobe crew can also assist with under-dressing or over-dressing to speed up a costume change.

Try hard to get your actors used to their costumes ASAP, not last-minute, to enhance both comfort and character.

MAKEUP Strict hygiene routines are essential in applying or removing makeup. The cost of fresh eye makeup beats a rash of Pink Eye every time, so forbid sharing eye makeup and require your students to wash their hands after each person's makeup application. Stage makeup (e.g. Ben Nye, Bob Kelly, Mehron, Stein) is all hypoallergenic. Baby wipes work great for removing makeup. If spirit gum is needed, keep it only in small containers to minimize the disaster of the inevitable spill.

SPECIAL EFFECTS There are plenty of toys out there for your special effects team. With a gobo projector such as the American DJ LED Gobo projector or the Chauvet Gobo Zoom LED, anything printed out from a computer onto a transparency, in b/w or color, can be projected onto your stage. Fog machines are often handy for effects but beware those available in party stores as they break down easily. Theatrical supply houses can rent or sell you more reliable brands. Be sure to get the right kind of "juice" to make the fog…and test that it won't set off your school's fire alarm system. Dry ice creates a low lying fog, but it's very finicky and can be dangerous to handle. LCD projectors and computers can create all sorts of images of whatever you need, these days. And avoid pyrotechnics unless you and they are properly licensed for their use in the theatre.

Auditions

When choosing a play to produce and direct at your high school theatre department, it is important to match the demands of the production to the talent that you have. If you are thinking about a musical, first talk to your choral director, who will tell you such things as whether there is a tenor to sing the lead and whether your prize soprano is a belter or a classical singer. Keep in mind that non-musicals usually make less profit, but they impose less pressure and are less specific in terms of talent requirements. In any event, once you choose your play, the fun really begins.

The Process

It may behoove you to coincidentally teach a unit on monologues and résumés in all your theatre classes during the month before you schedule your auditions for the first play of the year. That way, your students will be prepared for your approach to, and style of, auditions and be ready to perform at their best. Another tactic is the preparation workshop which is essential for the school musical and helpful for any kind of production. A couple of weeks prior to auditions, hold a workshop in which students can learn the basics: slate (name, character name, title of play, playwright), focus-technique, suggestions for variety in gestures, facial expression, movement, pacing and intensity, and saying "thank you" after the audition monologue. Be clear about how you want students to dress for an audition (it shows respect for the artistic process), the kinds of behavior that can help them to be cast, as well as behavior that could get them "excused" from an audition (e.g., talking while someone else is auditioning or while the production staff is giving instruction). Your theatre students should excel because of the additional training they receive in class—and they should be less nervous during the entire audition process.

Who Auditions?

As director, you get to decide which productions are open to A) Everyone in the school; B) Your school's theatre students only; or C) Theatre students from your school and from your feeder middle and/or elementary schools (usually limited casting for these lucky younger students who get to grace the high school stage early). There are other considerations in the audition process, based largely on the types and varieties of stage productions in your school. For example, even among your own theatre students, you may wish to limit auditions for the children's theatre piece in February to freshmen and sophomores (you could allow seniors to direct). Or you might wish to allow your advanced theatre juniors and seniors the exclusive privilege of performing in a classical main stage production that you would research and rehearse during most of the second semester.

Who Is in the Audition Room?

The only people who should be present in the audition room should be the auditioning group of students, the director(s), the stage manager, and any colleague you have invited to be part of casting. *Do not allow parents to be present for auditions.* This creates a sense of favoritism and can interfere with students' focus. Allowing a parent to be present for auditions also makes it more difficult for you to exercise your authority as the artistic leader of your department. After all, parents are not always the most objective of judges of their children's acting potential. You must resist the temptation to allow even the nicest, most hard-working, wonderful parent ever to be part of the audition process—their presence in the room creates a whole can of worms that you definitely do not want to open.

The 4-1-1

Whatever play you choose, you will have to let potential cast and crew members know about the audition dates and expectations. Hopefully, you have a theatre department bulletin board (callboard) at your disposal. Train your students to use it and see it as a perk for being in your class: your students get the freshest 4-1-1 directly from *you!* A flyer of some sort is essential to announce your auditions—even better if it has bright colors or an eye-catching logo. Post it on the callboard, around the school, and on the school electronic flat screen announcements (you might have to get it approved by some school administrator first). If you have enough lead time, put an ad in the school newspaper. Post an electronic notice on your theatre booster or department website, as well as on Blackboard. Repeatedly talk it up in classes and personally ask kids if they are auditioning. Don't lead anyone on with expectations or hints at parts—that's unethical—but encourage students to come and audition. The artistic growth and confidence your students will get from "putting themselves out there" will be worth the effort, whether they are cast or not.

The Pre-Audition Permission Packet and Schedule

Put together a pre-audition packet that requires parent signature and includes the rehearsal schedule, as well as some kind of theatre code of ethics (see our sample in the Production Contract in the appendix, as referenced below). It's important to document the tone of your department by clearly communicating expectations for behavior that will positively facilitate the collaborative art of theatre. Take nothing for granted and include a sentence that reinforces your school's honor code or student rights and responsibilities policies. Attach the rehearsal schedule to the parent/student signature page and no one can say, "I didn't know about this conflict because I didn't know exactly when I was expected at rehearsal." Include all performance dates and times! Believe it or not, students get ready to audition and realize that the performance dates are a conflict!

Put your expectations in a document that everyone reads aloud during the first rehearsal and turns in with student and parent signatures that verify their understanding. If your play will include stage combat or any other physically demanding activities, put that information in the pre-audition packet. If you need parents/students to sign that they are aware of the risks and accept them, this is the time to CYA (figure that one out yourself). This is also a good time to have them sign off on allowing photos to be taken for production publicity

Appendix 📄 Connection

Don't get caught casting someone who won't get parent permission to do the show! Get a contract signed before you make final commitments. Take a look at the brief *Production Contract* in appendix N, and the much more complete *Production Packet* in appendix O. Feel free to use or modify them as you see fit.

purposes, get T-shirt sizes and solicit parent volunteers. Don't forget your techs—they need a parent permission form, too, in order to use power tools and/or paint. It's a mountain of paperwork, but you'll be glad you did it when a student has an allergic reaction to sawdust or latex paint; at least the parent can't say they didn't know their child was involved in tech work.

Rehearsal Etiquette

You are an educator, and things that seem natural to you are often things that your students must be taught. Respect for the artistic process must be taught, so be very clear about what behaviors during auditions, rehearsal, and performance signify respect to you as the director of the play. It should include not talking in the auditorium while actors are auditioning or rehearsing, including backstage. Of course there are moments when you can relax and discuss context, motivation, etc., but when a scene is running, everyone in the space should be silent and attentive. Don't allow students to use cell phones in the audition/rehearsal/performance space—if they have to make a parent or emergency call, they can leave the space and go out into the hallway. This not only helps them to focus on creating art, but helps to avoid the unwelcome electronic commentary on someone's developing acting or an unwanted photo during rehearsal that becomes a source of embarrassment or bullying. Rehearsals should be a safe, closed community of the artists involved—not fodder for Facebook. Hopefully, this will also train students in *good* audience etiquette—there's nothing more distracting or disheartening than to see audience members on their electronic devices during a performance for which students worked so hard! It also equips your students with basic knowledge that will serve them well in other audition situations.

Specify Your Audition Expectations

For full-length mainstage productions, you'll probably want students to memorize a one to two minute monologue from a published play. If you want monologues from specific playwrights, make a list of them available to your students. If you accept random monologues from whatever sources, make sure students know your expectations include being appropriate to a school setting. For musicals, consider choosing specific songs from the show to teach the students at a preparation workshop, and then ask them to sing a particular section of a song that suits their vocal range. Instead of wasting time listening to their version of "Happy Birthday" or a student-choice song in a key not remotely close to anything from your show, requiring specific preparation gives students a sense of the commitment necessary for a mainstage production—and you need to know who has the work ethic and the "memory gene." Your music director should make sure of student range and ability to match pitch. If you are doing a dance-heavy musical, have your choreographer or dance captain teach a short combination at the preparation workshop, one that will be repeated at auditions. Give advanced dancers an additional opportunity to strut their stuff with some extra measures in which they can improvise.

Cold readings work well for callbacks, when you need students to read together in scenes. Callbacks allow the director to see chemistry between cast members, as well as more specific characterization choices. Create a sign-up sheet for your call-board so that students know when to arrive for their audition group (each group should consist of five to ten students). Announce on the sign-up sheet what your expectations are for how students should dress: for example, business casual, without cleavage or distracting designs on shirts.

Process and Patience

If you have smaller productions aimed specifically at underclass participation, such as children's theatre or an evening of one-act plays or sketches, cold readings may give your newbies an opportunity to get involved without extensive preparation. You can also use guided improvisation in auditioning shows that are particularly animated, in order to determine how well your students work in ensemble settings. Be aware of the trade-offs you make in your audition methods: improvisation reveals creativity, but memorized monologues demonstrate not only an ability to memorize but allow the student with a reading disability to shine. If you suspect that the cold reading process might be obscuring the skills of a talented actor with a learning disability, give that student a line or two that s/he can quickly memorize and see what happens. It's easy to promote the talents of those students who bring the whole package to an audition; other hopeful hearts may need your patience and prodding to discover their own hidden abilities and to experience the joys of theatre.

Casting

Both the bane and beauty of any educational theatre director, casting is always an adventure—especially if you are open to the truth. The junior that you hoped would "bring it" to auditions either doesn't show up or reads horribly. The talented senior decides not to prepare for the role you were hoping he'd nail. A talented freshman surprises you with the best monologue of the day but looks too young to play Tevye. Whether you bravely cast alone or ask a colleague to attend auditions for a second opinion, there are bound to be surprises.

Give the Speech

If you hold a preparation workshop for auditions for your show, and even at callbacks, you should give "the speech." This is the reality check for the students, attempting to psychologically prepare them for the brutal process of casting. You'll make up your own version, but it goes something like this:

THE SPEECH

DRAMATIS PERSONÆ

DIRECTOR, *person seen as having the power to cre-*
ate stars or crush souls
STUDENTS, *people who all want the lead part*

The SCENE *is a drama classroom*

DIRECTOR. Let's talk a moment about casting. Are all of you going to get the part you want?

STUDENTS. No.

DIRECTOR. And we know that going into this process, right?

STUDENTS. Right.

DIRECTOR. The way I look at it is this: life is full of things that you control and things you don't control. You do your very best with the things that you control, and you have to let the things you don't control go. What do you control in casting?

STUDENTS. You control the preparation for your audition.

DIRECTOR. That's right; you can make your audition a little gem— a show that is all the best you have to offer. So you choose a great monologue, you work on it way ahead of time, you prepare your song (if the show's a musical), and you rehearse whatever dance combination you are given. You get plenty of sleep, you arrive early, wearing nice but comfortable clothing that allows you to move well. You set yourself up for success. Those are the things that you control. What are the things you don't control in an audition?

STUDENTS. The director's vision of the play, how tall you are, your chemistry with other people, your age, etc.

DIRECTOR. How many leading roles are there in this show?

STUDENTS. Two.

DIRECTOR. Can we do the play with just those two people?

STUDENTS. No.

DIRECTOR. Correct. So every role is important or we can't do the play—we need everyone. Being part of the production has to be enough, no matter what role you receive. If you don't get the part you want, you are allowed to be disappointed; you vent to your family and/or close friends privately—not on the Internet—and then you get over it. You come to the first rehearsal with a positive attitude, grateful for this opportunity to grow. The great thing about theatre is that it forces us to be unselfish—we come together to create a gift for our community. You either come to theatre with your whole heart, or don't come at all.

STUDENTS. OK. We get it.

(STUDENTS *exit leaping, inspired and motivated.*)

The structure of theatre productions doesn't really promote taking turns or giving every senior a chance to play a leading role. Casting must be truthful, but it is not necessarily fair—in fact, it is usually brutal. However, someone has to play each role or there is no play. Several "someones" need to create an ensemble group in musicals and plays in order for the production to be complete. The audience sees everyone in the cast at some point, which makes everyone invaluable.

The art of theatre is the art of collaboration. Even if students don't get the parts they want, they must understand that being part of a theatre production is still an opportunity to grow.

Parents and students involved in your department must understand that everyone is important to the creation of the show. Communicate this to these stakeholders by posting the names of your stage manager, tech director, and your lighting, set and sound designers and other technicians on your callboard, along with the cast list. Get suggestions from your students about what activities can best unify the cast and make the production process fun for everyone: buddy bags, pizza or ice cream socials, paper plate awards, etc. Help parents understand by speaking to them at a theatre boosters meeting; speak to your students about the structure of a production in class. This is an intellectual understanding that you will have to constantly promote, along with a paradigm of the goals of educational theatre.

You get the idea. In the midst of casting, it's important to remind students why they came to the party. You could also ask students to state why they want to be part of the production; it all helps with perspective—and there's nothing that will mess with a student's perspective like casting!

The Truth

Casting is about finding the best cast possible for this script, according to your artistic vision and the talent available to you. That means you've done your homework: read/researched the script, studied the characters, chosen scenes for callbacks or cold readings that allow you to see how students respond to the language, characters and chemistry. Open your mind to the truth that is presented to you in auditions, regardless of which kids you love, which kids irritate you, which kids work hard, which kids "deserve" it, which kids have parents who are leading booster volunteers—regardless of all these things and more. As Oprah said: "When someone shows you who they are, believe them."

There are five major elements in casting, aside from the proverbial song and dance evaluations necessary to casting a musical (be ready to talk with your music director about whether a great voice outweighs the other elements). RESPECT the process:

REMEMBER to do your best to

EXPRESS YOUR...

SUITABILITY for the role speaks to your vision for the role. It can involve a multitude of other factors that relate to the student or the role. For example, the student's vocal and dance training and ability may not match the needs of the character. Similarly, a student's height, maturity, gender or other limiting factors may not match up well with your image of that character. And in many cases, you need to determine if a student's preparation and energy can overcome any of these shortcomings.

PREPARATION conveys respect for the process and work ethic. A student's degree of preparation can indicate how much you are going to enjoy working with them and what kind of role model they will be for other cast members. It's also the element that a student can control the most. Seniors who feel entitled to a part but who haven't put in the necessary preparation for it have lost many such parts over the years.

ENERGY is indispensable; in fact, some acting teachers have chosen energy as the defining quality for acting. A hard-working, energetic actor goes a long way onstage.

CHEMISTRY can be vital, but can often be arbitrary as well.

TALENT may often be packaged with some smugness, but talent does save you a lot of teaching time in rehearsal.

In casting roles in educational theatre, race/culture really should not be a factor unless the play is basically all about race/culture. Even then, be ready to defend your ethics in choosing that play in the first place, as well as your casting decisions. In educational theatre, students may often have opportunities to play roles they could never play in the professional world.

Real-World Moments

A young, first job theatre director had grown very close to her Thespian president, who had her heart set on playing Juliet in the upcoming production of *Romeo and Juliet*. Sadly, the sweet, senior Thespian was not the right match for the role. The theatre director called her prior to posting the cast list and asked the senior Thespian to be assistant director for the production. Midst tears, she accepted and thanked the director for calling her. The freshman who played the role was obviously the right choice, the production was a success and the senior was a wonderful example of unselfish leadership. A few years later, she invited the theatre director to her wedding.

Doing so can help them to grow in perspective and empathy. Remember that you are a theatre educator, not a Broadway director. You want a good show with truthful casting, but your real goal is *growth*; usually, one reinforces the other.

Who is deserving? Everyone who shows up with a well-prepared audition piece is worthy of consideration for casting. Usually the training, experience, and maturity of upperclassmen make them more appropriate choices for larger parts, but occasionally there's a sophomore or even a freshman who unexpectedly shines or is more suitable for the part. When this happens, don't be afraid to cast authentically—the person who is best for the role should get it. Unless you know something about that person's reliability, go with your gut and cast truthfully. If, however, you have equally qualified applicants for a role, age and experience should break the tie. Communicate this to your students and parents so that they know what to expect. Your casting cannot become a matter of earned politics.

Addressing the Aftermath

So you've posted the hard copy cast list on the callboard outside your classroom and you've sent the electronic version to your website or Blackboard. If you're smart, you'll do this on a Friday evening so that kids and parents have the weekend to move on emotionally and psychologically. Then it begins:

- "This is Johnny's mother. We are ready for him to have a bigger role. He's very disappointed—he's in his room crying. He's been so dedicated to this department for the past three years."

- "I thought seniors got leads."
- "I can't do this part; our family vacation is production week—sorry. This won't hurt my chances next time, will it?"
- "Can Ellen and I switch parts? She really wanted my role, and I really wanted her role…"
- "This is your booster vice president. I'm not sure I'll be able to help with front of house for this show; it has nothing to do with the fact that my daughter wasn't cast."
- "Lisa is upset because she got the role as the mother—she wants to be the cute daughter…"

And on and on….

It is important that you address these concerns via phone or email, so that when you start your first rehearsal you have a clean cast list that will not distract your dedicated actors from being excited about the show. Some "tried and true" responses are:

- "Mrs. Smith, is Johnny aware of the size of this role? He will have a lot of stage time and I'm sure he'll enjoy being up there with his friends. I'm sorry he's disappointed, but he has a part that will really give him an opportunity to shine onstage. Please ask him to contact me as soon as he has made his decision. I need to know by Sunday. Thank you."
- "Mathematically, it's not possible for every senior to get a lead. It's a shame you won't be in the play—I think this role is perfect for you and it would give you a great opportunity to grow as an actress."
- "I hope you'll look at the rehearsal schedule that I attach to the audition form next time."
- "Thanks for the idea of switching parts, but your roles are based on my evaluation, not on your preferences."
- "Thanks so much for letting me know—we'll miss you!" Or, if you know the booster better, "I understand and we'll miss you. I just want you to know that I could tell that Cindy worked very hard on her audition piece; she's really growing artistically. I appreciate all of her wonderful work, but she just wasn't quite ready for any of these roles. I really enjoy having her as a student—she's a terrific contributor in class."
- "Thank you for calling. The role of the mother is the leading role! Your daughter has worked so hard for the past three years, I know this role would give her a wonderful opportunity to grow and shine onstage. She's such a leader in our department—it would be a shame for her to miss this opportunity. However, if she doesn't contact me by Sunday, I'll have to put her understudy in the role. Maybe

your daughter would feel more comfortable working on publicity or running crew, so that she can still be involved in the production."

Most kids and parents just need a perspective shift and some comforting words from you, the director. Usually, everything falls into place by the first read-through. Remind parents that as the director, your job is to create the best cast for this show—your casting must be truthful in fulfilling the needs of the production. Assume that most parents and students simply need to understand the casting process and know that you care about their concerns. As noted earlier, if there is a tie in casting selection in which all things are even other than age it is a good policy to choose the older, more experienced performer. If, however, the younger student is simply more talented or better suited to the part—and seems to be dependable and committed—then that is the student you should cast. The most important thing a director must do in casting is to create a cast that will make the show successful—then everyone wins. Hopefully, your honest communication and comforting words will win people over to share your "big picture" perspective; if it doesn't, resist the "drama." Deal with any extreme situations quickly and professionally, then get on with the process of putting together a show. Lead and teach.

From the beginning of your tenure as theatre director, it is essential that you establish a tone of "theatre for all." This is roughly equivalent to the "there are no small parts, only small actors" mantra. Educational theatre is not about training the Broadway stars of tomorrow, although you may be fortunate enough to have a few of those gifted artists over the years. Educational theatre is centered on growth. Simply by being involved in a theatre production (and being fully committed to excellence in any role, acting or technical), students are bound to grow. They will not only grow artistically, but they will grow as leaders, organizers, communicators, team-players, sacrificers, time managers, discoverers, problem-solvers, critical thinkers, harder workers, stress-handlers, negotiators, and prioritizers—in other words, they will become persevering, more confident, more courageous, more sensitive-to-the-needs-of-others human beings.

Being involved with the arts expands our humanity. The great thing about theatre is that it provides a plethora of opportunities from which to choose for participation; whatever the role, committed participation will result in growth. This is the paradigm that you must foster in your department with both parents and students.

Tips on Directing

Your directing style will likely have evolved from those directors you have worked with in college or semi/professional productions. But younger student actors are their own breed and require some special handling. Here are some suggestions:

Get Ahead of the Game

Try to front-load as much of the production process as you can. Why not collect bios for the program and take measurements of your actors at the first read-through? Get a draft of the program done the first week, and your program crew will only have to do updates during crunch time before opening the show. Demand rehearsal props from the first day on stage. These early starts will pay huge dividends.

Motivation for Memorization

Although professional actors benefit from focusing on character development instead of memorization well into the rehearsal period, student actors still on book tend to look like they're in their private libraries the whole time, with chins down, zero eye contact and hands unavailable for gesturing. Students will wait until the last minute of a deadline to complete almost anything, so set a very early deadline for getting off-book (say, after twice through the initial blocking). Enforce it by making them call "Line!" for each and every prompt after that, and permit no prompting once into tech rehearsals. Frustration (and embarrassment) is a strong motivator for those who don't meet these deadlines.

Don't Forget the Techs

Unlike those in professional or community theatre, members of your tech crew will have had precious little experience at their jobs. Therefore, start with them right away on design choices and a plan for execution of those choices. And begin using lighting and sound (especially body mics) as soon as you get into the theater to rehearse. You want everyone in the show to be comfortable and confident about what they have to do. No one should have to succeed on a wing and prayer.

Understudies

Some would rather not be cast at all than lose the role they wanted, while others just want to be part of it all. But all are going to have rehearsal conflicts. Developing a culture where understudies are valued provides more people with opportunities for artistic stretching and for demonstrating dedication—and keeps things rolling along when a regular cast member is missing or if disaster strikes. Understudies also take much less time than double-casting, but do throw them up there at random rehearsal moments.

Blocking

Let blocking, the basic traffic patterns of movement that help tell the story, follow the general rule that physical distance should mirror psychological distance. Actors can often tell if their character is trying to persuade (approach) or avoid (retreat), is angry or scared (fight or flight), etc., and that can help drive their (and your) choices about blocking. Most young actors will also make light gestures at meaningful moments—encourage them to follow those instincts but enlarge the gestures to a stage-worthy size. Make a point of keeping most of the action forward, despite young actors' inclination to creep upstage as they continue. And pull forward those carrying the storyline from the background characters around them.

Avoiding Bad Habits

Familiar young actor movements include the "ninth grade cross-step walk," an unconscious "grapevine" step while in the midst of a monologue or speech, and the "firing squad," when a group of actors unconsciously line themselves up in a straight row without even realizing it. Break them into clusters of three or so, and discover the value of triangles and levels to create better visual pictures. Viola Spolin's side coaching phrase, "share the scene!," is effective (briefly) to remind students to both stay open to the audience as well as to keep projecting.

Script Homework

Your students are likely to be reluctant to look up definitions of words they don't understand in a script. Push the importance of due diligence, since it's impossible to make clear to an audience what is not clear to them. Team up actors with their understudies to help clarify and learn lines. Teach your actors how to "score" their text, marking pauses, emphasis, etc. For poetic passages or Shakespearean text, rewrite the lines in contemporary speech.

Articulation and Enunciation

Worry more about articulation and less about projection. Consonants carry the meaning of a line, and vowels carry its emotion. Lose those final consonants and we hear "sore" instead of "sword," "Beauty and the Bees," "great beard" becomes "gray beer," etc. Record those misspoken phrases and use them for daily vocal warmups.

The Hygiene Talk

Being in charge means you get the joy of saying the things that must be said…that no one else wants to say. This is bound to come up, so here's one version of how you might deal with it:

"OK, guys…as we head into the tech phase of rehearsal, we need to discuss some important stuff. We will start using our costumes, makeup and the dressing rooms soon. Be prepared. How? Listen up:

Dear Cast,

You really need to hear this. Really!…

You're going to be sharing a small space with a lot of people. Whether you do at present or not, it is now time to shower every day. Every day. Shower. Really. And use deodorant. Not so much or so strong that those with asthma will be sent to the hospital to recover, but not so little that those with or without asthma will be sent to the hospital to recover. Let's face it: you're adolescents, and you boys sweat—and you girls perspire—in a way we can smell. So please, shower. *Every* day. And use deodorant *every* day. You are welcome to keep some in your garment bag. Those around you thank you.

You only get one set of costumes for this show, so that means you'll be wearing them over and over. Guess what? They will stink. And trapped as they should be, in your garment bag between rehearsals, they will stink even more. So *please* talk to the costume folks about when it's OK to take your stuff home and get it laundered. Some items they are responsible for, but others—like the ones that are your own stuff, that you bring in from home—you must take care of.

Please let's keep up our sense of ensemble, of supporting each other in positive ways. So if you know there's a cast member who is stinkier than the rest, that perhaps never needed deodorant before, and no one at home is helping them figure out what to buy, or perhaps we have a cast member who just sweats a lot, that is *not* a call to tease or humiliate them! Come on! Either let someone have a quiet, private word with them or ask me to, and I will encourage them to make the world a better place for us all.

And if you are the person receiving that encouragement, please take it in the spirit in which it is intended. Welcome to the more grown up, more mature you. There is more personal hygiene in your future, starting tomorrow. See to it. Your ensemble is depending on you."

Teaching Kissing

Oh, how many first kisses may take place because of a theatre production! Is there any more awkward time? And yet, kisses overtly define relationships, and so the gap between being actual strangers/classmates/peers and being related to/in love with another character simply must be bridged sometimes if the storyline is to ring true. Make sure your students are aware of the necessity for this kind of physicality prior to auditions by discussing the play or making a statement on your audition form—and then move forward with sensitivity and professionalism.

Variety and Awkwardness

There are, of course, many kinds of kisses—and when to use what tells an audience a whole lot about the characters and their relationship, from a fatherly kiss on the top of the head to his child, to a peck of a cheek kiss from a visiting aunt, to a parental "temperature kiss" on the forehead to check for fever, to an air-kiss among socialites, to a full-on mouth kiss that lasts as long as it takes for the lights to fade.

Never presume a student is experienced. You may need to clear the room to make the training less of a public event, but never leave yourself alone with a student and don't demonstrate by actually kissing your student! Pay attention to the full body language, avoiding the triangle of nervous kids keeping apart except where they "have to" touch. Remind them that lust is fast, but love is slow. And discomfort shows. Savoring a moment is very different from "getting it over with." And try to get past their reluctance early on in the rehearsal period—waiting until show week is a terrible way to get characters to look comfortable with each other. Try starting with some trust falls and basic appropriate body contact points (e.g. touching foreheads, chins, noses or cheeks) just to get them used to being close to each other.

Creating Technique With Specifics

You may need to remind the couple to each tilt their head to the right (or left) to prevent crashing noses. Plan out how quickly the approach and withdrawal will be from each other. No tongues are needed. Remind them to hold eye contact after the kiss. It can be helpful to build up to the full kiss by either moving to within a fraction of contact while *not* completing it, or by kissing cheeks instead of lips and moving closer and closer to lips each time. But make no mistake: kissing air instead of a real kiss looks just like kissing air, and *not* like something real people (except the socialite thing) ever do.

All in the Timing

You can demonstrate timing and intensity to a student (male or female) by shaking hands, that is, holding (and releasing) their hand as you want the kiss to be, hard or soft, quick or slow, etc. They can also practice duration and intensity by kissing their own hand (also a good way to practice making the smacking noise).

You can count out how many Mississippis long a kiss should last. For a long embrace, be sure to keep the story progressing—a frozen pose looks just like that, but a kiss that adds a hand sliding up an arm to go around the neck...then the other's arm around the waist...then her leg "pops" at the knee, with the toes pointed, can really clarify how "into it" each character is, even though you may have to choreograph each of those moves very mechanically and specifically. Remember that these gestures are only useful to an audience when visible on the downstage side.

Remind students that these are the characters being intimate, not them. The more professionally you approach this aspect of physicality onstage, the more likely you are to get professional focus and attitude from the students. Parallels to professional acting situations can also be useful: personal sexual orientation should not factor in to an actor's ability to convincingly play romantic roles. Professional actors want to work and be versatile. Kissing is just one more tool for the actor's proverbial toolbox—student or professional.

Injuries and Illnesses

It's going to happen. After weeks of hard work, you're just about to open your production and disaster strikes. How will you replace a cast member at the last minute, or quickly modify your show to compensate for an illness, injury or absence you could not have anticipated? How will you maintain your cool in the midst of the drama your students are creating around this crisis? Be sure to project that authority, calm, and progress toward a Plan B that will reassure your cast and crew; keep your own panic well hidden.

The Show Must Go On

This basic dictum of theatre work must be taught and reinforced. Do your best to accept no excuses for missing a rehearsal and to make very clear that missing a show is simply unthinkable. We've all got tales of folks who went on despite illness or injury, let alone unhappiness—share them. Yes, true emergencies do happen. But lack of fair warning by a student—so an understudy can be brought up to speed—or a *created* emergency, should probably be seen as the end of that person's career in your program.

Real-World Moments

Bobby, the lead in *Crazy for You*, was played by a kid who went into a diabetic seizure during Act I. As his fellow actors held him up and the dialogue kept coming out of his mouth on automatic, the director went backstage and had the stage manager call an early intermission. They made it to the end of the scene and he collapsed backstage. As he was tended to, the understudy was poured into his costume—and his hair sprayed brown— a song was dropped, a plan for an upcoming set change was developed, and several hysterical girls were calmed. The show went on and, by the actual intermission, the lead had recovered and swapped back in. Both Bobbys took their curtain call, and the night was a roaring success!

Understudies

If you don't already post an understudy list as part of your cast list, we urge you to do so. If there are not enough students auditioning to create an understudy list, consider your options: ask another student in the show to assume a larger role and recruit from available students in your classes to fill in the casting hole you just created. Better to send on a kid with a script than to cancel an entire show, unless you must. Always ask the nervous understudy if s/he is up for the challenge. Better to cancel than to stop mid-show.

Illness

It's often a judgment call whether to permit a willing student on stage if they are truly ill, especially tricky with a failing voice. You don't want the rest of the cast infected, but you may be able to isolate your ill actor when they're off stage…or have a bucket ready in each wing, if that's what it takes, and then send them home ASAP. They can soldier through a sore throat, but if that voice is really fading, you may need to cut a song or even have them lip-synch to someone else or reassign some lyrics. Whatever it takes.

Injury

Again, a judgment call. If the injured (say…in a cast or wheelchair) character is described before their entrance, modify the dialogue to include the cast/wheelchair/etc., and you'll get a laugh, but then everyone just accepts it, and the show does go on. A mid-show injury can

Real-World Moments

Molly, the female lead in a high school production of *Brigadoon*, accidentally slipped on stairs about 20 minutes before the end of the performance, bravely finished the show, but was in anguish by curtain call. A trip to the emergency room revealed that she had literally broken her leg. Molly was determined to perform the final matinee performance that was being critiqued for possible awards. At four a.m. the *Brigadoon* director was typing up guidelines for actors to use in adjusting to new blocking that would accommodate a wheelchair and/or crutches. At twelve-thirty p.m. the director met with the cast and went over the new procedures. At one p.m. the leading man rehearsed the adjustments with his leading lady, while parents prepared decorations to make the wheelchair suit the time period. At two p.m. the show went on with a sincerity and unified focus it never had before.

Her newly disabled actress became a character with a disability. Members of the cast who were in the same family as this character became caregivers in the imagined world of the stage story, doing double duty in the real world. Some audience members thought the wheelchair was the director's artistic choice! There really can be wheelchairs in eighteenth century Scotland!

really bring the house down, of course, but it's still your call whether to have that sprained-ankle kid sit out in the wings or go home, or whether you need to stop the production and ask if there's a doctor in the house!

Imagination

Many of your conflicts will be about much less critical things. Why weren't you at rehearsal? Oh, it was my birthday…I had homework…I didn't know I had to be there…Someone said it was canceled…I forgot…etc. You must decide where to draw the line, and then do so. One sacrificial lamb to show that you really *will* cut someone from the cast (beware the parent backlash), and the word spreads like wild fire. Suddenly the number of missed rehearsals plummets. How about that?!

Judging a Play's Success

Every production is really two productions: the one you work on (the "process play"), and the one the audience sees (the "product play"). And they are very different.

The Process Play

The play you work on has in it all the things you struggle with along the way, and all the goals you set for yourself and those involved. These can include "finding" the character to bring it alive, figuring out how to accomplish that technical trick, getting up to speed on scene changes, hoping the lead will recover their health before opening night, or that the understudy won't be noticeable as such. The list goes on and on. Some things come together right away during rehearsals and stay that way through performance, and some you experiment with, and nurse, and pray that things will click—even if it is at the very last moment. Every single person involved in the play has his or her own version of how the production went and whether they met their own goals or not, that night. This is all about the process of a production. You are evaluating the production based on the whole of the effort—the changes you made or didn't make, the things that went well or didn't go well, the things that you all learned and the things that you still need to learn. And you can be very successful indeed regardless of how the audience responds or how many people there are in that auditorium.

The Product Play

The other production is the one the audience experiences, and those who have worked on it can rarely experience this version at all. It is the one where the audience doesn't know and doesn't care about what came easily and what took months to get right. This is the live theatre that brings the audience a new story that its cast has known for months, the one where the characters don't wear costumes, but simply the clothing that makes sense for the story. The crew works terribly hard to make things unnoticeable, like ambient sound or daylight or set decoration—all the things that register subconsciously with an audience and fill the space with atmosphere, but they are careful not to draw attention to themselves. The authenticity of props, the balance between the fierceness of a fight and the safety of stage combat, the aging of an actor into a character so much older than the kid portraying him, and keeping the brightest part of the stage where the story is being told—when done well, all of these things are invisible. What the audience gets is your version of the story the playwright is unfolding. So, trust the script. And trust your preparation. Try to hear the jokes and the serious moments anew. Listen to the silence and the laughter and the applause. They generally don't know if a line was dropped or an entrance was early. Many, many, things from the process play can go awry, and still this product play can be a roaring success if the characters delight the audience with the story they tell.

Each viewer sees a play as part of an audience, of course, but primarily as an individual. The story may truly touch one person yet leave another cold. Some may get the jokes, while others may not. You hope the audience sees the play the way you want them to see it. But every audience has its own personality—you've got to trust the script and your preparation.

Defining Success

So how do you know if your play has been successful? If you met your process goals? If you sold a lot of tickets or made a lot of money? If people are talking about it the next day? If the audience was responsive? If everyone stayed on pitch, and no one got hurt during the big fight scene? If you were nominated for or won some prize, or got a great review from a critic? Your students will look to you to tell them if their show has been successful. Think about it. How will you know what to say?

Focusing on the Process

If you have a growth paradigm that permeates your department, then asking students how they grew, or commenting on how actors or techs grew, is a compliment—a sign of your approval.

Educational theatre should focus on growth, not performance perfection—leave that to the professionals. A focus on growth also takes away focus from the lamp that burned out halfway through the show, a line missed or a stage drape that closed too slowly. You must assume that everyone is doing their very best in performance—you've communicated that expectation, right? If there are any students with special work ethic issues, speak to them privately—reward the group with your approval and mention specific ways in which they grew or made artistic discoveries. If there are any glaring issues, don't ignore them. Instead, mention them after you've praised everyone for their hard work and artistic growth, then devise quick fixes for mistakes that should not be repeated. Run the scene again, run the set change again—schedule time to improve specific problems before the next show. And of course, get your students' feedback on how they thought things went. You may be surprised at some of their comments!

Appendix 📄 Connection

Before heading off to play time in Chapter 5, you may find it helpful to note some selected *Online Resources*, for both class and production, in appendix T.

Finding the Balance

Remembering to balance the importance of both the process and the product will help to keep you and your students focused on growth. Of course you have minimum standards of what you will put on your stage, and you should communicate the expectation that everyone will do their best, redefine it, then exceed their best again—but if you engage in an organized, disciplined and nurturing process, the product should take care of itself.

You cannot control what individual audience members expect or receive from your production, but you can lead students to develop character, tech, and ensemble as they collaborate respectfully and learn the ways of the theatre. You are the person who provides them with the opportunity to discover the artistry and discipline that ultimately is most meaningful to them, as they create a production gift for your community. This is where the unseen process and the final product come together.

For Reflection & Discussion

Doing a show brings its own issues, not just within the cast and crew but in collaboration with administration and community... even the weather.

1. Backstage, your young assistant stage manager tries to quiet a group of actors nearby, only to be told "Shut up, Freshman. We don't have to listen to you!" What's your best course of action?

2. Your paint crew has finished applying the base coat to the set, and numerous actors arrive and declare it looks awful. Now your painting crew chief is so despondent she wants to quit. Your response?

3. You are not comfortable with some of the pre-show rituals that your students have come to hold sacred. How do you handle this?

4. You discover a consensual fight club among those offstage between scenes, and their fans. What do you do?

5. Your guidance counselors want to schedule an information session for parents in the theater the day before your show opens, a time the cast usually has the day off. They only need a little stage, the house, and a microphone. What considerations should guide your reply? What if it was the senior class, wanting to do a talent show that night?

6. To avoid a conflict with State Honors Choir, you push your musical show dates ahead a week. Now they conflict with the beginning of the IB testing season. What kind of heads up about this new conflict can you provide to students, colleagues and parents, and what level of leeway (e.g. students missing final rehearsals or tech sessions) can you live with, the week you open, from those with imminent high stake testing?

7. You choose your shows, announce and publicize them, and the principal receives a call that one of your choices is totally inappropriate for your community. You have not cleared your choices ahead of time with the administration. What's your best next move?

8. You schedule a show during the winter and, indeed, the big snow hits and wipes out the week leading up to your show dates. Or the weekend of the show. Discuss possible options.

5 **Enrichment Activities**

RELATED APPENDIX DOCUMENTS

- Field Trip Prep Checklist (Appendix U, p. 337)
- Field Trip Letter to Parents (Appendix V, p. 339)

As you settle in

to your classes and productions, you may find additional opportunities to enrich the theatre lives of your students. There are probably plenty of them, and some take less time than teaching—but of course, others don't. Oh, well!

For most of these activities, plan to spend significant time on logistics, collecting forms, communication with students and parents, travel plans, fundraising (for some), red tape, nagging for payment, and playing out what-if scenarios in your head. Also plan to hear your students rave about these experiences for the rest of high school, proud that they were in that select group that got to participate.

School Events

Broaden your students' experience by arranging participation both in school-wide events—discourage drama snobs—and by bringing into your school some events that can be enjoyed by others, not just those on your roster.

HOMECOMING PARADE Fight the us vs. them, theatre arts vs. the world cynicism by joining in on school-wide events, such as the homecoming parade. If you can, have everyone in the parade dressed in costumes for your next production. Will they let you distribute leaflets or post-cards along the route? Wouldn't it be amazing if the homecoming king and queen were two of your theatre kids? Stranger things have happened!

SPIRIT WEEK Why not buy in? Dress up to match the day's theme, decorate your door as part of that competition, and maybe even volunteer to be on the faculty drill team in some competition. At the big pep rally for the athletes, maybe you can get your student "act-letes" introduced to the school, too!

GUEST ARTISTS Sometimes you bring in guest artists to address your students on things you don't know enough about. And sometimes it's just so they can hear an expert say exactly the things you've been harping on for weeks.

STAGE COMBAT Safety first, so fight choreography is best taught by someone certified to teach it. The Society of American Fight Directors (www.safd.org) can lead you to someone who can come to you. Prices are often negotiable.

IMPROV Be it TheatreSports, Comedysportz, some Second City wannabe, or other, there are some terrific improv troupes out there. They can really help your kids to polish up the skills that you've been teaching them.

TECHNICAL THEATRE SPECIALISTS It can be fun—and useful—to bring in someone with professional skill in stage makeup, sound, lighting or whatever. After all, your tech kids deserve some special treatment, too.

CLASSICAL ACTING If there's a college or professional theatre within reach, they may well be all set up to do community outreach, and that's you! For example, The Shakespeare Theatre in Washington, D.C. provides tickets to their matinee equity shows for $10 for students—and they first send you a guest artist to do a full class session workshop to help prepare the kids for the show (which is also followed by a talk-back session with the cast and dramaturge). Local colleges may send you someone to help with almost any sort of theatre problem including technical theatre, often a weak link in schools—it's a terrific recruiting tool for them. Win-win!

Field Trips

Field trips are always a welcome break in the routine for the students and, although they can be a headache to arrange, they can be great fun for the teacher/coach, too. Some may be obligatory (play competitions following the district/region/state pattern of sports events come to mind). Many are totally up to you, your motivation and the artistic, academic or other payoff for your kids and your program. So while you may well have your hands too full to plan field trips your first year, do find out what's around, what other schools do, and figure out whether and when it's time to venture out and about.

THEATRE CONFERENCES AND COMPETITIONS If you're close by, or can arrange travel to a theatre convention, your students can pack a year's worth of workshops and plays into a few days. Often there are also college audition opportunities and always there are theatre vendors, ranging from scripts to new lighting equipment, to check out. This is definitely worth your time and (hopefully your department's) money, but you might want to go alone first, to really check it out, and then attend with students as spectators before bringing a show of your own. SETC (SETC.org), the South Eastern Theatre Conference, is one of the largest and draws from several states' individual theatre conferences.

ITS The International Thespian Society (SchoolTheatre.org) has statewide chapters all over the country and sponsors many state festivals, often held on college campuses. ITS offers your students an exciting chance to be around a college without the pressure of an admissions visit. Workshops, short and full length play presentations, social events, and other tightly organized activities will keep your kids learning, busy, and happy. And it's a perfect time for you to meet your local-ish colleagues and swap stories, get advice, etc.

ATHLETIC ORGANIZATIONS The statewide organization that sponsors your school's athletic events may also sponsor a short play competition that, as with sports, has winners advance from the district to the regional to the state level. You should also be able to get the same funding (bus for travel) that the sports teams get when they compete. This is the organization that school principals know best, so success here can carry real weight with them (you may even be required to participate). Ask your Athletics Director or Director of Student Activities for more information. For an example of such an organization, see www.vhsl.org.

Appendix 📄 Connection

To help you get organized to travel with students, you will find in appendix U our *Field Trip Prep Checklist* and in appendix V a template for a *Field Trip Letter to Parents*. Feel free to use or modify them as you see fit.

PROFESSIONAL PRODUCTIONS Taking your students to see professional theatre is a terrific way to meet course objectives since their actors model the behavior you're teaching. Professional shows can really inspire both your actors and your techies to a higher standard. Many theaters offer matinee performances, often with a post-show talkback with the cast, at reduced (or at least group) rates for tickets. Check whether you are permitted to charge public school students for events that happen during the school day. If not, perhaps your drama boosters could come up with the money to pay for tickets or receive donations to help offset this cost. Transportation to these productions can get pricey quickly unless you can organize parent or student carpools. And of course, you may well need class coverage for part of the day, either from colleagues or by hiring a sub. If you get tickets to a show outside the school day, be sure to have all your ducks in a row anyway (parent permission, emergency care cards, transportation arrangements, etc.). If something goes wrong, you'll still be held responsible.

COLLEGE VISITS Encourage your students to learn as much as they can about their theatre-related options beyond high school. They can talk with representatives at theatre conventions, attend the ITS conference held on a college campus, visit alumni of your theatre program who are now in college, take classes at a nearby college, or travel to one of the many colleges that offer summer programs for high school students. Be sure to have them inquire about scholarships or theatre-related work/study options. Also, have them check out the annual college edition of *Dramatics* magazine.

WORKSHOPS Professional and semi-professional theatre companies in your area may offer workshops during the year (or during the summer) that your students can hook into. Local vendors may also offer short courses in stage makeup or lighting or other skills. Those folks are also potential guest artists in your own classroom. Some professional theaters have extensive workshop programs, bringing free guest artists into your classroom multiple times and culminating in a performance at their venue. If yours is an IB school, know that the International Schools Theatre Association, the group that trains teachers for IB Theatre, holds student workshops throughout the country (and the world!). Find them here: www.ista.co.uk.

COMMUNITY CONNECTIONS Virtually every community has something special to offer to theatre students (and if not, sooner or later you should create something!). Discover your community and its resources. For example, in Washington, D.C., the Folger Shakespeare Library runs an annual Student Shakespeare Festival for student performers to take to their stage for a day, sharing their performances of cuttings from the Bard's play(s) with other schools, being entertained and taught, getting feedback and having a terrific time. This event can be a highlight of the school year (and perhaps a perk for signing up for your class). What's near you? Check out online postings, local newspapers and other publications.

Cappies

The Critics and Awards Program (www.cappies.com) is an international program that trains high school students at participating schools to become theatre critics (and adults to be their mentors). Each school can select one of its shows to be reviewed each year and the reviews are vetted by an editor/mentor, with the best reviews passed along to their local media for publication in print or online. Students who review enough shows get voting privileges at the end of the school year for categories that mirror the Tony Awards, and awards are presented at a huge ceremony of the chapter to which the schools belong.

The Cappies program is very well organized, with handbooks of the rules for critics, mentors, and directors, along with an online presence and ready advice from the national governing board. The board meets annually to tweak and improve the program as needed. Each area chapter has some flexibility to tailor the program to fit its particular circumstances.

For your students, this is a wonderful chance to give shy writers a chance to shine or to send your real theatre addicts to see lots of shows for free. Having a review published looks great on a college application, too. It's also a way for students to get to know each other, to share an interest/passion, and to see what they can learn from watching others in similar situations. (Gee, it really *does* matter if people are enunciating clearly!) For schools, it's a chance to raise the bar and to make your principal happy if you are nominated or win something in one of the 35 or so categories. And if your school does well repeatedly, the Cappies are a way to quantify the reputation of your theatre department. For the school system/chapter, it's a way to show teenagers doing excellent work by focusing on collaborative, creative efforts, and bringing quality entertainment to the community. Win-win all around.

Find out if your new school participates in this program or if there is a chapter in your area. If there is none, wait until you're not so wet behind the ears and then apply to start a chapter. Other than getting set up really early in the school year, the program takes very little of a teacher's time, and some schools identify a fellow teacher (the creative writing person, perhaps?) to handle the mentor's job and a booster parent to host the critics when it's your turn to be reviewed.

This is a terrific, student-driven program, well-supervised by adults, which can enhance the quality of your school's theatre program and bring kudos to your whole school. As with any competitive awards program, it is your role to teach students perspective about recognition and how much it should or should not define their artistic work. A discussion about how professional critics affect the success of Broadway shows and the differences between professional and educational theatre can create wonderful teachable moments for discovery and reflection.

Travel

Your school may have many rules and regulations related to travel with students, as well as to the collection of money associated with such travel and events. However, once you clear those hurdles (often easier said than done), there are wonderful things out there for your students if you've got the energy (and/or sufficiently organized and supportive parents) for it. Distance travel is a lot to undertake while you're still getting your feet wet at a school, but it may already be part of the established culture of your program and it can be a real draw if it's considered a perk of taking your classes.

Of course, these types of opportunities will necessarily involve fundraising over the course of many months (see the section on fundraising), and tons of paperwork and planning sessions, to assure that everyone will be safely supervised the whole time, including at the hotels and while in transit.

NEW YORK CITY Every student travel organization on the planet will be delighted to arrange a weekend or week-long trip for you and your students to The Big Apple. Find out whether your school only approves certain companies for this purpose. Ask your theatre colleagues for their recommendations, including not just theatre tickets but workshops with professionals, talks with the performers, etc. Expect to travel free with your group if a certain number of students sign up (as few as six, in some cases), and get a chaperone free for each additional threshold of participants.

ENGLAND How about spring break in London? Take students on an educational field trip with an approved company, and you travel free. Same as above but pricier (and hopefully not riskier).

ISTA The International Schools Theatre Association (www.ista.co.uk) leads multi-day IB Theatre workshops around the globe. Feeling ambitious? Or maybe they're going to be just down the street from you. ISTA provides top notch teachers; and your kids will make friends from afar that they may hang onto for life.

CRUISE SHIPS Especially for singing and dancing groups, there are opportunities to perform while on a cruise. Check out disneyyouth.com, starsatsea.com, rocktheboat-cruises.com,

SCOTLAND The American High School Theatre Festival is a travel company (Worldstrides) that vets established high school theatre programs (you have to have taught there for at least three years) to travel and perform at their venue at the Edinburgh Festival Fringe (www.ahstf.org). If nominated and your application is approved, you will spend a major chunk of the school year planning for this once-in-a-lifetime experience, joining thousands of others performing all over the city as it nearly erupts in celebration.

Real-World Moments

The state ITS convention was a very successful weekend, and the snow didn't hit until the evening before departure. By morning, it was so bad that the school system couldn't send buses to fetch everyone home until the next day, with 300 kids at the Howard Johnsons Motor Lodge, and no more programming. Luckily, the motel had the room to keep everyone the extra day. Many phone calls to principals were made to assure that expenses could be covered. Many phone calls were made to parents to update and reassure them that all were safe and staying put, like it or not. TheatreSports to the rescue, and a day of improv fun in the lobby and theatre games in many rooms. Thank goodness for bringing that school credit card "just in case" and for having the contact info to reach the administrator at home.

Field Trip Travel Tips

Here are some particular bits of advice culled from our experience that may help you avoid a difficult situation or two, when traveling with students.

- Always double-check exactly how many seats will be available on a bus—you do not want to leave one weepy child in the parking lot because there was no seat left. Does the driver automatically claim one for his/her stuff? So the question is not how many seats there are, but how many will be available for you to fill.
- Who pays for chaperones? Will they generously pay for themselves? Do you have enough drama fund money to cover their costs? Can you figure those costs into the per pupil price you charge each participant? Be clear what is and what is not covered, beforehand!
- You know that good behavior contract everyone signed to go on the trip? Only the nerdy kid and your wannabe pet read it. Try a choral reading in full unison before you depart.
- Carsick kids? Bring them to the front of the bus. It's a less popular location, but sure beats smelling vomit for two hours of travel. Most buses will have trash bags available, but bring your own to keep handy!
- Have a system for taking attendance on the bus. That one quick last-minute trip to the bathroom should never turn into leaving someone behind at a truck stop

Real-World Moments

It was a 13 hour trip to the ITS National convention, and a hot day, too. When we finally arrived at the hosting college campus, and got off the bus, everyone was exhausted. But one girl really had had too much, and passed out right on the sidewalk next to the bus. To make matters worse, when she went unconscious, her bladder relaxed, too. The kids were freaking out, someone went for the campus police, and someone summoned medical help. When the EMT's arrived, we were *so* glad to have those emergency medical care cards right at hand, to answer their questions. It all worked out fine, but what a start to the week-long conference!

because you "thought" everyone was accounted for. Buddy clusters work pretty well—everyone can spot the few kids that make up their own cluster (four is a good number). Counting filled seats is OK, but have someone double count. Try calling out your roster of names, and let each kid respond with the time of their next check-in with you (for example, when they are supposed to be back on the bus). Hearing that reminder 50 times works pretty well!

- Bring DVDs you can vote on to show during the trip if the bus is equipped to do so. Beware of titles that parents may object to upon your return. You just don't need the grief.
- Watch to assure that the odd kid isn't the odd kid out. Everyone wants to be included, but some gentle shepherding by you can make this happen seamlessly.
- No matter how much you warn them about it, someone *will* leave behind something they need, on or under the bus seats. After the bus empties out, personally go from back to front. Every time.
- Kids who misbehave get to stay glued to a chaperone after that. Pick a painful duration, so they'll get the message, but try not to destroy the whole trip.
- Is the driver supposed to get a tip? How much? Was this figured in to your price by the travel agent, or are you expected to hand over some cash? What is your finance person's take on this?
- Do you need to reserve/pay for a room for the driver at your motel? Does the deal with the bus company require the driver have a full eight hours off between shifts? What if you get back to the motel after midnight, but have to be back on campus

for your assigned 7:30 breakfast? Be clear about the requirements and limitations of your bus company; your director of student activities is a good source of information, as they plan many trips for student athletes.

For Reflection & Discussion

Arranging special events with students can be terrific fun—and multiple disasters waiting to happen.

1. What performing organizations for theatre students are there within an hour of where you are? Within the state/region?

2. What if your school *always* participates in a competition that is in the fall, but it's your first year teaching and you are overwhelmed? How can you manage this? Who do you talk to?

3. A representative of a student travel organization visits you. They *promise* to take care of *everything*. Just sign on the dotted line... What questions do you need to ask?

4. You've scheduled a stage combat workshop, but school is closed that day due to inclement weather. Your guest artist was available and expects to be paid anyway. Your finance person says, "No school. No visit. No payment." What now?

5. You've planned your weekend trip to the state theatre conference for weeks, got all your ducks in a row, but the weather is bad the morning you are to depart and the school system cancels all field trips. Your options?

6. Your whole group is gathered out front, boarding the field trip bus... except three kids. Do you leave on time as promised?

7. Some kids are missing, reported to have gone off with kids from another school. Is that OK? If not, why not? What if it's with "townies?"

8. You forgot to count bus seats, and you really are short a couple. The driver will not let kids squeeze together to fit. How do you handle it?

9. Kids are caught drinking in their rooms. Or *smell* like it. Or it's a rumor. What level of response is reasonable? What follow-up is required, and with whom? You're with these kids the rest of the year—is it OK to cut them some slack by violating your agreement with the school to follow the rules?

10. Your kids are not only angels, they win all sorts of awards at the competition. Whom do you crow to first? How?

Part II

Winter

6 Paying Attention to Professionalism

RELATED APPENDIX DOCUMENTS

- Response to Patron Complaint About Show Content (Appendix W, p. 341)
- Use of Weapons on Stage (Appendix X, p. 343)
- Recommendation Request Form (Appendix Y, p. 345)

Hopefully by now you will have a chance to breathe a bit—and maybe you'll be able to pay some attention to a variety of other issues that have or will come up. What about your seniors who need you to write them a college recommendation? Or their parents, who may be worried that their kids will become starving artists? Or your administrator, who will be coming around to observe your classes? What if you get sick and need a substitute? There are plenty of good examples—and mistakes—out there to learn from. So, learn away!

College Recommendations

If you enjoy writing, you will probably enjoy composing college recommendation letters. Whether you enjoy the process or not, writing college recommendations is part of your position as theatre director on the high school level. You can make a difference in the life of a student. As you seek to convey the true gifts of each student for whom you write a recommendation, trust that good college recruiters, particularly those involved in selection for competitive programs, will recognize the difference between a strong recommendation and one which seems to have omissions, or "damns with faint praise." You want to make sure that your recommendations are consistently meaningful and authentically helpful to the admissions process. In doing so, you are also developing a reputation for yourself as one who can accurately assess the prospective students you recommend to them.

The first order of writing college recommendations is to meet deadlines. Perhaps you have a special white board space in which students can write their names and dates when their recommendations are due. You may also wish to grant the privilege of "permission to bug" (otherwise known as encouragement) to remind the teacher that the recommendation deadline is approaching. This is entirely appropriate, since students should take some responsibility in this aspect of the college application process which is to their benefit. You may also ask students to provide you with pertinent anecdotes from class or productions—details that may reveal positive qualities to college admissions people. If you have a large theatre department, a form or list of requirements may be helpful to your process. Use or modify ours, found in Appendix Y.

Another choice that presents itself is whether you prefer the online or hard copy (old-fashioned paper) recommendation process. At this writing, there is still a choice, although most theatre directors wind up doing a little bit of both. Even if you choose to submit your recommendation online, you need to have copy on file. Keep one for yourself and give at least one copy to the student's counselor. If the online process for a particular school is not user-friendly, go with the traditional paper printout from your word processor. However, the next school may have a more friendly online process, so save your recommendation electronically so that you can cut and paste it into that online space.

As the recommendation writer, you can decide whether to reveal the contents of your recommendation to your student. Most students decline their right to read the written recommendation, but some teachers will still give students a confidential copy of the recommendation for their files, directing them to share it only with parents. The advantage of this approach is that the student has the choice of whether to use the recommendation or not and no one can accuse you of keeping their child out of college. A side benefit is that hardworking parents deeply appreciate the accolades often present in a college recommendation, especially if you have taught their child for four years and watched them grow up.

The difficulty of writing college recommendations for your students is, of course, that they are not all equally talented or qualified to go to college. College recruiters for theatre

Appendix 🗎 Connection

To help guide and organize your students who want a recommendation, we have included a *Recommendation Request Form* in appendix Y. Feel free to use or modify it as you see fit.

Real-World Moments

Mary Beth has been in Mr. Sanford's theatre classes for four years but plays for several sports teams and does not have time to participate in the after-school theatre program. Mary Beth took theatre class through the years to have fun, be with her friends, and because she didn't prefer another elective. She is neither an exceptional participant nor volunteer. When she asked Mr. Sanford for a recommendation for college, he was surprised—he asked Mary Beth if one of her coaches could write the recommendation. Mr. Sanford felt guilty at turning her down and asked her about the recommendation a couple of weeks later, but she had already gotten someone else to do it and was fine.

training programs and conservatories are generally quite adept at reading between the lines. For example, you may refer to one student as simply being "reliable and responsible," but you may then describe another student as one who "brings to life a multi-layered, fully energized, human character onstage." You are being positive, telling the truth in each case, but you present very different pictures of these two students. For your students who do not want to study theatre after high school, "reliable and responsible" may carry them a long way for colleges that focus primarily on grades and test scores. On the other hand, your glowing recommendation will likely mean much more to the gifted student who truly has a flair for theatre and may even have a shot at Broadway someday.

In considering the potential impact of your recommendations, be aware that not all students track well with the "four-year formula" of high school—or even college. There is no way for you to know if Johnny, who was an underachiever in high school because of a difficult home life, might well mature and become a star of stage and screen in a few years. You can only write about what you see in a student's work as you know it—but never tell a student that s/he just doesn't have what it takes to make it. Maybe they haven't developed their talent or skills to the level a conservatory wants to see this year, but there is life after high school and beyond! Many students blossom in the months and years beyond your recommendation. Johnny may very well have what it takes, but you just can't see it right now. Write about what you have seen in your time with him.

If you truly cannot write a positive recommendation for a student, it is usually because s/he has not appeared to be as committed or involved in your program as you would like them to be; it's okay to tell them that. It's okay to say, "Are you sure there isn't someone else who knows you better? You just haven't put the time into the after-school productions, so it is difficult for me to write much of value in a recommendation." It's also okay to say, "No." The individual reasons will vary, but telling the truth in a kind manner is the best path.

Make the college recommendation writing process work efficiently for you. If you worry about losing the stamped envelope that the student may give you to mail to the college, don't accept it. Give copies of your recommendations to the school counselor, who has to be involved in the process anyway—if you are determined to keep them all private. If you are comfortable with giving the students their recommendation, charging them to be mature and to keep the forms confidential, then give them each an envelope with several signed copies to sort and mail themselves.

In addition to your written narrative, some colleges and other programs may require you to submit forms in which you "rate" your students on a number scale or similar basis. You probably should keep these forms totally confidential and not share them with your students. There is very little nuance in a numerical rating, and revealing such a rating can be unnecessarily hurtful to the student being rated.

Hopefully, the final product you create for students will be something you are satisfied with, and even proud, to put in your files. It is one piece of reflective documentation of your journey together—a journey in which you and your students have both undoubtedly grown.

COLLEGE ADVICE TO PARENTS

A Short Play

DRAMATIS PERSONÆ

DIRECTOR, *a person seen as having the power to create stars or crush souls*
PARENT, *a person who wants to divine the future success of their child*

The SCENE *is a drama classroom.*

PARENT. Have you got a moment?

DIRECTOR. Yes, sir. You're So-and-So's dad, right?

PARENT. Yeah. Listen, she's been talking lately about applying to college to major in theatre, of all things."

DIRECTOR. Oh…?

PARENT. Well, that sounds to me like a great way to stay broke forever, with all due respect.

DIRECTOR. How can I help you?

PARENT. What I want to know is this: is my little girl really good enough to make it? I mean, I don't want to spend all that money just to have her never get any work. Has she got what it takes? What's the good of a major in theatre?

DIRECTOR. I have two answers for you. The first is that it's too soon to tell if she's got what it takes. She may be capable and talented, but in college, everyone will be coming from the top of their high school theatre programs. Will she stand out? It depends on who else is there and what shows they choose. Will she work hard? Will she strengthen her weak links here, in preparation? Concentration? A good ear? Taking criticism (or whatever the case might be for that kid)? And you're right, a life in the theatre is hard. How thick is her skin? Can she handle being turned down 49 times for every one job she gets? 'Cuz that's the average. Professional acting is about sales, perseverance, self-confidence and luck, as much as it's about being able to do the job once you get it. If theatre truly is her passion, and she is willing to put in the work and face the realities, then nothing either of us can say will dissuade her. Now, she's ready for more training. But I can't say what the result of that training—and four more years of maturing—will be.

PARENT. Hmm…what's the other answer?

DIRECTOR. Theatre is a lens much like any other humanities subject. It's a way of investigating the world, who we are, who we have been, what we're like, what makes us tick, and how to treat each other now and in the future. Like history, psychology, sociology, or political science, theatre can help us to discover our humanity. And it's really effective at that, especially if she comes to it with a love for the process and a hunger to learn more.

PARENT. Yeah, I guess I can see that.

DIRECTOR. As with any other college major, she will have to read, analyze critically, and write clearly. She will learn to research and apply that research in very practical ways. And it's better than the other soft sciences, I think, because it incorporates and develops skills that are tremendously useful in the real world: the ability to communicate clearly, to collaborate with others, to use critical thinking to solve a wide variety of problems. Those aren't skills just useful on Broadway—they are useful in practicing law, in sales (now there's a ton of jobs), and in pretty much any business setting you can think of. Theatre develops discipline and a determination to always keep working toward excellence.

PARENT. I never thought of it that way. She just wants to be on Broadway.

DIRECTOR. Will she become a star? I don't know…people win the lottery every day, despite the odds being statistically against them. Will she be able to make a living? If she has the grit, passion and determination to hang in there, stay mobile, live cheaply, network like a fiend, and keep at the top of her game, she might well do so. Will she benefit from a theatre major even if she gives up on acting professionally? Absolutely. The college degree itself is more important than the subject or the school, as you know. And the things she will have learned? Priceless.

(PARENT *exits, still troubled, but enlightened.*)

Choices for College Theatre Education

A.A., B.A., B.F.A., B.S. and beyond. It may be helpful to explain to parents the general differences among the types of undergraduate degrees available in theatre education. They'll still
have to deal with the specifics of the schools in which their child is interested and that they
can afford, but at least you can give them a starting place for making choices for theatre. Parents need more assistance than you might suspect—and you are viewed, rightly or wrongly,
as the educational expert!

Associate Degrees

You need to show respect for the local community college as a starting place for higher education; don't assume that every parent can afford the more traditional four-year college campus experience or that every student is ready for that experience. Ask parents and students
about the schools that they are considering. For economic and/or personal reasons (maturity,
academics, health concerns), living at home and pursuing an associate degree with an emphasis on the arts/theatre is a viable option that can ultimately provide the first two years of
a Bachelor's degree. Some states have special arrangements between the prominent community colleges and their four-year colleges/universities for easy credit transfer and admission.
You can offer community college information and still discuss four-year degrees, since most
parents will want a Bachelor's degree as the educational endgame for their child.

Bachelor of Arts

The B.A. degree at most colleges is designed with a liberal arts philosophy in mind, which entails a belief in a strong foundation of required general education courses. Students typically
spend much of the first two years of a B.A. degree program fulfilling the general education
requirements, with minimum enrollment in their degree emphasis (major/minor). Theatre
majors can still audition for productions outside of class, hopefully developing and using
time management skills to balance their class work with their love of theatre. For some students, the B.A. program offers the opportunity to major and minor in different subjects. By
comparison, the Bachelor of Fine Arts degree—B.F.A. (see below)—tends to be more pre-
scriptive and requires more complete focus on the theatre program. In terms of ultimate
employability, both the B.A. and the B.F.A. offer respected undergraduate resume credits;
the choice depends largely upon the needs and wishes of the student and the specifics of the
degree program at each college/university.

Questions to Consider in Comparing College Theatre Programs

- Does the college prohibit theatre students from auditioning their freshman year? Do they require it?
- Are students required to contribute stage crew hours?
- Are students able to take theatre courses before fulfilling their general education requirements?
- Can non-theatre majors participate in productions? Can they take theatre classes?
- Is there a non-major theatre production company? Can theatre majors participate?
- Is there an alliance with a professional theatre company? How does that work? Does it limit or expand opportunities for undergraduates?
- If there's a music program, what is the relationship between the music program and the theatre program? Are they independent? Cooperative? Collaborative?
- If there is a graduate program, does it undercut the attention given to undergraduates? And if so, how much?
- Are undergraduates taught by professors or graduate assistants?
- Which are the stronger and weaker areas of the theatre program?
- Is there a student improv troupe? Who can participate?
- Is there a film production program? Does it interact with the theatre department?
- Is there a dance program? Does it interact with the theatre department?
- What do the student newspaper and the alumni magazine have to say about the current issues on campus (these are likely to be less biased than the brochures available)?

Bachelor of Fine Arts

The B.F.A. is the newest of the four-year degree programs commonly found for undergraduate theatre offerings. It is the logical child of the M.F.A. (Master of Fine Arts), which largely replaced the Ph.D. in the 1980's as the terminal degree for college professors who teach performance, rather than research, in theatre. The B.F.A. is a departure in philosophy from the B.A.; it focuses more directly on the arts. It requires fewer general education classes, which creates room for more content-specific classes with an emphasis on performance and practicum. The B.F.A. performance degree is the fully-accredited college's answer to the programs offered by independent conservatory programs (see below).

The B.F.A. in Theatre Education degree is the prospective teacher's version of applied practicum, since it is designed to integrate the science of education with the art of theatre. B.F.A. Theatre Education students receive training that specifically focuses on the unique aspects of teaching Theatre Arts—their collegiate study is viewed through the lens of a theatre teacher. It is best suited to students who are quite certain that they wish to pursue theatre education.

Most B.F.A. Theatre programs are highly concentrated—there is little flexibility for majors or minors in other subjects due to program performance and/or practicum requirements. Perhaps the greatest example of this is the Musical Theatre B.F.A., which requires study in all three performance areas: dance, music and acting. Since the B.F.A. is a legitimate four-year college degree, its value is equal to the B.A. in terms of the graduate's employability and future options.

Bachelor of Science

Although we generally think of theatre as an art, theatre may be considered to be either a science (does that make teachers mad scientists?) or an art, depending on the school. Some schools offer a Bachelor of Science degree (B.S.) instead of a Bachelor of Arts (B.A.), even though the required curriculum may be almost identical for both degrees. As is the case with the B.A., the B.S. program will necessarily include a large number of general education courses, limiting the number of theatre content classes that a student can fit into a schedule. The B.S. in Theatre Education does not usually include an integrated approach to theatre and education—often the education classes do not address the unique needs of the theatre education classroom. It is left up to the student to determine how to apply the best educational practices in the theatre setting.

Five Year Programs: B.A. + M.Ed. = Teacher Certification

Since many states no longer require full licensure for theatre education, but are satisfied with minimal certification programs, the B.S. in Theatre Education is less and less popular. Some students are not prepared to make the decision to teach when they graduate from high school, so the B.A. degree is an appropriate starting place. In the place of full theatre education licensure, some colleges offer a five year program that covers the requirements of both the B.A. and a Masters Degree in Education (M.Ed.), culminating in teacher licensure in theatre.

The M.S./M.Ed. program doesn't incorporate the fully integrated theatre education training of the B.F.A. Theatre Education degree, but it is a viable alternative for many students, and is more widely available. It may also offer students the opportunity to achieve certification in more than one subject area—theatre teachers often begin in part-time programs that require them to teach another subject for full-time employment. The Master's in Education may also provide greater marketability to the graduate, since many school systems may prefer this level of professionalism and offer higher pay for it.

Conservatory Training

What if a student is completely certain that they must follow their passion to pursue acting or technical theatre immediately after high school? Where can they get additional training that will prepare them for, and connect them with, the professional world of theatre? The studio training of a theatre conservatory—usually in an urban setting—provides an immediate step toward fulfilling their dreams.

Most conservatory programs are valuable in terms of local connections, networking and training for professional theatre. Depending upon cost and the reputation of the conservatory, this is a viable option for students who seek professional theatre training and are not concerned with the backup plan versatility that is offered by a college degree. Caution should be exercised, however; this training at a studio type conservatory can be costly and may not translate into any helpful credentials to put on a job application unassociated with theatre.

Conservatory programs that do not culminate in a college degree may or may not offer some college credit. Some conservatory programs offer a certificate that may translate into college credit at some schools, but this may vary from school to school. It is safe to say that most parents would prefer to spend their money in the college arena, assuming they support their child's passion for a career in theatre; although the total cost is usually more than the typical two year conservatory program, employment opportunities available with a college degree are of a broader scope. It all depends upon what works for the individual student.

Politics and You

"All education is politics" may be a cynical way to look at things, but there is some truth in there. Even though you may be alone in the classroom with your students most of the time, you will also be interacting with many other people whose opinions differ from yours and who want your policies to reflect their opinions, not yours. When they feel that your statements, behavior or other choices (such as your choice of show) are incompatible with their own ideas, you are likely to be called on the carpet to justify your choices or even reverse them. How you handle those moments can bury you in aggravation or keep you captain of your own ship.

It's important to remember that, basically, we are all after the same thing: for students to have the best possible experience in school, learning and growing in a safe environment. So, from that perspective, you are always on the same side as that angry parent. It's also true that some parents will totally back up their kid no matter how guilty or wrong the student may be, and some will interpret as your bad action anything that their child finds uncomfortable (like not getting cast). These moments can rarely be handled successfully by email—they must be face-to-face moments, where tone of voice and body language (you understand all about those!) are relevant and useful elements.

The principal must often balance support for the faculty with the demands of the other stakeholders, including those who set policy for him/her to implement, the students, community, and sometimes the angry parents who want him/her to reprimand you or reverse a decision you made. If you smell trouble, give your principal or other administrator(s) a heads up—along with your version of the situation—before they get that angry phone call about you and the "outrageous" thing you have supposedly done. No one wants to be blindsided—but don't be surprised if someone goes straight past you and the principal, and right to the school board to complain about you or your policies. It happens.

When a parent greets you in "mama bear" mode, emotion is ruling the day rather than reason, so take a deep breath and be sure to have a third party present, such as a guidance counselor or administrator. Remember at the outset that it's hard for people to argue with you when you are agreeing with them. So begin with an an apology for whatever the misunderstanding may be, then add in a smile and let them know that you hope you can clear it up quickly.

Remember that the issue is how you are going to make the situation better for the parent and student, so avoid getting defensive. Do provide what explanation will untangle misunderstandings, and be ready to modify your behavior, but calmly stand your ground if the situation requires it. For example, your casting decisions are irreversible; in that case try to shift the discussion to the value of working with the parents to help the child develop resilience, a hugely valuable quality much harder to learn after the child has left the safe nest

Appendix Connection

When you field a complaint about foul language or other questionable content in a show you selected, you may find it helpful to refer to the *Response to Patron Complaint About Show Content* in appendix W. Feel free to use or modify it as you see fit, and do give your administrator a heads up *before* that patron reaches out to them.

of home. Empower them to make their child stronger. Being challenged on a decision does not necessarily mean you have to reverse it.

Dealing with volunteers, like your drama booster parents, requires acknowledging your appreciation of their assistance. You simply must not take them for granted, no matter how routine their help may become. Keep people in your corner by recognizing that they are providing invaluable service to you, their child, the theatre program, and the school and community. Yay, Drama Mamas and Drama Dads!

If you are sharing a performing space with other teachers, or requesting assistance of your colleagues, be as diplomatic and understanding of them as you would want them to be when making a request of you. Everyone is working hard. And everyone has that "other life" outside school that we often know precious little about. Be warm and generous, but be clear about what you need, and hopefully, why it would benefit both of you to get it. And if they just won't help, you'll have to decide whether to let it go, or whether it's worth making this issue a battle you want to pick and move it up to the next level/administrator. Of course, escalating the dispute will likely engender ill will, so save it for something really, really important.

What about the hot water that can come from students pushing the envelope when it comes to including/selecting scenes that contain questionable language or behavior? Try explaining it this way: "If you're doing a scene in class, and you use language or behavior that makes your classmates turn to me to see if I'm going to object, then it means you have caused your audience to "break character" and stop watching the performance. In that case, that language or behavior should be omitted. But, if it is truly likely to draw the (class) audience further into the moment of the scene, then leave it in."

This guideline means the threshold of what's acceptable changes with different age groups or venues. A more mature audience can handle more challenging material. You may be able to perform material at a theatre convention that you could not perform at your own school— yet another reason to include a "rating" or other warning on your publicity materials if mature themes or objectionable language is part of the show.

With your students, politics means not playing favorites, but letting policy trump personality. You will be making choices that seem personal even when they are wholly professional, and teenagers are *very* sensitive to being slighted or treated unfairly. When your cast list goes up, some will ask you not just why they didn't get cast, but "what was wrong with me?"

Appendix Connection

If you do a show involving prop weapons, be sure to refer to *Use of Weapons on Stage* in appendix X. Feel free to use or modify it as you see fit, and keep your administration in the loop.

Real-World Moments

The Drama I student was oh, so easily distracted, and just would not stop talking during attendance. He was a football player, so in an effort to regain his attention, the teacher called his name and tossed the grade book into his lap. Two hours later they were in the principal's office sitting next to an "angry bear" mother who demanded to know why the teacher had thrown something at her son during class, practically assaulting her baby boy!

How you frame your reply is essential to their continued support and their self esteem. You may want to note items to improve as you watch auditions. Those kids who are obnoxious or needy want the same treatment that they perceive others getting. "Why do you always like the kids who do all their work better than me?" is a question asked with sincerity.

Your influence on your students is a given. As such, your own views on issues of the day should be kept fairly close to the vest—you know, that great triumvirate "sex, politics, and religion." It doesn't mean you can't discuss current events, but be careful not to open yourself up to charges of telling your students what they should think. If your statements run counter to what Mom and Dad have been teaching their children, you could be in for it.

If there is a contentious issue at your school that has gone (or could go) public, you are advised *not* to talk to the media. Let the administrators (or lawyers) weigh in—you stay out. You will never be seen as a private citizen, only as a representative of your school, no matter how much you insist that you're giving only your personal opinion.

Learning diplomacy and politics takes time. Reaching out to parents and helping them calm down and see the wisdom of your honest efforts (or at least the honesty of your efforts) is a skill that evolves through experience. Stay calm, think before you speak, be honest and generous, and you will get there.

Recertification Check

The requirements to teach in a private school are established by the particular school; they can vary from just your knowledge of the subject and your passion to teach, to evidence of years of experience, training and a certification process created by that school. But to teach in a public school, you must always be certified according to rules established by that state's Department of Education. Typically, that requires that you document you have sufficient coursework for the type of certification you seek. There may be different levels of certification, and the duration of that certification can vary from one year to lifetime certification (increasingly rare), depending on the state. In addition, you may be "endorsed" to teach only in a particular subject area(s) in which you have shown sufficient training. Although it may be possible to be hired while short one course or two, your time to complete the state requirements is limited.

Here's a horrible scenario: you get a new job that you love, and you get so wrapped up in it (that's *easy* to do) that the one required course you needed to be properly, officially certified to teach slips off your radar screen. The next thing you know (probably the week before your show opens), you're informed that the State Department of Education (or whoever) has disqualified you from continuing to teach the following year... and it's too late to fix it.

Most teachers are hired on a single year contract, which may eventually (three years is common) become a continuing contract, but even those require proof that you are still pursuing professional development in your field. Teaching licenses vary in duration—five years is common. In order to have your license renewed, you will need to be recertified before the term of the license expires. During that time, you must earn enough recertification points or education credits or you will not be able to have your teaching license renewed.

How do you work toward recertification? Dig back into all that paperwork they gave you when you started, or ask your teacher's union, or ask some older, wiser teacher or your administrator. There may be forms to fill out, things for them to sign, categories to fill (e.g. attending training sessions, publishing, presenting at conferences, taking classes, etc.). But definitely do this as your first step: *Make a folder for documentation of your continuing education and recertification activities.*

Put your continuing education and recertification folder where you cannot lose it, unless this information is all stored online by the school system. Be totally vigilant about accumulating the records of anything you do that might count in your favor so, when the time comes, you don't have to scramble to take a class that you have *no* time to take, and you don't have to search frantically for proof that you really have been keeping up your skills and professional development. However disorganized a person you may be, you need to take care of yourself by taking care of this.

If you should change schools (say... someone with seniority bumps you out of your happy new job), be certain to take these records with you. You will still need them!

Evaluation

As a student teacher, you know you will be watched and evaluated by your mentor teacher and directly or indirectly by the professor in charge of your education program. But as a new teacher—and periodically throughout your career—you will be evaluated by your administrator, too. From place to place, evaluations vary widely. At one end of the spectrum, an

Real-World Moments

My student teacher was a musical theatre major with an education minor. She was all energy and enthusiasm, ready to sign on and work hard. Her college (in another state) had assured her that she was well prepared. But in the state where she did her student teaching—and wanted to work—the requirements for certification were different, and her coursework didn't satisfy the requirements for certification. She was devastated (and angry with her college advisor)... and ended up teaching math.

evaluation could be merely a "rubber stamp" that guarantees future employment unless you do something bordering on criminal. Or, it could be a formal process consisting of a series of pre-conference, announced and unannounced observations, and a post-observation conference. You will then be rated you against whatever scale has been set up by the school system, resulting in documentation of your abilities and recommendations for improvement (they must find something in both categories). You may have an opportunity to add your own explanations or rebuttals to the evaluation.

What does your observing administrator know about theatre? They may well judge your value based on the success of your productions, the most visible evidence of your leadership (even though you're barely paid slave wages for all that after-school time, and it's your *classroom teaching* they are supposed to evaluate). Will they expect to see students sitting quietly at desks taking notes on theatre history or some aspect of acting? Will they want to see your daily lesson itinerary on the board, with the standards and indicators from your official program of studies identified? Do they want your class structured tidily into "What we're going to do; now we're doing it; here's what we did" format? Or L.E.A.R.N. format (see below)? Will they be listening for edu-jargon?

You have no control over observer expectations... unless you can get them to visit your class a few times prior to the official visit(s) and chat informally about what they observed before it counts. Try to remember that it's in everyone's best interests that you be successful, and that you're teaching a subject that is designed for audience consumption. So if, during an observation, you feel like *you* are on stage, performing for your students—and the evaluator— just do what you do, and try to learn from their feedback.

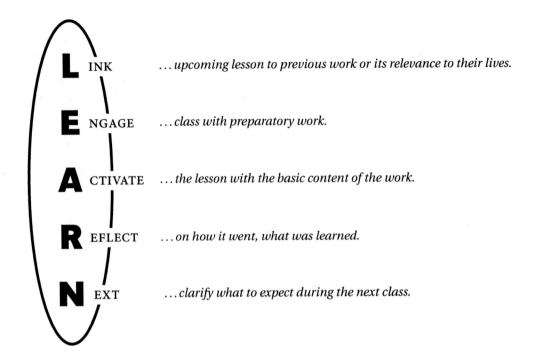

LINK   *. . . upcoming lesson to previous work or its relevance to their lives.*

E NGAGE   *. . . class with preparatory work.*

A CTIVATE   *. . . the lesson with the basic content of the work.*

R EFLECT   *. . . on how it went, what was learned.*

N EXT   *. . . clarify what to expect during the next class.*

Staff Development

A school or school system that fancies itself progressive will constantly be pushing its teachers to try the next new thing in education; to meet expectations from the school system, state and federal education institutions; and to encourage its employees to improve their skills and incorporate best practices into their routines.

Staff development can take many forms. You may be required to take an online course (or view video clips) and answer questions about sexual harassment, safe online/Internet use, dealing with bullying, preparing for disasters of various kinds, etc. Your teaching recertification may depend on completion of these required courses.

Your department meetings at the school or area level may include the sharing of information about best practices, the collection and productive use of data, introduction and training on new software you are required to use, etc. Teachers may have an opportunity to introduce lesson plans or techniques they have found successful. Guest artists may be invited in to demonstrate or lead the group in some new activity.

Faculty meetings are typically required, and sometimes even informative. They don't usually count as staff development, but it all depends on who is planning what (raise eyebrows here).

If you teach at a school offering the International Baccalaureate program including courses for theatre, you will certainly want to go to one of their staff development workshops (the longer the better—go for at least a long weekend if you can). These are led by ISTA (International Schools Theatre Association) and are terrific at recharging your batteries and at clarifying all aspects of the IB Theatre program. If you are working toward a Master's degree (or sufficient advancement leading to a possible pay bump), staff development opportunities may provide credits toward that goal.

As of this writing, the current trend is for members of the same department to meet for professional development. Ironically, this push for Collaborative Learning Teams (CLT) and a Professional Learning Community (PLC) is not very compatible with being the only person who teaches theatre in a school, as is most often the case. And theatre people are such a collaborative bunch, it's a shame not to collaborate. If you have the chance to meet with theatre educators from other schools in your school system, jump at it. Everyone has something valuable to share, and networking alone can make it worth your time. Contribute your own ideas, tactics, and lessons that work whenever you can. Make contact with those who can assist your professional development, whether formally or not. If you attend a conference, arrange ahead of time for staff development credit toward teaching recertification, and document which workshops you have attended to prove that it is justified. If yours is an IB school, offer to host a regional meeting to network with other IB Theatre teachers. Such sessions may be funded (including substitute pay and refreshments) by your IB program and are always of tremendous value to both new and experienced IB teachers.

Substitute Teachers

From time to time, you're going to miss class. Whether for illness, family emergencies, professional development, or field trips—it's going to happen. Now is the time to keep in mind how you treated the substitute teachers when you were in school. (Ouch!) So it's worth giving this some thought, because now you are the one who will be returning to class after that absence, and you don't want to regret taking it.

Create an emergency lesson plan for each class, and teach the students in that class how it works. A round robin of improvisation or a set of theatre games can be a welcome break from regular work. It should be something you try out ahead of time so your students can basically fill the class period, even if a sub never shows up—it happens! But emergency lesson plan aside, it is much more productive if your students are able to carry on with ongoing classwork, including show prep, when you aren't there. It can be a test of your students' maturity and theatre-mindedness. After all, you want to create a culture where the kids don't need someone to say "OK, begin," but know to get started on the current work and keep it productive even in your absence.

If you are ill, the question is always, "How sick is too sick to teach?" The longer you're out, the more catch-up will be accumulating for your return, the more "off" your kids will be from your intended lessons, and the fewer sick days you will have left before pay is deducted from your check. On the other hand, coming in to spread disease is no kindness, either! So while the mice always behave better when the cat is *not* away, you're going to have to balance the benefits of absences with the costs. If you do come in feeling under the weather, at least warn your students at the start of each class so they can keep their distance or not take personally any snapping at them which might not be justified.

So let's say you must miss all or part of a day of school. How do you get a sub? If you only need to miss a piece of the class day, you may be able to get coverage from a fellow teacher in your department or building (and then, of course, remember that you owe them one). Where do subs come from, anyway? Wannabe teachers, retired teachers, part-time teachers, and others can end up on your school system's official roster of substitutes. But if possible, find some *theatre* subs! Start building a list of possible subs you might use, and keep those numbers handy. Often, they will leave business cards in the faculty lounge or mailboxes. Word of mouth recommendation is often the best. Be certain your substitute has been approved by your school system—it's not OK to have some actor friend or kind parent stand in for you when you're out. This person bears the same legal responsibility as you when students are in their charge.

Whenever possible, arrange for a sub ahead of time. There are likely to be standard forms to fill out, the hidden bottom line of which is "Who is going to be paying for this person?" Is it some administrative fund, to cover your professional development day? Your paycheck, if you have exceeded your allotted number of sick/personal days? Your drama department (ticket receipt) funds? There may be a code number to indicate the source of the funding. If it is a last-minute absence, you may have to fill out this paperwork upon your return.

Schools and school systems vary in their procedures for substitute teachers. You may be responsible for getting your own sub directly, or there may be an internet site or phone number to contact to make such arrangements. If you know the person that you want as your sub, find out if he or she has an ID number that you can enter into the system. Your administrator (or secretary) needs to know if you will be out, and who to expect. They will arrange to have your classroom unlocked, and will verify that the sub showed up and should be paid for the day.

So as a theatre teacher who should sub for you? Ideally, it's someone who understands your job, and can keep the class moving forward. Someone who just babysits may be danger-ous at worst, and even at best, leaves you having to play catch-up with your class. A sub who covers all classes probably has not covered many classes where kids are not sitting at desks most of the time, and could get a lot of push-back from your kids if they try to assert more control that the students are used to.

Make sure you provide an extra copy of your detailed sub plan—procedures as well as content—for your sub as far ahead of time as you can. Be *very* specific about what should be read aloud to the class, what level of supervision you want, how things should be left at the end of class (e.g., where do props/costumes go?). Are there procedures you use (e.g., how you call attendance) that the kids expect and the sub could use, too? Catch-phrases of yours that will be shortcuts your students understand, and will make the sub appear more in the know? Leave copies of needed materials in easy-to-find locations. Request detailed feedback about how each class went, what got accomplished, etc.

Can your sub stay and supervise after-school rehearsal? Probably no, since they're no longer on company time, even if they're willing. It's that liability thing… you'll have to cancel, or have someone who is qualified to supervise kids take over.

Fixing Problems

To err is human. And for all the time you are going to spend anticipating and nonetheless dealing with the consequences of the errors of your students, your own humanity is going to shine through also, from time to time. Below are some specific situations you might run into and some more general principles to keep in mind as you try to stay as error-free as possible. Fixing mistakes and dealing with problems will be easier if you set up a theatre education program with a culture of planning ahead, of being proactive.

* Paint on clothing? Use rubbing alcohol, but don't delay!
* Paint on carpet? Try Woolite.
* Sore throat? Throat coat: hot tea with honey; most effective: limit use of voice, get rest, and stay hydrated.
* Touched stage lamp? Try cleaning it with rubbing alcohol.
* Lost rented script? Pay for it and add to your inventory of plays when it turns up.
* Fire Marshall complaints? No choice but to do what he says.
* Casting error? Live with it—switching horses midstream is a route to even greater disaster.
* Public release of casting notes? Lay low, then try to move on as fast as you can.
* Lost (by you) homework/test? Assure students it doesn't lower the overall grade.
* Provided building coverage for your own event? A conflict of interest that could get you fired (if you get paid separately by two organizations for the same event).
* Omitted a name in the program? Post a sign in the lobby, or do a program insert.
* Omitted an ad in the program? Post a sign in the lobby, and send back their money.
* Cast someone without parent permission to do the show? Use all your diplomatic skills to talk those parents into approving after all, but find some kid to understudy/save the day if they say no.

Parent Permission

Among all the mundane items that you would like to forget, permission slips may actually be one of your most important tasks. Technical theatre students, acting students and anyone planning to participate in your program should fill out a parent permission slip, get their parent's signature, and return it the first week of school or as soon as possible. This will not protect students from getting paint on their clothes or splinters in their fingers, or from burning their hands on lighting instruments or an over-worked drill bit, but it will protect *you* from parent and/or administrative prosecution. This documents your efforts to work with parents and be clear about the activities with which their children will be involved. Permission slips also set a tone of serious intentions, and they effectively communicate information to the parent who otherwise might say, "No one told me they would be handling power tools." Make it part of your department culture to require all student volunteers for tech days to get a signed permission slip and emergency care information returned for you to keep on file. This will keep you protected and provide critical contact information should an accident occur.

Integrity and Responsibility

When things go wrong, be a role model of integrity. Model for your students what you are trying to teach them—take responsibility for your actions. If you or the kids spill paint on the auditorium carpet, clean up what you can and confess the rest to the building custodian. Offer to help, ask what you can do to make it right and apologize. Most building supervisors or engineers will appreciate anyone who honestly brings their attention to an accident, rather than having to discover it themselves without any explanation. The shared use of facilities at most schools makes it inevitable that spilled paint will be apparent to all, so you are wise to set a good example by accepting responsibility.

School finances require the most care of all. Stay in close contact with your school finance officer and department chairperson for anything involving money. Make sure that you learn all that you can about finance procedures at your school and get confirmation that you are doing things correctly. Your paperwork error can become a nightmare for a finance officer or building use coordinator when the auditors show up, so it's important to realize that you really are part of a school "village" in which your actions affect many others. As you fall into productive, validated patterns of financial procedures, you will earn trust and respect from both colleagues and administration.

Casting Errors

Unfortunately, if you make an error when posting your cast list and the wrong name goes on your department website, on Facebook and on the callboard, you have to live with it unless there was an obvious formatting error. You cannot recall a cast list once it goes out, except to

Mistakes You'll *Really* Want to Avoid

- School money unaccounted for or processed incorrectly
- Incorrect calendar dates for building use (e.g., auditorium reservations)
- Incorrect cast and/or production team list
- Inappropriate touching of a student
- Leaving a student behind on a field trip
- Neglecting to take roll
- Neglecting grading deadlines and requirements
- Unprofessional language, topics or clothing
- Missing the state recertification deadline
- Exhibiting a negative attitude

add names that were omitted—not to change roles. Admitting your error would only make things much worse. So suck it up and encourage the heck out of whomever you cast. Maybe there are problem-solving ways you can manipulate or creatively change your approach to the play, but you must not revisit casting unless the students make changes that give you an opportunity to make your own changes. The worst thing you can do to a student is to show a lack of confidence in them once they are cast. Remember that every student can grow—your job may be harder, the play may be different than you originally envisioned, but none of that matters next to the self-worth of a child. If it's a matter of talent, forget it and go for work ethic. If it's a matter of work ethic, have an honest discussion with the student about what your expectations are for this role. Give everyone an acting contract that clearly defines your standards and hope for dedication and growth. The results may surprise you—challenges are also opportunities for you to grow.

Thinking Ahead, Staying Humble, and Working it Out

Honesty, critical thinking, communication, and a proactive outlook are tools that every teacher must possess, especially theatre educators. Don't wait until the fire marshal points out the music stands or platforms obstructing part of the backstage exit. Make a habit (and communicate it to your other performing arts facilities users) of keeping the exits clear at all times. Include your students in your proactive habits; it will make them proud "owners" of the space. If your casting notes wind up in the wrong hands, bravely be the first to communicate and apologize as necessary. Next time you'll make sure that doesn't happen—you'll take more time and be more patient with the process and yourself. Another proactive casting policy is to cast understudies, preferably from the ensemble. If you make a mistake about casting a student without parent permission, you have your backup ready to go.

One of the hardest mistakes to correct involves scheduling of building use since there may not be an easy solution. If you think a space is available and it turns out to be in use by others, there isn't much that you can do at that time. One way to avoid this is to check in with your building use person on a weekly basis to get confirmation on the dates you believe are on the schedule. However, if you've messed up, go directly to your building use person and explain the issue; that person may have additional information that can help you resolve the conflict. If it means you have to reschedule, then that's what it means. Apologize, claim your humanity, communicate the changes, and *move on!*

For Reflection & Discussion

It's when the unexpected takes place that your professional judgment is put to the test.

1. What if you feel you can't write a good recommendation for a student you have taught for four years and who is very involved in your department?

2. How do you keep track of all of the students who want college recommendations, the deadlines and those pesky stamped envelopes? How can you keep your opinion secure and private?

3. What difference does it make if you post your cast list first thing in the day or last, or only online after school?

4. A gun has been found at school and the local news channel is outside at the end of the day, interviewing whomever they can find. Do you tell them what you have heard about the situation?

5. A pair of students has been working on a scene for several weeks, and now, the week before the final performance, one of the parents strenuously objects to the material, demanding that it not be used. What do you do?

6. Your cast list is up, but a parent claims that it wasn't fair and his daughter deserved the role, is devastated, and may do harm to herself if she doesn't get it. The principal wants you to help prevent a tragedy. What do you do?

7. Your drama booster board presents you with a list of shows they think you should do for the coming season. They make it clear that their continued support depends on your support of their efforts on behalf of their kids. Now what?

8. What activities are you likely to pursue as professional development? What do you need to know more about? What counts toward recertification?

9. What will you reply when your observing administrator asks "if you will be teaching" on the date they'd like to stop by?

10. What are the pros and cons of having an "observation lesson" ready to go whenever the unannounced observation takes place?

11. How can an administrator know the great things you've done that are not observable in the classroom, like leading an in-service workshop for your peers, or presenting at a conference, or receiving letters or emails of praise from parents or patrons?

12. You wake up feeling like death warmed over. Whom do you call to tell that you're not coming in? What do you do to assure there is a substitute teacher watching your little darlings?

13. You have arranged for the same sub to cover several dates. After the first one, your students complain that the sub was horrible. What do you do?

14. You discover that the quiz you left for the sub to administer was taken with all the students sitting in one (easy to "share") clump...or given to one class but not the other ("Oh, I didn't find that quiz you left until the second class. My bad."). Now what?

15. You've arranged for a sub, but your field trip gets canceled at the last minute. Do you keep the sub and have a great free (or work session) day? How does one cancel a sub?

16. Your sub reports that the kids have been holy terrors. How do you deal with that? What if it's just a couple of them? How do you respond?

17. Is a "mental health day" a legitimate reason to take a day off? As often as needed? Is it OK to take a personal day and call it a sick day?

7 Branching Out and Bringing Them In

RELATED APPENDIX DOCUMENTS

- Playwriting Lesson Plan Templates (Appendix Z, p. 347)

It's amazing how quickly planning for the next school year begins, but for many schools, it starts in the winter. That means you need to learn about the enrollment process and calendar for your program. You have to promote your classes for next year to your potential students. For your older students, it's time to keep the ball rolling. On the other hand, it may also be the perfect time to let your younger students have the limelight with a small performance and/or bring in younger audiences and give them a preview of the theatre program to get them interested and excited about it.

Enrollment—It's Your Job!

Theatre is almost always an elective class. As such, you are competing for enrollment with all other electives that your school offers. There is no guarantee from year to year that you will have enough students enrolled to support you and the theatre program. Thus, your job security may well depend on your ability to build and sustain student enrollment in your program. By winter, next year's course selection forms have been printed and guidance counselors are beginning to enroll students. You've got stuff to do!

Become Articulate About the Benefits of Your Courses

Put together a list of elements and benefits that your program can provide to students, and use it to generate a sales pitch (Schooltheatre.org has materials available that can help with this). What content and skills do you offer? Prepare your sound bite version. What expectations are there in your classes? Is there much homework or reading? Why should a student take your acting class if they can try out for the plays anyway? What does each successive course offer that hasn't already been covered?

Your Productions vs. Your Classes

Your productions are the public face of your program. "Good productions?...you must be a good teacher!" Even if your classes cover totally different material, many people will only know about your theatre program because of your productions. And realistic or not, they will make assumptions about your classes based on their reactions to your shows.

Make sure you have a clear policy on whether theatre students must do your shows. Do you require your theatre students to participate in your shows? If not, be aware that a misguided counselor may turn away potential theatre students who say they don't have the time after school for your productions. Make sure your policy is clear.

Know Who Promotes the Electives

How do parents and students know what electives are available to them? When? Is there a place on the school's website that identifies and explains the electives? Who makes changes to it, and when? Is there an electives fair for the various classes to be promoted to the students? Is there a meeting for parents to explain the options? Who represents theatre arts? Could you? This is extra time worth the investment. Volunteer! Prepare handouts or a display. Pull out every stop!

Know the Guidance Counselors

Plenty of kids have no idea what class to take to fill an elective slot, so the advice of a counselor can make all the difference. How supportive of the arts is each of your school's guidance counselors (it may vary a lot)? Do they know the difference between acting and "acting out?" Do they see theatre as frivolous, or as a dumping ground for students who don't have another strong elective interest? How much of a relationship can you build with them so they get an accurate idea of who you are and what your program offers? Just like casting, the goal is to find the best match between the student and the available classes. Make sure that they become familiar with the various elements of your programs. Get them to visit your classroom, support spaces and backstage. Find out if they have ever come to see your shows. You may need to send out some invitations—and free tickets—or take some folks to lunch.

Real-World Moments

Low theatre enrollment in one school we've heard of just didn't reflect the enthusiasm for the drama teacher's class. The teacher was baffled by the low enrollment, so she asked around. She came up with 35 more students who claimed to have asked for her next course but were not enrolled. It turned out to have been a clerical error: the secretary had filed their requests without entering them into the system! When the error was fixed, it saved the teacher's job.

Get to the Rising Ninth (or Seventh) Graders

Once your students are in your program, they generally stick with it—thanks to your program choices and your leadership. But looking to the future, you really need to hook the students from the school that feeds into your school. If you draw from several feeder schools, how will they become familiar with, and attracted to, your program and classes? What can you do to encourage these young-uns to look into your program? Can you offer free tickets to your shows to potential students? Would it make sense to do a children's theatre production to get your younger community familiar with your program? Can you tour a small show to your feeder schools? Can you send over a delegation of enthusiastic students to promote your class? Can you do a holiday or vacation drama camp or summer program (a win-win for both you and the community)?

Make Extra Room for Electives

If a student's schedule is full, there may still be ways of fitting theatre into that schedule. For example, a student might take a course during the summer, or online, to free up space during the school year for your elective. You may be the only one to suggest this kind of an alternative—don't presume that others have done so.

Be Exclusive and Inclusive

Be exclusive—the exclusive appeal of a class open only by audition may build enthusiasm that an open enrollment class can't achieve. Watch how the music department does this. Also, such a class is a treat to teach, since you know the students are willing to work.

But also be inclusive—students who have already worked with you on shows, or others with no theatre experience, may be ready to jump over a Theatre I class and bolster the enrollment of your Theatre II class.

If your school offers the International Baccalaureate (IB) program, make clear that no previous experience is required to enter your theatre program. IB is much more concerned with how much a student can learn than with how skillful or talented they are to begin with.

Consider teaming with an ESOL (kids learning English) or other special needs teacher. Theatre is a terrific way to learn both socialization skills and language skills. You may find some great talent there!

Maintaining Momentum

As the first semester draws to a close, students often need to regenerate the enthusiasm that was so prevalent at the beginning of the year. There are many things you can do to get these kids motivated, most of which can help you and your program in the process. It's a great time to offer some high interest units for your classes that will make theatre class even more fun and encourage students to sign up for class next year.

High Interest Units

In general, movement, warm-ups, improv, and theatre games should be regular components of your class work. However, students typically love classes or units that focus intensively on one or more of these components. Here are some examples:

STAGE MAKE-UP Offer to order individual kits for your students, and get parent permission slips.

- Standard stage makeup application
- Special effects—scars, burns, bruises
- Facial hair

STAGE COMBAT Consider a SAFD.org certified guest artist.

- How to fall safely
- "Victim initiation" and control
- Slaps, choking, hair-pulling done safely and dramatically

CREATIVE MOVEMENT Responding physically to music and ideas

- Focus on liberating physicality
- Solo and ensemble work

- Include gesture and facial expression

IMPROVISATION Creating characters and narrative on the fly

- Competitive team improv, like TheatreSports
- Long-form improvisation (current events based; "park bench" scenes; etc.)
- Include gesture and facial expression

MUSICAL THEATRE When dialogue just isn't enough!

- Choreography
- Evolution movement game (see Glossary)
- Acting out scenes—use scripts you have collected over the years
- Musical scenes—acting out a song in exaggerated style
- Visual Project: go online to explore websites of musical theatre publishers; create a hat, mobile, poster that represents a musical; create and share a fantasy cast (people dead or alive!) of a musical

MASK MAKING Low ego, high energy expressiveness; great construction project

- Commedia dell'arte (Renaissance Italian improv stock character types)
- Ancient Greeks
- Mardi Gras celebration

PUPPETS Creative construction and uber-human expressiveness

- Create paper mâché "Bunraku" puppets
- Buy professional puppets and put on shows
- Perform for class, local pre-schools, or pyramid elementary students

CHILDREN'S LITERATURE Develop vocal skills or dramatize the tales

- Students bring in their favorite children's book
- Read aloud to the class as if reading to a child

MELODRAMA Go large or go home!

- Melodrama "Cue Story" (see Glossary)
- Short plays or scenes—*Plays* Magazine

Guest Artists and Field Trips

The middle of the year slump is the perfect time to hire a guest artist to come in and teach your students some specialized theatre skill, such as stage combat or specialized stage makeup. A session of some different theatre games or improvisations will be more impressive led by a different voice and face. Some college theatre programs promote themselves by sending senior students or professors into the local theatre classrooms. Investigate which colleges/universities in your area have these theatre programs; send an email to the head of the department and inquire.

Field trips can add a lot of variety to your program, exposing your students to professional or college work. Before their intense end of year tests begin, arrange for your students to attend a play outside of school—even if it's on a weekend—or tour the local elementary schools with a children's play from your Theatre I classes.

Children's Theatre

Children's theatre can be a highly beneficial aspect of any theatre program. It allows your students the thrill of instilling a love of the arts in their young audience members. This, in turn, can generate a supply of future theatre students for your program. On the high school and middle school levels, it can provide another public opportunity for your school to provide local, reasonably priced, quality family entertainment for your community. You can even use one of your standard theatre class units that includes playwriting and a performing tour as a resource for your pyramid elementary schools. Children's theatre can be a valuable aspect of your theatre program that makes the collaborative art more accessible to all.

For Fun and Funding

With supportive publicity, you can attract a substantial audience for children's theatre. This means you need to produce plays that are written for a young audience, performed by your middle or high school students. These productions are typically shorter than a regular main stage production—anywhere from 45-90 minutes, with an intermission. Your target audience is largely elementary school students. Some shows will also be appropriate for preschoolers. You will need to make sure that your publicity accurately reflects the target age group. The shorter length and less sophisticated characterizations that usually accompany children's theatre will provide special opportunities, such as:

STUDENT DIRECTORS Children's theatre is more within the grasp and skills of your students, so it provides a chance for them to try their hand at directing.

ORIGINAL SKITS OR PLAYS WITH A THEME This genre lends itself easily to the creation of original material, sketches or themed plays you may create or find.

UNDERCLASSMEN CASTING EMPHASIS Let your older students direct the younger ones.

FUNDRAISING Many communities are hungry for family-friendly entertainment, so the chance to enrich your department's coffers is strong.

DISCOUNTED TICKET PRICES To encourage bringing the whole family to see these shows, consider discounted prices for children or families or groups.

For simplicity's sake, you may not want your children's theatre production to be a musical, unless you have ready access to talented student musicians who need additional creative opportunities. While there is value in choosing shows with recognizable titles or subjects (fairy tales, folk tales, etc.), your production can take on whatever form you like. Be sure to get the word out to every school in your pyramid, as well as local private schools and daycare centers. If you advertise your children's show in the program for your other productions and present it at the same time every year, families will look forward to the consistent, easily accessible entertainment that your department has to offer.

Classroom Unit

While there are plenty of scripts to choose from in the professional world, children's theatre by its very nature may lead your students to try their hands at playwriting.

Let's assume that you're giving your class a known fairy tale and asking them to develop a children's show from that fairy tale. You can begin with student groups for improvisation and have them present the "fairy tale in a minute, thirty seconds, fifteen seconds, five seconds." This gets the creative camaraderie going—students will soon be asking you if they have to adhere to the original plot and characters of the fairy tale they have chosen. After the hilarity of this exercise, allow students to think in terms of a ten minute play that expands on their improvised piece. Subsequently, set timelines for written work, requiring that each group submit a plot outline and character list to you—one per group. Monitor students to keep them on task and in their groups; even if only one person is doing the actual writing or

Appendix 🗎 Connection

Our Playwriting Format Template and Playwright Project Outline worksheet can get your class started on becoming playwrights. These templates can help keep your students on track and accountable during the process of playwriting and give you opportunities for preliminary process-based assessments. See appendix Z, *Playwriting Lesson Plan Templates*.

typing, everyone should be contributing their ideas to the ensemble. The written work allows you to accomplish "formative assessment." Preliminary presentations keep students on task and accountable, as well as providing them an opportunity to give and receive constructive feedback for improvement. Final presentations may include props, costumes, programs and publicity flyer designs—more categories for a "summative assessment" rubric. Since this is children's theatre, you'll have to remind your students of what is developmentally appropriate for the target audience which is ages four to ten.

There are also some structural strategies to children's theatre as a genre that are helpful:

- ACTION, ACTION, ACTION!
- Chase scene
- Audience participation
- Audience volunteers
- Upbeat plot
- Break the fourth wall
- Actors who play musical instruments
- Gymnastics or dance
- Puppets
- Masks
- Banners, flags
- Costumes (complete or just accessories)
- Props

You can decide whether you want students to choose several of the above components to include in their final presentations. If the quality of these little shows reaches your standards, contact the elementary schools in your area and schedule a field trip day for your class to present their shows. Another option is to recognize groups who really did a great job with their children's project by asking them to perform at an evening of one-acts or other performance opportunity outside of the school day. Whatever you do, you should assign a reflective writing piece to your students when this unit is completely through. You may be surprised to find out how meaningful the ensemble, original work was to all of your students. The usually quiet student may be set free by a puppet, mask or use of a cape—confidence soars as your students make artistic discoveries and share their work.

Performing for little kids is an opportunity you want your students to have! Little children see teenagers as super cool and view stage characters as practically real; let your students feel the gratitude and adoration of a younger audience. For a public performance, allow time for the actors to come out in costume and sign autographs or pose for photos with the children. It doesn't hurt to give a reminder speech about appropriate language and behavior around younger children. And you'll need to monitor these aspects, of course, but chances are you'll be smiling while you do so.

An Evening of One-Act Plays and Scenes

Most parents want to see their child onstage performing. Don't forget, all of those kids in the music department are required to perform in multiple concerts, so parents may expect theatre students to perform, as well. So do consider a performance opportunity for every student you teach—above and beyond the productions that are part of your regular season.

An evening of one-act plays and/or scenes can be an annual event that lets parents see what their theatre students have learned. You need to announce the date at the beginning of the year so that families can save the date, but also have an alternate assignment ready for the one or two students who just can't commit. This could involve reading a play and researching some aspect of it (such as character, time period, playwright or set design), building a model of a set or of some props, or designing a small unit of study to teach to their classmates. In many school systems, a school cannot charge for a required, graded performance, but donations are usually acceptable as long as a dollar amount is not specified. Your evening of one-act plays may not be a money-maker, but it might give you some job security and will likely provide invaluable student memories.

Original student work is appropriate for this occasion, as well as professional short plays and scenes from published works. Be sure to consult with the plays' publishers about royalty requirements—most playwrights and publishers still require royalty payments (and certainly credits) for any kind of performance, whether you charge admission or not. Don't get sloppy with these details just because this is a smaller event; you can still get in trouble if you don't follow the copyright rules. Make sure that whoever is putting the program together for the evening has all students' names spelled properly and all copyright information in place.

The best time for this event will be during the second semester, when students have gotten their creative feet wet and have something to show for all their hard work. Since you don't want this show to go on all night, it may be wise to choose a short offering from each class. If you have a larger theatre program, you may need two evenings of class presentations.

Fundraising

As a theatre teacher, you're going to have expenses that go far beyond books and stationery supplies. You may be lucky enough to come into a department with plenty of money at your disposal, but more likely you'll find that there's never enough. You'll need to raise additional funds somehow. Here are some thoughts.

Accountability

No matter what money making scheme you come up with, a foolproof method of tracking every penny is drop-dead essential. Auditors are not in the business of trusting anyone—they need to see the paper trail. Be certain to follow your school's procedures for handling money (and when/if students may handle money), or you could be out of a job. Get the names of purchasers, date of sale, amount, and check number or cash. Give and get receipts, keep your copy, put a duplicate of your list of transactions somewhere—transparency is key. Make your school finance officer the ally who keeps you on the straight and narrow.

Boosters

In many schools, the primary function of a parent drama booster club is to raise money. Some of them are very good at it, too. Others are not. And you may feel that the boosters can help most by getting as many "bottoms in seats" as possible, so the hard work of their kids gets as much appreciation as it deserves. One advantage of booster fundraising is that their bank account is likely separate from the school accounts and so has far fewer restrictions on how it can be used. Even if the boosters may not have restrictions on their funds, your school system itself may limit the money and other support that the boosters can provide. Find out the particulars from both boosters and your finance officer!

Competition

Fundraising efforts should be coordinated around the school, but that doesn't always happen. Nonetheless, if you select a scheme previously claimed by a different club or sport—for example the sale of lollipops, or running a car wash—unnecessary conflict can result, and that's to no one's benefit. Find out who sells what, when, and where, before undertaking an effort that could pit your kids against someone else's. Check with your school's student activities director and/or finance officer.

Ticket Sales

Advance sales really pay off, but you don't want kids wandering the halls or their neighborhoods with tickets in hand. What if those tickets get lost (or put through the wash)? Even if the understanding is that the kids are responsible for their tickets, you'll spend hours with the parents defending their little cubs, since *you* gave them those darn tickets in the first place. As for collecting the money for those tickets, remember: students should never have cash that really belongs to the school. You could deal with this issue by printing ticket order forms that purchasers could drop off or mail to the school. An online ticket vendor solves many of these problems, and it lets parents use credit cards, too. If your school doesn't allow an online vendor, your booster group may be happy to sponsor one, and then transfer the revenue back to your department.

Sales "Opportunities"

Whether by mail or by walking into your classroom, there are vendors out there who want you to hire them, to use their sales program to make or save you (i.e., your department) a lot of money. They want you to sell their products, for which you will receive a percentage of the proceeds. Oh, beware! Even if they are totally legit, theirs is a minefield of potential catastrophe. What if items arrive broken? What if students lose them? Who will collect the money, keep track of it, collect it from the slackers, etc.? What if you can't return any unsold items? What if you can and do, but they never arrive back where they came from?

Never sign a contract with a vendor. That's your principal's job, since they represent the school, and you are a mere underling—and here, that's a good thing! Your school system may well have restrictions about who can do business with whom, or approval of contracts, so acquaint yourself with the procedures unique to your situation.

Beware of selling food items in particular. They vanish easiest of all. They are a *lot* of work for a minimum of profit. It may also be that only your cafeteria can sell consumables during the school day. But if you do go ahead with an item sale, be sure that when the items arrive you double-check your inventory vs. your order; keep everything locked up tight at all times; have a plan for dealing with lost or broken items or money; and track every penny according to your school's finance procedures.

Raffles and Such

A simple 50-50 raffle (someone wins half of the money collected) during intermission may seem an easy way to pick up some additional revenue—but gambling is prohibited by many schools and localities and, even if sponsored by your booster group, a special permit is usually required. The kids don't usually understand why this is so problematic, so you'll need to explain it patiently.

T-Shirts and Other Garments

T-shirts and similar items can have both publicity and souvenir value and, with a reasonable markup, they can be an effective fundraiser. You can use them to publicize specific shows or just your program. Designing T-shirts is easy these days, since online vendors can let you see just what your shirt will look like before you ever place your order. If you're not publicizing a show, just doing a fundraiser, think about not putting a date on your shirts—it's hard to sell shirts that have a date on them if that date has passed. In fact, try to avoid having any leftovers by only taking orders in advance, and not purchasing extras. In any case, when the order arrives, make sure that the numbers and sizes you receive match the ones that you ordered. Discrepancies are not uncommon. And before you start distributing the shirts, put a strip of masking tape with the purchaser's name on each garment. It can minimize problems from people not remembering what size or quantity they ordered. Finally, have a sign-off sheet and be sure each purchaser signs off that they've received their purchase.

Good Ideas

- Go with your strengths: use performances and theatre ticket sales as your primary fundraising tactic.
- Peg prices just under local movie ticket prices.
- Run a weekend, vacation, or summer "kids day out" or drama camp . This can be a huge fund raiser in which everyone wins, since it also builds awareness of your program in general.
- Hire a touring company to perform in your theatre (e.g., the national political satire group, The Capitol Steps). Use the event to give your tech students an opportunity to practice their skills so you can avoid facility rental charges. But professional performers do cost money, so you need to make sure you publicize their event thoroughly, and make sure your ticket sales will cover their cost, if possible.
- Repeat successful events so your community can come to anticipate them, and they become part of the culture of your program.

For Reflection & Discussion

Your own program is the best sales pitch for building future enrollment. But how can you best assure that you will have the resources you need? What can—and can't—you control?

1. Last year the band sold lollipops at a buck apiece, and they seemed to be quite popular. As long as you make arrangements first, why not have Drama sell them this year?

2. You hire a performing group to use your theater, and you will get a percentage of the gate receipts. Then the snow hits, and school is closed. The group expects payment anyway. What recourse do you have?

3. How expensive should your tickets be? Should you offer senior discounts? Free faculty tickets? Group rates? Early bird sales prices? Family tickets?

4. Who will track incoming funds, and how? A responsible student? You, in all your spare time? A parent? When? What are the requirements regarding the handling of funds, frequency of deposits, record keeping, etc.?

5. Is there a cap on enrollment for a class (when it is full, no longer accepting students)? Can you request that the cap be lifted if a new, highly motivated student really wants to be in your class?

6. What kind of student is the best match for taking a theatre class? Who is not a good candidate?

7. Why might a parent consider theatre a good elective choice for their child? How can you communicate that to them?

8. What does the typical student want in an elective that theatre classes can offer? How will they know, so they will sign up for your class?

9. What are the possible advantages and disadvantages of working with ESOL or other special needs students in a combined class?

10. What theatre-related events would be most attractive to potential students in a feeder school?

Part III

Spring

8 The Show Must Go On

Ahhh, the season of spring... good weather, raging hormones, seniors drifting away (even if their bodies keep showing up), perhaps the big spring musical, and plenty of administrivia for next fall. And high stakes testing, state standards, AP or IB, and final exams. And all those end-of-the-year events, from senior awards to prom to graduation! So much to do!

Surviving Entitlement

One of the ugliest qualities at work in most schools is the perception of entitlement. Seniors feel they are entitled to certain privileges simply because they are seniors. This is often reinforced by the overall high school culture by senior early dismissal, senior courtyard, etc. While 3+ years of enduring high school may earn a certain status in the greater high school populace, your department is a different matter.

Entitlement takes on many ugly expressions. Often, a senior who feels that he or she has been unfairly deprived of a leading role is being reinforced by parents who don't know how to comfort their disappointed child. Parents who spend countless hours working for the common good are challenged to stay supportive when their child doesn't get the role they feel was deserved. Hopefully, you can diffuse the worst of the entitlement monster by frequently discussing and reminding students and parents of the structure of theatre (mathematics dictates that not every senior will get a leading role) and emphasizing that you expect seniors to lead by example.

Sometimes, despite your best efforts, entitlement can rear is ugly head, often in socially unacceptable ways. When it does, you need to stay strong and follow your school's protocols in dealing with it. For example, a student may post harassing, foul language directed

Real-World Moments

The new, young theatre teacher of a struggling department announces that casting for the musical will be on the basis of talent and suitability for the role, not seniority. If a freshman is right for the role, s/he will be cast in that role. Seniors are outraged and declare they will not audition for the musical—several relent and wind up cast in leading roles, with a talented freshman or two in supporting roles. The show is a success, gets the department out of debt and onto the local community map. The seniors who didn't audition express their regret later and audition for the next show.

at other students auditioning for a role that s/he desperately wants. Clearly, this type of activity must be short-circuited. Show the posting to your administrator and ask for advice. Usually, a meeting with administrator, counselor and parent will put things in perspective and—through the drama grapevine—send a firm message to the rest of the department. Revisit your Theatre Ethics document again with your students to make sure everyone knows that harassment is unacceptable. Your theatre ethics are supported by the school's student rights and responsibilities that transcend and reinforce your position as theatre director.

The hardest part of entitlement is to avoid becoming an entitled, defensive director who feels s/he has the right to inflict his/her own frustrations on students. You are only human—it's true—but try to stop before you engage in the rant that you may regret later. On the other hand, some firm speeches to a cast, crew or class may be necessary to convey what you are passionate about—what behavior you will and won't tolerate. Try to end even your fiercest speech with something positive—you are the builder of the program, not a negative force that tears it down. Examine whether your words are for the good of the show, the students and the department—not just your own need, however justified, to vent or assert yourself. Chant: "I am a professional" over and over again, if you must. Despite your human frailty, you are the role model; your entitled arrogance or helpful humility will influence the culture of the department in which you teach.

Preparing for Next Year

Technically, the school year runs from fall to spring, and then things begin again in the fall. However, that new beginning next fall takes a lot of advance planning this year. Enrollment

Real-World Moments

A group of seniors is being very negative in the dressing room with a lot of unproductive talk and spiteful, poisonous comments. This comes to the attention of the director, who reads the whole cast the riot act, without foul language, but with plenty of her own intense frustration at the selfishness and disrespect of the seniors. As the director walks out of the room, one of the quieter seniors says, "Good job—you should have done that three years ago."

The juniors are a little rattled by the lecture, but understanding. They are loyal to the director and prove to be superior leaders for the theatre department the next year.

The bitter group of seniors performs and withdraws even more into their clique—thank goodness graduation is right around the corner.

for next year's classes might begin as early as February and probably has to be completed by April. April is when staffing decisions are made, although indeed changes may occur right up until the last minute next fall. You'll need to figure out what you're going to need in terms of textbooks and supplies. Then you must find out where to get them and what they cost, to make sure you have them when you need them. Then comes the paperwork and the waiting.

Ordering Supplies and Equipment

But how much do you have available to spend for your program? Your school may use some magic formula, a per-pupil amount that can be "adjusted" by your principal to assure that their priorities are intact. "Your" money may also be incorporated into a larger department (Fine and Performing Arts?) and subject to its overall priorities as determined by the department chair and administrator. If you're lucky, you will get a total dollar amount, perhaps separated into textbook money and supply money—will they let you mix the two? The book allowance never seems to be enough for, say, a full class set of textbooks. Can you spend textbook money on scripts? Will they let you supplement this order with your ticket receipt money? Will they cut back on your allotment because they know you have access to that other source of funds? One thing is certain: if you don't use all the money allocated to you, you are *very* unlikely to get that much the following year; apparently, you didn't need it if you didn't spend it.

Every so often it may be textbook adoption year for your subject area. That means there is a bunch of extra money, that one year, to be used for new textbooks approved for use. Claim it. Use it. It ain't comin' again for a long time.

Scheduling Your Theater

Theater scheduling is done well in advance, perhaps month by month, for the next year. This scheduling often takes place in the spring. You may well be competing for space and time with your colleagues in other departments. It may be first-requested-first-scheduled, or there might be a big sit-down negotiation between competing parties, or you might be asked for your requests and then the scheduling is all done by fiat from above. Don't play new kid—stick up for yourself and your students! It is essential that you find out when and how the system works and identify the decision-makers at your school! Don't be left out in the cold.

If you know you're sharing space primarily with the music department, for example, be proactive. Go talk to the music teachers before the scheduling date and find out their events and their priorities. Brainstorm with them to find ways to interact and to coordinate your events with theirs. For example, can you spike, strike and reset all their orchestra stands and chairs in exchange for stage use the afternoon between their classes and their concert? With some practice, this can be done pretty quickly and it will buy you some needed extra rehearsal time.

Meet with other regular users, too, and plan a strategy that will accommodate as many requests as possible. Then hopefully you can present the strategy with a united front to the official scheduler. Building solid, supportive relationships with those who also "own" the space will reap lasting rewards.

Next Year's Theatre Season

As the school year draws to a close, you will have choices to make. Do you select and announce your shows for the coming year? If so, you have more time to gather a design team and make some real progress during the summer. If not, well, you have the summer to read up on and find those shows that are a perfect fit for you.

Getting the Timing Right

If you choose next year's shows during this school year, you can hit the ground running in the fall. You might even be able to cast a show and give the script to your students to learn over the summer. That way, they might even show up in the fall ready to work "off book" on day one (hey, a person can dream!). On the other hand, if you do that, you lock yourself in and you prevent incoming students from being cast. It may not be fair to the incoming students, and you risk missing some brilliantly talented newbie.

Another approach is to select a theme for next year's season (e.g., "A Season of Discovery") and choose the titles of possible productions—just make sure you procure the rights to the shows prior to announcing them. This allows students the opportunity to become familiar with the shows over the summer and there are no excuses for poorly prepared audition pieces the following fall. This process gives everyone enrolled in your program—even transfer students—ample opportunity to participate in every production of the year.

Yet a third choice is to wait until the beginning of the new school year and hold a talent audition for the year or the semester; this is similar to what many college theatre programs do. If you have a couple of shows in mind, this option lets you evaluate whether you have the cast you need. It is rarely wise to plan a show based around the talent of one student. But knowing who is out there, and how well developed their artistic gifts are, can help you decide between show A and show B.

Big Picture: Seeking Balance in Your Season

As a theatre educator considering your season, your first priority should be to make show choices that offer a variety of artistic growth opportunities for the students in your program. If you have a plethora of young women in your program, choose shows with predominantly female or gender neutral roles—just make sure that the playwright's publisher/copyright licensure allows you to cast women in these roles. Your choices for shows should also reflect what your learning community will support, and you will also need to produce some money-maker shows in order to help financially support your department. Some principals require their approval for your play selections, so that creates a starting point. Make sure that your principal takes your professionalism as an educator seriously. Communicate in academic terms that focus on the students' need to be exposed to a variety of theatrical genres as part of your school system's theatre program of studies. Perhaps you will choose a family-friendly musical, then a more socially conscious, somewhat controversial one-act for competition. Or maybe *Chicago* is your musical of choice, followed by an awesome children's theatre production. Make sure your publicity team communicates mature themes well in advance.

Exposure to a variety of genres not only teaches your students about style and historical context, it also gives different kids different opportunities to excel and make artistic discoveries. The improvisation team might find out that Commedia is cool; that quiet kid in the back of the room might find children's theatre less intimidating; your serious dramatic students will need to know Ibsen, Chekhov, Williams, O'Neil and Miller; your physical actors will love the active choices of classical theatre, especially if you hire a stage combat guest artist. If you create an educationally balanced season with a variety of theatrical styles, it will be easier to defend each of your choices. If parents or administrators challenge your choices ("Why did you choose that play?"), emphasize that *you* are the professional who needs to consider *all* of the students' artistic/educational needs. Give examples of how your program does this effectively. After all, you went to college, just like the math, science, and English teachers—hone your professionalism and wield its sharp edge as necessary.

Awards and Recognition

The end of the year is a great time to have your thespian/drama club officers lead the way by organizing a final celebration. Make the event free of charge, potluck or minimally catered, so that all friends and family can attend—this is an event that can inspire parent volunteers and siblings that may be future students—even if you have to eat in the school cafeteria and then move to the auditorium or black box, and above all, have *fun*! Your Thespian officers can design and distribute invitations, decorate, organize the schedule of the evening, coordinate sound, lights and music, conduct new Thespian inductions and coordinate food with you and the boosters. It should be a meaningful way for your seniors to bid farewell to your program, and their fellow students.

Senior Recognition

Your school may schedule a ceremony to give out annual department and/or activity awards, and they will call on you to represent your program. Senior awards are common, but awards for juniors or underclassmen are out there, too. These events give you an hour or two to acknowledge your students' many accomplishments in so many areas besides yours—and, of course, to wait patiently for 90 minutes to have your 2-minute turn at the podium. And sometimes your prize actor turns out to be a top Latin scholar, too (how can some kids excel at so much when others can barely show up?). You will need to decide whether to recognize your top student(s) at multiple ceremonies or whether to spread individual recognition across departments, activities, ITS, Cappies, and other events.

Scholarships won by seniors are often announced in awards ceremonies or at graduation. If your students have won Thespian or other arts scholarships, be sure they get the recognition they deserve.

Graduation "bling" is a big deal in some schools. School academic award ceremonies may include a medallion to be worn at graduation. The National Honor Society gives honor cords that are worn over the graduation robe during the ceremony, but other honor societies—including the International Thespian Society—make such items available, too. Your school may, however, have a policy about graduation dress and adornments, so check with your principal first and be sure to lobby for inclusion of your special insignias, if they're not already approved. And do attend Graduation; your seniors will really appreciate it. And you may even have an opportunity to interact with your students' families—especially siblings who may become your future students!

Real-World Moments

A new theatre director was surprised to learn that part of the awards ceremony at the end of the year included seniors handing down notebooks from previous years that urged students to copy school keys. He was not comfortable with this tradition so that notebook disappeared, along with that particular tradition.

Reviewing Existing Traditions

As a new theatre director following your predecessor, get all the information you can about the previous traditions of your department, including the awards. Your active involvement in the awards process will depend on how much you can learn about the way things were done before you arrived and how comfortable you are with that process. If you're satisfied with the status quo, you can fit right in without much added effort. But if you think changes are needed you owe it to yourself and your program to lobby hard for your changes. If there are awards given out by students, find out what those awards are and the criteria used to decide on them, so that you are not surprised by something that may be inappropriate or negative.

Typically, a theatre department end of the year celebration includes:

- Thespian inductions and Thespian officer recognition
- Refreshments or a meal
- Theatre booster recognition and scholarships
- A slide show with photos from the year's productions
- Senior recognition and gift from the boosters
- Awards on which students vote
- Student scenes/songs as entertainment
- An activity, such as dancing

Your first year in a new department, you should ask to see and approve everything that is going to be part of an event. You need to learn all about school events that were conducted by or under your predecessor in order to know areas that you may want (or need) to change. After all, it is your department now, and you need to be comfortable with events held under your control. You also want to learn the traditions of the theatre department and areas in which you must tread lightly to avoid unnecessary conflict. Once the parameters of which

Organizing the Awards Celebration

Some questions to ask:

- Where does the awards event take place? Who reserves/acquires the space?
- How long does it take? Start time? End time?
- What is the suggested dress code?
- How much does it cost? Different prices for guests (including you), students, or parents?
- Who handles the finances? School theatre department vs. boosters group?
- Who hosts the event, presentation of awards, etc.?
- Do you need equipment to display a slide show, etc.?
- Does the event include Thespian officer inductions?
- Will you announce theatre booster scholarships?
- Who votes for awards and who is eligible to receive them?
- Are there other presentations or recognitions besides theatre awards?

you approve are set and met, they too will become tradition within a few years. Stand your ground. You must make sure that your theatre students do not engage in secret ceremonies or traditions that violate school policies.

Awards

While an awards celebration needs to follow your rules and the school's requirements, make sure that the event is—very simply—*fun* for everyone! Here's a check-list of awards that may come to mind, somewhat modeled after American performing arts awards in the professional world.

Before setting up your awards, you'll need to decide: Who should vote on them? Should you limit voting to enrolled theatre students only (except for ensemble awards)? Or should voting be open to any student who worked on any of the year's productions? Or perhaps you want to limit voting to inducted Thespians only? Although these choices may depend upon the size, culture and traditions of your department, discuss the implications of your decision with your students. There has to be recognition that at some point, theatre awards should be given to students who commit to the entire program through taking classes—not just engaging in the after-school program. A helpful comparison may be to note that music department awards are almost always given to students enrolled in music classes.

Typical theatre department awards on which students vote:

EXCELLENCE IN ENSEMBLE ACTING

EXCELLENCE IN ACTING   Female/male

- Leading roles
- Supporting roles
- Comedic roles
- Featured or cameo roles

SINGING AND DANCING AWARDS   Obviously, these address the musical, so you decide whether they are appropriate.

- Student Choreographer
- Excellence in Dance
- Excellence in Singing

TECHNICAL EXCELLENCE

- Student Director
- Stage Manager
- Tech Director
- Lighting Designer/Technician
- Sound Designer/Technician
- Set Designer
- Master Carpenter
- Costume Designer
- Costume Crew
- Stage Crew
- Run Crew
- Assistant Stage Manager
- Set Decorator
- Paint Crew
- Publicity

EXCELLENCE IN CREATIVITY

- Playwriting
- Music Composition
- Program/Poster Design

Class Awards

In addition to the awards that the students vote on, you should also give some director's awards and class awards. These awards enable you to recognize the unsung heroes of your department, some of whom may not have been eligible or included in the popular voting. Since every year is different, reserve the right to surprise everyone with the numbers and subjects of your awards. These awards should cover areas that are uniquely within your purview (You don't want students—or parents—to be comparing your choices with theirs). For class awards, consider:

- Most Improved Theatre Student
- Highest Theatre Student GPA
- Excellence in Participation
- Excellence in Creativity
- Excellence in Ensemble Work
- Warm-Ups Leader Award
- Excellence in Improvisation

Make sure that your comments are more about the *we* than *I*. Express your gratitude for all of the hard work that the parents and students have done—emphasize your success in working together. This is *not* the time to make caustic comments or bring up negative issues; let this be an evening of camaraderie and celebration.

If you choose to announce your season for next year, make sure you already have the rights to all of the shows you mention. Be sincere, short, sweet and grateful to all who have contributed to making your school's theatre department a positive place where kids can grow.

9 When the World is Bigger Than Theatre

Every now and then, something genuinely overwhelming takes place that affects your department, your school or the outside world, for which no one can be fully prepared. It might be a horrible storm, a traffic accident, a lock-down incident at your school, a death, or who knows what else. At times like this, your maturity, experience, and ability to be a true leader will be essential. Those drama kids of yours will be desperately looking to you to help them figure out how to react, and perhaps to restrain them from reacting in unhealthy or unsafe ways. At such times, it's not just about the class or the show, but rather about binding the community you have created into a family that can huddle, hug, grieve, or forge ahead as one. And at such times, you're not just one of that family; you're the mom or dad, the sympathetic rock to guide them to safer shores.

Do you stop class/rehearsal to have a group discussion about what's going on, or do you keep going with "business as usual" to provide the reassuring familiarity and normalcy to the school day? Depending on the event, do you try to handle the issue yourself, or do you bring in administrators, guidance counselors or other trained specialists? Do you try to keep a cool exterior, or do you show your own humanity and pain so your students understand that you really do empathize with them? When so many are depending on you, how do you manage to remain outwardly calm to your students, even though you may have the same urge to run screaming into the night as they do?

Though no one likes to dwell on tragedy and how to cope with it in the school setting, we are including that topic in this book because it has become an ever more important aspect of life as an educator. The world is an increasingly unpredictable place—you must be the strong, calm, protective, predictable, reassuring teacher who helps your students to get through any crisis that may present itself at school. Experience has taught us that it is folly to assume that "this will never happen to me." Recognize that these things can and do happen in life, and children are affected, wherever they are. Your job is to deflect as much of the potential hysteria, speculation, and drama as possible, in order to help keep them safe.

As theatre educators, we are surrounded largely by students who wear their emotions on their sleeves, so to speak, and are ripe for overly dramatic reactions to stressful situations. Because of the bonding typical among theatre kids, they tend to establish and reinforce a group mood very readily and strongly. For yourself and for them, exercises in slow, rhythmic breathing as a way to calm the body and mind can be most useful. Make these exercises part of your daily warmups; you never know when they may come in especially handy. Like any other good teacher, reach out to school resource personnel to help both your students and yourself. And by all means, learn and rely on your school's established procedures—those annoying fire drills and lockdown simulations can and will actually make a difference.

As educators caught in the classroom during the unfolding of climactic world or community events, the best you can do is to stay calm and follow procedures, acknowledging student reactions as we reassure and nurture. You don't have the option of indulging your personal feelings or reactions. Your duty is to keep the kids safe, both physically and emotionally, until they leave school. You can answer questions up to a point, but you need to leave the detailed responses to administration and parents. If you are unsure about what to say or do, call on reliable colleagues and make use of school resources that are designed to address emergency situations. In emergency situations, the school as learning and teaching community can be at its best.

How bad could it get? Below are a few stories from our past. We hope you encounter very few experiences of your own to add to these.

National Crisis

For those of us old enough to recall the 9/11 destruction of the World Trade Center Twin Towers in 2001, we all remember where we were, who we were with and how we received the news. For me, it was Morehead Elementary Cultural Arts Magnet School, on the cafetorium stage with a class of young faces looking at me. My principal walked in and handed me a note that said something like this: "The World Trade Center has collapsed and smoke is coming from the Pentagon." As she handed me the note, her words, as I remember them, were: "Don't react."

Looking back, this seems like a scene from an absurdist play, telling the theatre teacher not to react as she is handed a cryptic note containing information of high dramatic import. However, I cannot even imagine being the principal of an American school in the mid-Atlantic region on that day, as parents came to retrieve their kids, their dearest possessions, wondering whether the world was coming to an end. For my part, I played the role of teacher as best I could, maintaining an apparent calmness that denial imposed on a mind without many details.

What I did know was that I did not want to upset the children under my care. As soon as class was over, my observing college interns rushed to my side. They told me that although my body reflected calmness, my face had revealed some kind of upheaval—one that I could not share with them until the theatre class was over and the children had been escorted from the stage to their regular classroom. As soon as the children left, the interns and I dashed to the school library television across the hall to encounter a world that had been forever changed.

Lockdown

It was spring, and I was directing an after-school rehearsal for *Oklahoma!* when one of our administrators entered the auditorium, accompanied by the school police officer (SRO/School Resource Officer). They told me that a sniper was in the area and that the police were still pursuing the possibility of a second sniper on the loose; I was told to lock down the auditorium.

I calmly paused rehearsal and made sure all doors were locked, asserting that no one was to come in or out of the facility until we had administrative permission to do so. Since we were stuck in the auditorium anyway, I continued to rehearse for a little while, but then information began to filter into rehearsal as parents called to make sure their children were safe. We learned that two police officers had been killed at the local station, along with the shooter, who had just graduated the year before: some of my students knew him. Although he was not a close friend to anyone in the cast, he was part of their world—someone they had often seen in the school cafeteria and elsewhere in daily life. For many students, this became their first—and very personal—encounter with an acquaintance gone bad, one who took lives and lost his own in the process.

Through tears and disbelief, my students struggled to grasp a situation that seemed so surreal in its violent assault on their previously-predictable world. The school was in lockdown in our auditorium within minutes, thanks to modern technology. The sanctity of my classroom and rehearsal had been necessarily superseded by public safety and school administrators. Parents began to arrive at school to pick up their frightened kids. School administration decided to allow early dismissals. Given the tenuous situation, we needed to step back from our daily schedule and wait for further information.

When we finally learned all the facts about the confrontation and casualties, our grief at the losses was compounded by our connections to the victims and perpetrator. Many of our school security officers were former policemen who knew the victims personally. They were not just anonymous casualties, they were friends.

As a theatre department, we eventually needed to find closure; after all, all of us in the class were affected by the event as it happened. Because of the timing of our rehearsal and our lockdown, this tragic community event became an intimate moment in all of our lives as theatre people. Before our spring musical opened, I asked for and received special permission to collect donations for the surviving family members of the police officer victims. At the end of each of our *Oklahoma!* performances, the cast came out with buckets, similar to Broadway Cares efforts. We were able to give almost three thousand dollars to the police officers' families and address our own feelings of helplessness. Our classic spring musical became a source of community healing that extended way beyond the auditorium doors.

Suicide Watch

"Joan" had always been a nervous, twitchy student, but that year she slid into depression. Many hours were spent huddled in corners with a friend, trying to work out whatever it was that seemed to be pressing down upon her. She was even hospitalized a few times but she returned to the theatre, which was her haven, as soon as she could. Since it was clear to all that she was still under tremendous stress, I asked a couple of her close friends to keep as constant an eye on her as possible.

During one evening rehearsal, Joan had seemed particularly distressed. At the end of the rehearsal, when the company gathered for its routine end-of-rehearsal notes, someone noticed that Joan was missing. We quickly checked all our dressing rooms and work areas, but to no avail. Panic spread like wildfire. Before I knew it, 80 kids wanted to run (some still in bare feet) into the night in all directions to find their friend before she did something desperate. Clearly, that was a horrible idea and I needed to take charge of the situation. I kept the cast and crew in place, sent one student to find the emergency care card that would help us contact Joan's parents, and asked another student to fetch the parent volunteers that were nearby. I ordered the cast to get out of their costumes and told them that we would then regroup and formulate a plan. It was nearly time for the custodians to lock up the building—not a problem for the students—but I decided that this situation did not need the custodial staff to extend their shifts.

Some parent/student teams were formed, with specific areas to go searching, and the rest of the company was permitted to either head home with their parents or wait in the theatre. Joan's parents were contacted and they came over to the school. The drama kids, fearing the worst, needed to be constantly reminded that nothing critical had happened, only that we didn't know where she was. "Let's not jump to conclusions; people are out looking for her." About a half hour later, Joan was located at a nearby shopping center and she was returned to her parents' care. Social media were very helpful to swiftly calm the crisis: "She's found and OK." The search teams returned to collect their things and head home, and to reassure those who had left already.

The next day it was clear that this traumatic event was still overshadowing all other considerations—I had to address it so we could try to move on. I brought the cast/crew back to the edge of the stage and acknowledged their fears. I reminded them of the importance of grounding their actions on information instead of just raw emotion. I told them that I understood, to a degree, what Joan was struggling with from the personal experiences of one of my close family members. I praised their loyalty to their friend but explained that some things are beyond the reach of caring alone; that some healing requires professional attention. They could no more "care her well" than they could cure her of an allergy or physical ailment. Caring is good and admirable, but keeping the secret of a friend contemplating suicide, or trying to ease the pain of medical depression is simply beyond the limits of what a teenager should or can do. Yes, it's hard to feel helpless, especially when your friends are the most important things in your life, but lifting a friend out of sadness is not the same as treating one for depression. Their support has limits and they should feel good that they did everything they could do. Now it was time for those with professional training to apply *their* skills to help their friend get well.

It was a tough talk, and a lost rehearsal, but it really seemed to help. Some kids were surprised at my personal disclosure about a problem that felt like theirs, and some appreciated being let off the hook for trying to make Joan better without knowing how. They had been given a chance to vent and express their own fears and concerns and, finally, were able to move forward. The show must go on. And it did.

As for Joan, she dropped out of the theatre department and away from those friends whose lives were entangled with hers. She did get professional help, and eventually she pulled her life back together and headed off to college as a much happier and more stable young lady.

Westfield Wounded

"There are some things more important than theatre." My students do a double-take when I say this sentence because they know that I hold theatre as sacred. There are, however, moments when life looms larger than the art which emulates it. The following is a personal essay I wrote soon after the Virginia Tech shooting tragedy on April 16th, 2007. I was one of two Theatre teachers at Westfield High School in Chantilly, Virginia, from which not only two of the 32 victims had graduated, but also the shooter. As you read, note the school procedures that assisted students through this horrific event, as well as the special, healing gatherings that were created by the staff, parents and administration of the high school learning community. The Reema Samaha Cabaret and Erin Peterson Tournament continue to be annual, positive community events as of this writing.

★   ★   ★

It began on a Monday. By the time we knew the worst, indelible scraps of memory would be imprinted upon our minds, flashbacks of our grief. Mine would be a psychological photo of my younger daughter standing at the top of the stairs, the phone in her hand, tears streaming down her face: "Reema is dead."

I could not grasp it. My answer was "No, there must be some mistake. It can't be true."

I could not wrap my mind around it. My fourteen year-old handled it better.

My older daughter came home from a night class with wet disbelief on her face.

"Of all the people I know, she deserves it the least. Why?" She was angry.

She walked hesitantly down the basement stairs, past the photo on the wall of Reema in a play, together with another friend who had just called my older daughter's cell phone. She said it was strange to hear a great big baritone in tears.

Tuesday we wept together, many of us in the theatre department at Westfield High School—many of us who had known Reema's smile, grace, dancing, joking and beauty—others who had seen her on the stage in *Fiddler On the Roof, Arsenic and Old Lace* or *Oklahoma!* The loss was very personal.

We were not ready for television cameras or news reporters; our wounds were too raw.

Even the sight of the news crews, planted across the street from our school, was painfully invasive.

The theatre director arranged with the school principal to allow students to come to the black box theatre classroom any time that day to mourn. The counselors in Student Services were prepared to receive the students; the school psychologist was prepared to receive the students—as well as the teachers.

The morning brought more tragedy: Erin Peterson, another sparkling spirit at Westfield, had also been killed at Virginia Tech. And then the other news: the killer was a Westfield graduate from 2003. We did not know him.

We knew Reema and Erin, 2006 graduates, active and friendly just a few months prior, spreading their positive energy through the halls and classrooms, gyms and auditorium of our Westfield world. We knew them well. We knew their families because they were active parts of our school and community family. We had seen them at the plays, the games, the meetings, the graduation. We had hugged, laughed and cheered with them. Now we wept for the parents and their daughters.

They wept and went on not only to endure the impossible, but transcend it with their courage and unrelenting faith. Both the Samahas and the Petersons were inspirational in their strength, their love and their positive communication with the press.

While we went through the halls of Westfield numb on Monday and Tuesday, the storm clouds continued to gather. While we gathered at churches for candlelight vigils, so full of sadness that most high school students are never asked to know, the outside world gathered its arrows.

My younger daughter found out how cruel kids can be as she played in a school sports competition at a rival school.

"They breed killers at Westfield!"

The taunt pierced her fragile fourteen-year-old defenses and brought her to tears.

The appropriate authorities were notified, apologies made. Too little, too late.

The young man who threw his casual cruelty onto the court had not known Reema or Erin. Since he did not know our pain, he chose to add to it. He could not know, as we did, how much the educational structures and people at Westfield had given to help monitor, educate and nurture students with special needs. Once the high school support system was left behind, guns were easier to get than help.

On our street, kids from the theatre department were making tie-dye shirts in Virginia Tech colors. Reema loved tie-dye. They wore her love on their hearts in shades of orange and maroon. A world of sadness had to express itself somehow.

On Friday, the fifth day of our mourning, our principal called a special assembly in the school stadium, the only facility large enough to hold over three thousand people. He stood with the two other principals in our seven-year school history, joined by a student from Virginia Tech.

Three thousand voices were never so quiet, so full of focus and unity.

Banners of our achievements, the district, regional and state titles, academic and artistic excellence, hung on the fences surrounding our football field, reminding us that we are a school of superior artistic and athletic talent, work ethic and intellectual pursuit. We are competitive and intense, but loving and energetic, graceful and kind.

Reema and Erin represented the best of us.

Butterflies were released in memory of our lost achievers.

Words of encouragement, of pride, of strength and truth pierced the air.

And we heard them, taking up the chant: "We are Westfield."

The memorial services began, followed by funerals.

Just as the sun finally broke through the clouds that weekend, some of the significance of the tragedy broke upon my mind and heart as I heard the words of Joe Samaha reveal the meaning of Reema's last name: forgiveness.

In the halls of Westfield, we began to put one foot in front of the other. We began to hope that we would laugh and smile again, feel our world healing, if not whole.

Less than two weeks after that awful April sixteenth, Westfield's theatre department students, alumni, teachers and Drama Booster parents created and performed "Remembering Reema," a tribute in song, dance and spoken expression. Since Reema's most memorable acting role was one of the aunts in *Arsenic and Old Lace*, we improvised a scene with the actors who had surrounded her in that play—a scene in which Aunt Martha is on a trip and Aunt Abby gathers with the other characters in the play to say how much they miss her. My oldest daughter had been Aunt Abby onstage with Reema; it was hard to watch her now onstage, clutching the photo of her friend and stage sister, with tears in her eyes—creating the farewell that none of us had been allowed to say.

The first Reema Cabaret was tearful and cathartic, beautiful in its raw emotional clarity and sincerity—terrible in its necessity. We could not let her go without our own dramatic ritual from the department who knew her artistic soul. It was two hours of heartfelt, soul-wrenching therapy which we shared with Reema's family, raising our spirits and money for scholarships honoring our favorite Lebanese dancer. The final piece was Reema's theatre teacher, reading her reflection paper from the year before, in which she expressed how much theatre and dance meant to her. We listened and cried, even as we marveled at the candor of her words, her voice still living in our minds.

The tributes and memorials continue, at the Kennedy Center Cappies Gala, in the rooms and halls of Westfield. Student faces smile again, going on as they must.

Worn adult faces smile in response to teenage energy and need, hoping we will be swept up in teenage resilience, letting them teach us about life in 2007 as we teach them from what we hope is the wisdom and training of our experience. One of the best parts of teaching high school kids is how much we help each other. That learning community concept actually works. We go on, looking out for each other, doing what we must do to succeed, learn and progress, growing beyond today into a tomorrow we hope will be better. But we will not forget. Ever.

We are Westfield. (2007)

Part IV

Summer

10 Summer Stuff

With all the momentum from a hectic school year, you may wonder what to do next, during the summer months—how to make some extra money perhaps, or how to enhance your program even further by reaching out to new audiences. In planning for the summer, some of your students, now entranced with the theatre, will surely ask you for advice about where they can get more training during their vacations. You and your students might even want to stick together during the summer for some crazy new adventure in a land far, far away.

Summer Drama Camps for Fun and Profit

If you are a "theatre-workaholic" for whom there is no greater joy than building your school theatre department, consider establishing a summer theatre program at your school if one does not already exist. If your booster (or other) organization already has a summer theatre program up and running, find a way to connect with them without stepping on the toes of the founders or organizers. The beauty of such a program is that it links your department even more closely to the surrounding community, serving the needs of many of your future students and their families. However, the camp should also be open to anyone else who wants to attend or audition. In the short term, you will accelerate your relationship-building and knowledge of your current and future learning community (and earn some extra cash); in the long term, you will fill seats in your classroom and theater.

If no summer program for theatre exists at your school, ask why not—and find out what you have to do to establish one! The director of student activities office or administrative assistant (AAs rule the world!) is usually a good place to start. Your school may require your summer program to be sponsored by an ongoing booster organization or PTSA. Theatre boosters are, of course, preferable, since you are already connected to them and the summer program can become a major fundraiser for their school year budget. If you are hired to be the director of the summer program(s), be transparent about finances and the payment that you expect to take home. If the director of another successful summer theatre program is willing to share her/his budget and experience with you, take the offer. Local precedent is usually a good thing. It enables you to jump right in without reinventing the wheel. Establishing a summer theatre program is essentially like running a small business, so make sure you obtain reliable, specific information from the school system facilities manager and your finance officer before you publicize any event or establish your prices.

There are two major formats for summer theatre camps: 1) training/classes that focus on theatre process rather than a final product, and 2) production camps that consist of casting, rehearsing, producing and ultimately performing a show. A short youth theatre camp and a month long teen camp can be highly beneficial elements of your summer theatre program.

Planning Your Camp

In order to make your camp a reality, you will have to submit some kind of plan or proposal to a supervisor in your school system. Great ideas often fall victim to the perpetual paperwork that the field of education usually requires. However, paperwork can make you create a framework that reinforces your accountability. It can also help you communicate your rules and your vision to all concerned. As you plan out your camp and prepare to apply for permission to do the camp, make up a promotional flyer that contains this basic information:

- Ages of children eligible for the camp
- Dates of the camp
- Cost of the camp per camper
- Contact information for the camp director
- Registration form
- Name of the sponsoring organization

Also, create a proposed budget for your camp which includes expenses such as these:

- Professional staff compensation
- Student technician compensation
- Camp counselor compensation
- Guest artist compensation
- Projected costs for equipment and supplies
- Royalties, script rentals, props, costumes, photography
- Estimated income (charge per camper)

- Other income (e.g., projected ticket sales)

There are usually school system guidelines for how much different camp positions are paid, so expect to make a little less than you make teaching during the school year. But don't be afraid to ask for the largest salary if you are the director of both the camp and of the culminating production. Students are paid less than adults and guest artists are paid somewhere in the middle, depending upon what they charge and the number of hours they spend at your camp.

Students are usually paid by the hour, with hourly pay guidelines provided by the school system—usually a little higher than minimum wage. But the kids are also getting invaluable experience as counselors or technicians, so you can give your upperclassmen the opportunity to make some summer money and build their resumes. Summer camp staff already employed by your school system are often required to go through the established payroll system, so check with your finance officer for details on how you will report the hours and submit the weekly paperwork/pay sheets for everyone involved. If you are the director of the camp, you may well be the person responsible for making sure everyone gets paid.

Timelines

The timeline for summer theatre camp usually begins in January or February. The first step discussed at that time depends on the type of camp you'll be running. For "process camps," you will usually focus on the theme: what aspects/skills of the theatre process will you be teaching at camp? For "production camps," you will begin to discuss what show you plan to have as your concluding production. You will work to secure licensure for that show if necessary, obtain commitments from staff members, and begin to recruit student counselors and technicians. If you work with your boosters, you should get written approvals of all the pertinent details and make sure they appear in the meeting minutes so that there are no misunderstandings later about what was or wasn't approved. If your boosters assign parents to work with you on the paperwork, welcome them and set up a time to meet with them. You must make sure that all required paperwork (contracts, invoices, budget, etc.) is ready to submit to the powers that be by March 1st, or whatever date is required by your school system for necessary paperwork for camp approval.

Securing a license for a musical before you know whether your camp is approved can be a little tricky, but you should talk to the licensing representative over the phone to get a sense of any restrictions on the show and how likely you are to get that permission. This also may motivate you to get your theatre camp paperwork in sooner, rather than later. Once your camp is approved, you can complete the licensing process and advertise the show, which will in turn attract prospective campers and promote ticket sales.

For your production camp, you will need to hold auditions as early as April or May to enable students to have time to find out whether they made the show. Older students may decide to enroll in the camp only if they got the part that they really wanted. Where possible, you should publicize summer camps sooner, rather than later, since many families start to make their summer plans early in the year. If you wait too long to publicize your summer program, you may lose potential campers.

A successful summer camp can raise significant funds for your theatre boosters to use in their budget for the upcoming school year, and you will have earned it through a shared theatre-related experience instead of selling pies or knocking on doors.

Process Camps for Younger Children

Parents are always looking for summer activities for their elementary aged children, so a week-long, half-day process camp for rising third through rising sixth graders can work well for all concerned. If you are the camp director who conceives and directs the theme, lesson plans and structure of the camp, you can hire trusted upperclassmen in your theatre program to help teach the classes and keep costs down. A 9 a.m. to noon schedule works well, especially if you divide each day into three one-hour-sessions, with rotating groups of students roughly divided by age. Hire two high schoolers to team-teach each rotating session. This gives you a team of six counselors; if you enroll as many as sixty students, you'll still have groups no larger than 20 and a one to ten teacher/student ratio.

Use the unique talents of your high school camp counselors to best advantage. For example, if you have a student who juggles, offer a session in juggling. If you have a trained dance student, offer a session in dance or creative movement. Your improv team captain might be the perfect camp counselor to teach a session in drama games—but definitely stay away from unstructured improvisation with little children; it can quickly degenerate into unproductive chaos and inappropriate comments. Use a structured improv game such as, "What are you doing?" instead.

On the last day of children's camp, invite the parents in for the last hour and stage a whole group sharing presentation, in which students can share their week's activities through a creative dramatics presentation or game-playing. You can even ask parents to participate in a creative movement activity! Introduce the camp counselors, say a few words about how much you have enjoyed watching everyone grow, and pass out flyers about any upcoming productions appropriate for kids in this age-group to attend in the coming school year. Keep it low pressure and simple so that everyone feels successful and appreciated.

Production Camps

If you choose to direct a teen production camp, think in terms of rising seventh graders through this year's graduates. This makes your camp experience available to a large span of ages, but the younger kids will feel cool to be with the high school students and understand they may even form the larger percentage of the ensemble. The summer production gives your high school students one last chance to grow under your direction in a musical theatre role. Sometimes that student who wasn't quite ready for a lead during high school hits their developmental stride just after graduation and puts on an amazing performance that summer. Because most aspects of camp life are less restrictive than in school, you will have to establish specific guidelines for behavior and maintain your standards of theatre ethics during the summer (for example, how much coarse language is acceptable among high school vs. middle school campers). Hold your auditions in the spring, but publicize them as soon as you have program and production licensing approval. This gives potential campers time to get excited and prepare a great audition.

Make sure you assemble a team of people with whom you enjoy working, and who have the necessary expertise to handle the accelerated schedule of a summer production. *This is critical to its success and everyone's enjoyment.* If your school choir director is willing, able and fun-loving, their involvement will make a great beginning for your production team. As much as possible, choose people for the production team with whom you have worked successfully before, to ensure an amiable working atmosphere. You will be eating and breathing this show and creatively interacting with your team for a solid month, so do everything in your power to choose complementary and cohesive personalities who can handle the schedule and the stress.

Choosing a Show

Hopefully, you know your community well enough to know what will appeal to them. Some learning communities can draw crowds for shows like *Chicago* and *The Producers* at any time during the school year or in the summer. However, other learning communities may prefer family shows like *Seussical* or *The Sound of Music* for all their productions. Our experience is that just about everyone will want to be in or see fun shows like *Grease* or *Footloose*, no matter where you live, and those happen to be relatively inexpensive shows to produce; consider them if you haven't done them before. If you have a bigger budget, consider a Disney musical or Junior musical, which always draws a crowd. The biggest factor for choosing the summer show is your limited time frame, usually four or five weeks. Even if your camp hours are from 10 a.m. to 3 p.m., five days a week, you will still be challenged to get a full-scale musical up in one month. Unless you have a massive parent and student resource "machine" that is willing to be dedicated to the summer show for the entire month of July, choose a show that is not too technically demanding. Remember that the summer is also a time to relax and enjoy, so you may wish to focus on a show that is light and fun, and appropriate for both middle school participants and highschoolers.

How Much Should Theatre Camp Cost?

Apply your teacher ethics and philosophy to the issue of cost. Even though most theatre camps are designed to make money, they can provide you with so much more than that!

You can use the camp experience to build your audience base, and hopefully your enrollment base, while you serve your learning community. It is far better to create goodwill and positive energy in the community by charging a reasonable amount for your camps than to create resentment by being greedy. Make your prices competitive, but on the low end, and you will probably come out way better in the long run in both financial and personal/professional results. This also works to your advantage when you need to ask camp participants to provide their own tights or wear a particular kind of shoe for the production camp. It's obvious that you aren't fattening your pocketbook at the expense of the camp families. Find your competition and price accordingly for a week-long half-day children's camp and for the month long, five+ hour a day production camp. You can even include a couple of show tickets and a camp T-shirt for each camper as part of your summer theatre experience!

Once you have received registration forms and payments from all of your intended summer campers, send out an introductory letter to the parents, confirming receipt of their materials and giving them information about the camp, such as:

CAMP ATTIRE

- appropriate shoes (no flip flops)
- clothing suitable for dance/creative movement

CAMP SCHEDULE

- Dates of camp attendance
- Any days off
- Lunchtime arrangements
- Drop-off and pickup points and times
- Penalties for tardy pickup
- Production week schedule changes to accommodate pit rehearsals

EXPECTATIONS

- Items provided by the camp
- Items provided by each camper
- Behavior and ethics
- Limitations of camp staff

COMMUNICATION

- Ask parents to communicate any changes in attendance (doctor's appointments, etc.) ASAP
- Reminders about what is included in the camp package: T-shirt, comp tickets, etc.

- Medical issues that may need attention during camp hours

PERMISSIONS

- Secure form granting parental permission for publicity photographs of campers.
- Solicit permission/assistance transporting campers to off-site or after-hours events.

Final Details

Once your camp is completed, either you or your theatre boosters should send out a general "thank you" email to all involved. You can attach your high school production dates flyer to it, inviting them all to come and see your next show. The final task of your summer camp is to meet the deadlines set by the school system for turning in all required paperwork. This usually has a 10 to 30 day turnaround, so don't procrastinate or your camp may not be approved for the following year. This paperwork is sure to include your financial records of the camp, including all camp fees, personnel stipends, equipment/supplies expenses, and ticket sale income. Make sure that you keep good records as you proceed from your set-up process, so that you will know where to find all of your information when you need to submit it. Collaborate with your boosters—don't feel like you have to do this all by yourself.

Educational theatre summer camps can be wonderful vehicles for both building your school program and further integrating that with the local learning community. If you love what you do and don't need the whole summer to recover from the school year, the rewards of your summer endeavors will carry you through the following year, supporting and enhancing the high school theatre program and giving your students additional opportunities to grow.

Summer Enrichment Programs for Your Students

It's helpful to become familiar with summer training options that are available to your students. Just as with colleges, students and parents will be looking to you for sage advice in this area as well. In addition to any summer theatre program you may have at your own school, other area high schools, community theaters, community centers and school or state-sponsored enrichment programs may be sources of activity, training, and experience for your enthusiastic thespians. As you receive promotional brochures and hear about various options, compile and post the information where students and parents can easily find it. Look into these programs yourself and evaluate them as best you can. And do ask around for feedback about the differences and quality of these programs.

Since many theaters go dark during the summer months, their actors and technicians often offer classes to young (and not so young) wannabe actors. Again, ask around to help distinguish those places that have really good teachers of acting from those that merely have out-of-work actors. Some theaters (rarely, we know) may also offer unpaid internships that can provide your students "a foot in the door" to their local theatre world. You never know!

Similarly, many college theatre programs also offer teen versions of their programs during the summer months. Some are of excellent quality. On-campus housing may be available, too. The program can be a great promotional tool for the college and an exciting summer opportunity for the students. One notable example is the teen summer program at Northwestern University (nhsi.northwestern.edu/theatrearts), but there are plenty of them out there! Check out the annual summer theatre edition of *Dramatics* magazine (www.schooltheatre.org), which identifies or profiles over 200 summer theatre options for teenagers.

Summer theatre camps across the country vary enormously, from day camps to sleepaway camps that offer drama classes and/or productions. The theatre component of a camp may be as small as a single class among a host of other activities and as comprehensive as some intensive conservatory-style summer-stock-like experiences. Among the most famous of the competitive programs are French Woods Festival of the Performing Arts (frenchwoods.com) in upstate New York, and Interlochen Summer Arts Camp in Michigan (camp.interlochen.org/theatre-arts-summer-programs).

There are also programs in the major theatre centers of New York City and Los Angeles that let students brush shoulders with and learn from working professionals.

In deciding which program suits their student's needs, parents will need to weigh many factors such as cost, distance, facilities, housing, and experience of the staff. Your job is to find these opportunities and make the information available. By doing so, you will strengthen your own program when the students return bursting with enthusiasm to your classroom.

Travel with Students

One of the best experiences you can have as a teacher/director is watching the growth, personal and artistic, of those students with whom you bond as you prepare and experience travel afar. Here is the Who, What, When, Where, Why and How of it.

Who Would Do Such a Thing?

Actually, *you* might want to, especially after you're used to your school and students and community. Such a trip can be tremendously satisfying personally, professionally and artistically. Consider who you might take on such a trip: the students who are cast and/or doing tech in the show, if you're performing? The students who have been successful in your class(es) during the year? The students who can pay their own way on the trip (must they be thespians)?

What Will You Need to Do?

The list of to-do items will feel nearly endless when planning a big trip, but here are a few general—and a few specific—items to get you started.

- Open clear lines of communication among all the potential stakeholders (kids, parents, school, travel and transport agencies) and set meeting and payment times throughout the year.
- Pin down the particulars of transportation, housing, food, sightseeing, tickets, etc.
- Get parent support for the details parts that don't require your policy input, and to track the financial pieces.
- Set up fundraising opportunities, or permit others to do so, as long as you are in the loop.
- Select and rehearse any show you may be bringing on tour.
- Keep the energy up during the fund-raising season, when the trip feels very far off.
- Arrange for cell phones so all can keep in touch at any time with you, each other, and the home front. Rehearse the travel, load-in, strike, and "what if" scenarios.
- Assure that copies of passports, if needed, are in your hands *long* before any foreign trip.
- Return home safely with the same number of warm bodies you took off with in the first place.

When is the Best Time to Travel with Students?

There's no right answer here. Travel during winter and spring break keeps kids from missing school—and keeps you from being with your own family and friends. Check with your music department: if they take off school days to travel to competitions far away, that precedent should permit you to do the same. In the summer, there is time to both travel and have some time to yourself. More details are below.

When do you need to plan such an activity? Well, frankly, don't even think about it in or during your first year teaching, unless you arrive to discover it's already in progress (like, half the funds have already been raised). Otherwise, *plan ahead*. Waaay ahead.

Decide where and when you want to go. Will a colleague come along with you? How many kids would you be willing to travel with? What kind of administrative blessings will you need? What forms need be filed, and by when?

What will be your philosophy and policies (especially about money and refunds)? Will you have the option to turn away the kid you *know* will cause you and the others nothing but trouble? Is the main point to enjoy time away? To perform? To compete? To discover new places? To meet new people? To take workshops or see shows? Different priorities will lead to different decisions.

Real-World Moments

We were gearing up to tour a show to the Edinburgh Fringe Festival when world events got so tense that our school system banned all international travel. All our students and their parents were willing to move forward with our big adventure, though, so we held a very official meeting—including the principal—and severed our ties to the school system. One of the parents did the paperwork to incorporate our traveling group (separate even from our school drama booster group), collected funds were transferred over to a new bank account, future meetings were held off-site, and all publicity and paperwork disavowed any official ties to the school. Thankfully, the trip did indeed go off without a hitch and for subsequent foreign trips, we stuck with the incorporation plan to maintain our independence.

Whose permission will you need to travel near or far? Parents, certainly. Administrators, too. But do they also need to go higher up to approve such a trip?

Where Is There to Go?

You'd be surprised at how many places you can go! Here are a few examples: ITS runs a week-long festival in Lincoln, Nebraska, the last week of June. You all live in the dorms, eat in the dining halls, and can take zillions of workshops, see full length shows daily, tons of short plays, and do evening social events. Not a lot of sleep, but tons of fun, including plenty of colleagues for you to meet and swap war stories with…or pick up teaching tips from (schooltheatre.org for details).

Edinburgh, Scotland, hosts the world's largest arts festival, the Festival Fringe, in August every year. Anyone can go (if you're super-organized, and have the money), and there are more than 1000 shows a day, as the entire city turns into one mammoth celebration. The American High School Theatre Festival (www.ahstf.org) is a branch of the WorldStrides student travel agency; they invite high school programs to apply to travel and perform with them, if selected. A $2000 "deposit" also buys you, the teacher, the "fam"(familiarization) trip the summer before all of you travel, to see the Fringe for yourself, along with the other directors chosen. It is simply amazing!

Why not get adventurous? Numerous travel agencies will happily vie for your business, creating a custom trip for you or adding you in to one of the standard packages they already have ready to go. From New York City to London to…well…everywhere, the possibilities are endless. There is even a theatre festival in Avignon, France. Get enough kids to go (between six and twenty, depending on the company and the trip) and you travel for free. Be sure to get good references before selecting a company.

Why Do Student Travel?

Touring together generates a strong bond between you and your group, and within your group, that inevitably lasts much longer than the trip itself. You all develop a sort of short-hand for getting things done and keeping an eye on each other. As long as that traveling group doesn't consider themselves the entitled elite, they can become real leaders and great examples for the others back home. You are largely responsible for making sure that the "elite" status never takes hold.

Broadening students' horizons is enriching in and of itself. Seeing that the world they know is not the end-all and be-all of existence is a healthy thing. Getting a sense of history (or just redefining what "old" means), trying new foods, and dipping into cultures is valuable to their growth as individuals in a world oh so very much larger than their own high school.

Travel can help your students to realize that people who live in very different places and situations are still very much like themselves. This helps build empathy and understanding. Our similarities far outweigh our differences, and hopefully student travel will open their eyes to the universality we share.

On a purely practical note, a student trip not open to all comers can be a terrific enroll-ment enticement. If only the advanced kids get to go, or only those who do consistently solid work for you all year, students may enroll in your class with the goal of being part of that next great international adventure. On the other hand, you may really need some techies or others with just the right skills or traits to match the needs of your show. Just be sure your policy is very clear.

How to Travel with Students

Here are some general guidelines, questions to ponder and suggestions to help make your travel plans and trip with students go more smoothly:

> **BE INSPIRED** If you're not totally jazzed about going, the trip will fall apart for sure. What inspires you? A personal chance to visit someplace new? Showing off your talented students? Watching the wonder spread across the faces of the kids you've come to know and care about? Bringing new opportunities to those who have worked so hard during the year? Or even simply a chance for you to travel for free?

> **BE SPECIFIC** What activities will form the core of your trip? What agency will you work through to arrange ticketing and other logistics? Who can chaperone? Where will

you stay? Will food be included? How much will it cost? How will the money be raised? What clearances do you need? How can you best coordinate your travel with your school schedule and with your students'/families' schedules?

BE TRANSPARENT Does your school have rules about what travel is allowed, when or where, or who can participate? Who will provide insurance for the trip? What will be the rules and expectations during the trip? How will updates and changes be made available to parents? What is your policy about fundraising? Who will manage the money? How far in advance do you need to collect travel costs? What if someone has to drop out? Be prompt, upfront and clear about these things.

BE ORGANIZED Use a spreadsheet to track who has signed up, who has paid up, who has turned in a copy of their parent permission, health insurance card, passport and/or other required documents. Who will keep all the copies and forms and other materials? Who will carry what? Who will be in charge of what? Mistakes can be costly indeed!

BE PREPARED Forewarn your (and the students') banks of upcoming travel lest they lock those accounts due to what they consider unusual (international) activity at some foreign ATM. If touring a show, who will be carrying the set pieces, the props, the costumes? Who will explain what in the world those things are when you approach Customs and Immigration? What should students do in case of emergency? Who offers short-term cell phone rentals that will work over there and can be pre-programmed with everyone else's number? Whom should you designate as your official contact person at home and on the road?

BE ALERT Wear bright show shirts on travel days. Watch out for that one kid who disappears to the bathroom just as the group is leaving, despite your "buddy system," or the kid with diabetes who forgets to take his insulin kit along on the afternoon boat ride (yeah, that happened). Be aware of budding romances. Watch out for liquor breath. In the UK and Ireland, look *right* before left when crossing the road. Count heads often.

BE RELAXED You are traveling, after all, to have a good time. You may not get to go out for a beer, since you're working 24/7, but you need to enjoy and laugh along with everyone else.

11 Older and Wiser

Although it may often feel true that "the first year sucks!," it is equally true that the second year is *infinitely* easier than the first. You finally have a picture in your head of all the routines, processes, and personalities you have to deal with, and a much better idea of how to pace yourself, prioritize, and improvise to keep things moving forward. But you do need to take care of yourself if you're going to survive and thrive in this job. And over time, there are skills that you simply can't have at first but that you will develop to make your life easier. You will even get some feedback from your students and parents that restores your confidence and your faith in yourself and encourages you to come back more creative and determined than ever. Your learning never stops.

Recharging Your Batteries

If the show must go on, then so must you. Ideally, you will take steps to recharge yourself as you go along—eating right, getting enough sleep, exercising—which you should be doing anyway. Teaching skills (including patience, communication and enthusiasm) are tied to your physical condition. Despite a generally healthy lifestyle, however, you know that the nature of theatre education, with its production schedule demands and the committed hard work of teaching, can occasionally drain you.

The Basics of Staying Sane

Here are some suggestions for keeping yourself ready to do your best and still have a life outside of your job. Try to find the one you're *not* good at, and make it this year's challenge.

Cut yourself some slack if you're a perfectionist. And remember that your own family really *is* always more important than your job.

P.O.D. Prioritize! Organize! Delegate!

PREPARE EARLY Whatever can be done ahead, do it ahead.

TEACH LEADERSHIP SKILLS Train your students to be leaders, so you don't have to lead all the time. As they say, "The best way to learn is to teach." So let your students learn (and buy you some breathing time) by letting them teach some new material to their class.

RESPECT THE TIME OF EVERYONE INVOLVED One disciplined, committed run-through is better than two sloppy ones. Start on time and end on time for meetings and rehearsals.

WORK EFFICIENTLY Prepare and prioritize, to enable shorter or fewer work sessions.

DO SOMETHING TOTALLY DIFFERENT Outside of school, engage in an activity that has nothing to do with theatre (e.g., reading, kick-boxing, yoga, tennis, hiking, outdoor activities, games with friends—cards, chess, attending to a pet, etc.).

SET ASIDE PERSONAL TIME Have a social/family life. Compartmentalize school work vs. home time, and don't neglect important relationships.

REMEMBER THAT THE SUN WILL STILL RISE TOMORROW, EVEN IF... The backdrop isn't painted? The lead actor is too sick to perform? Your musical is snowed out? Think through a backup plan and know that you'll live through it. The bigger the "disaster," the better the teachable moment, and the better the tale to tell for years to come.

STAY POSITIVE Perhaps one of the most important ways to maintain your sanity is recognizing what you control and what you don't control. Work hard on what you can control; *let go* of the things you don't control. Stewing about the uncontrollable will do nothing but raise your stress levels, so let it go and move on.

Opportunities to Recharge

Professional ways to recharge your batteries may coincide with staff development activities such as conferences, peer meetings, theatre trips or even going to see a local production. Sometimes writing—and reading—educational blogs (like the one via SchoolTheatre.org) can be helpful to remind yourself that you are not alone with the challenges of being a professional educator. Theatre and teaching may inspire you, but they may not always be enough to refresh.

Sometimes the best thing you can do for yourself is to do nothing: nothing at home; nothing on a family trip; nothing on the beach, in the mountains or at Disney World. Teachers are invariably very hard workers, so it's not surprising that so many educators feel that they need to give themselves permission *not* to work on lesson plans and the like on the weekends or at vacation times.

Especially in an age of constant communication, it may be difficult to resist reading school email every day—but you don't have to do so if you're on vacation! Set up that auto-reply message saying that you're unavailable until whenever. Leave your emergency cell number with a trusted colleague and give yourself an offline break. Only you know how much time you need. Some people use an entire summer, while others can run a summer theatre camp and rejuvenate in two or three weeks. You will learn what works for you. Spend some time and attention reflecting on what you need, and then commit to it. If you don't take care of yourself, you won't be much use to anyone.

The Voice of Experience

The first time doing anything worthwhile is usually both the hardest, and the most memorable. And so it is with the first year of teaching. The tears at the end of each exhausting day will inevitably give way to your accurate anticipation of what the next day may bring, and how to deal with it. Here are some things about teaching theatre that come with experience and get easier over time.

Duration

How much material/rehearsal can you get through in a 45 (or 90) minute class? Start by having waaaaay too much material available (sure beats running out!), but eventually you'll find yourself saying, "So, I'll see you all tomorrow" immediately followed by the sound of the bell.

Lead Time and Deadlines

How long do you need to allow before it's too late for things? How much in advance must you select a show, apply for the rights, receive the contract, get it approved, return it with a deposit if required, and receive your scripts and materials—all before auditions? How far ahead must you request administrative leave for a conference—before that year's pot of money for such things is exhausted? When (and what) should you prepare for Back to School Night? These things vary from situation to situation, but some will become annual routines for you to follow.

Punting

Sometimes the best laid plans get shot to pieces. The materials don't arrive on time. The critical cast member gets sick. A tornado drill interrupts your momentum. The photocopy machine dies. You forgot it's testing week, and only half of your class shows up. The list goes on. This is why it is so essential for you to develop and maintain an emergency lesson plan. Your emergency lesson plan is necessary, of course, in case you need a substitute teacher to take your class. But on occasion, you may need to use the emergency lesson plan yourself when you encounter unforeseen obstacles to what you had intended to do that day. You will find that shifting gears abruptly when necessary becomes much less stressful after you have built up your bag of tricks from years of teaching.

Predictable Loose Ends

You may comply completely with all deadlines, but some folks are not as dependable or timely as you are. You'll discover who (students, vendors, colleagues) forgets things, like returning parent permission slips (including the high-stakes Federal Survey Form); bringing back receipts; sending invoices; cleaning up and collecting their lost and found after an outside group has used the theater. After a show closes, it's easy to move on, but there are always loose ends, like reconciling the value of the tickets sold against the deposits actually made to your finance office. Or sending a program to everyone who advertised in it. Or making darn sure all those props and borrowed costumes are cleaned and returned to those kind enough to lend them (or to rental companies who will keep the meter running!).

Penalties That Work

A lesson that you will undoubtedly learn quickly: only threaten those things that you can actually carry out. For example, while you might want to kick a kid out of your class for good, you just can't do that—but you probably *can* remove them from your cast. And you'll also find that some consequences don't seem like penalties at all to some students. You'll probably never get it totally right, but you will certainly get much better at it. And hopefully, as you build the culture and reputation of your program, you will minimize the need to threaten or impose penalties on your students.

Consequences can also be thought of as holding students accountable, or giving them what they need. The two girls who can't stop talking in class do need to be separated. Tell them the truth: they are showing you they need to be separated—at least for now. You're not the bad guy—in fact, you're the good teacher who is giving them what they need—and deserve.

Nuance

As more of your skills move to autopilot, you'll be better able to concentrate on and attend to detail. You'll begin to notice automatically the "slightly off" mood of a student who needs attention or encouragement, that ensemble member who is distracted. You will gravitate to the painted line on the set that needs touching up, or a reference you missed in a line of dialogue. The quality of your own work will increase over time because of your attention to detail.

What to Own, What to Loan

Being responsible for a class or show does not mean that you have to do—and provide—everything yourself. You will get better at figuring out what you can safely delegate to sharp (and not-so-sharp) students, to parent boosters, to guest artists, or to colleagues. And you'll also learn what things you need to reserve as your exclusive domain (like grading, show choice and casting). Even in class, you'll discover that it's fine to delegate some things to your students, such as by encouraging them to research a theatre tradition that you know nothing about. Delegating in this way may seem somewhat scary at first, but you will be helping your students to learn essential research skills and they, in turn, will teach new information to both you and the whole class.

Building a Library and Inventory

You may have inherited a collection of scripts and books, but undoubtedly over time you will add your own materials—such as magazines, texts, manuals, anthologies, and scripts—to that collection. You can also selectively retain lumber, stock units (flats, platforms, stairs), tools and equipment, and gradually build a supply of stage lights, wireless microphones, cables, etc. Over time, your theatre classroom and auditorium can become exceptionally well-equipped! Start right away to develop and maintain a reliable system to organize and index all these materials so you can locate that script or that cable when you need it.

Telling the Truth Diplomatically

When you make a mistake, own it. And expect your kids to do the same. Tell the truth about why you make decisions; just make sure that students, colleagues and parents are able to accept and understand the truth you tell. Sometimes you have to deliver a diplomatic truth—especially when it comes to casting. *How* to tell the truth will come easier with experience. A helpful, truthful phrase for the student who didn't get the part they wanted is: "S/he's not ready for that part." "Not ready" indicates an open-ended possibility in the future. And it's true—you cannot accurately predict how any student's talent trajectory will mature during high school. Teenagers are subject to change; who knows what they will be able to do next year, with additional preparation, training and development? Reminding students and parents that every part is important in order to create a great show—which is what we all desire—is the ultimate truth in casting.

Which Battles to Fight

Students, administrators, parents and the community at some point or other will call your judgment into question. You will gradually, over time, begin to figure out which issues can be easily dismissed, which ones explained, which ones ignored, which ones really merit a plan of action, and which ones, ultimately, justify putting your job or career on the line. The triage of issues gets easier as you develop more personal experience. Knowing what pushes your buttons, and what will do that to others, becoming aware of how you work—and how those around you respond—all of this takes time, but it comes. It gets easier to know which things to let roll off your back and which ones to take on.

Final Thoughts

Sometimes, your faith as a teacher, or as a person, can be shaken. As when…

> …there is no apparent resolution to student, parent or colleague conflict.
> …you don't get to see whether the good decisions you make outweigh your moments of simply being human and making mistakes.
> …you have visions of a bitter student going on a talk show and telling the world how horrible their high school theatre teacher was.
> …kids post unkind remarks on teacher rating websites.
> …kids who are immature and selfish as students grow up to be immature, selfish adults who can't understand how you tried to make a positive difference in their lives.

So, *move on!* Don't dwell on it; you're only human. Try your very best to find and use strategies that keep you in a positive, productive place. Focus on what is right and appreciate the good that is happening—because sometimes, even at the most unlikely moment, your faith is restored. For example…

> …a student writes you a note that conveys deep appreciation for what a difference you made in their life.
> …kids bloom and grow right before your eyes.
> …your theatre class gives you a birthday card.
> …the kid you coached, who didn't get into that distinguished summer theatre program, nonetheless gets into a college conservatory program.

…one of your kids wins an award and thanks you publicly at the Kennedy Center.

…the courage of an injured student inspires your entire cast, crew and director.

…the mother of a special education student tells you, with tears in her eyes, how important that ensemble role was to her child.

…the best theatre student as a senior turns out to be the one who argued most with you as a freshman.

…a shy senior transfer student develops confidence in your department and gains the courage to pursue college scholarships.

…your students hug you and thank you for the opportunity to grow.

…you are invited to a college graduation for a kid who nearly dropped out.

…one of your students makes it on Broadway.

…a kid who graduated two decades ago with an addiction problem contacts you and tells you that she's a successful teacher at a university because your department was a haven for her.

…a kid with few financial resources gets into college because you gave her the opportunity to audition.

…the transfer student from another country tells you that your class made him feel accepted.

…you are watching TV and suddenly see one of your former students on the screen.

…a student who graduated two years ago sends you an email that says he decided to be a teacher because of your example.

…it all just works out.

Life goes on. There are more students to teach and nurture. Get up again tomorrow and do it again. Grow.

Kudos From a Student

Here's one of those makes-it-all-worthwhile letters from a student. It was her college application essay (used by permission of the author). We hope you save all your "kudos" letters.

Describe a place or environment where you are perfectly content. What do you do or experience there, and why is it meaningful to you?

Mr. R,

I wanted to share this with you.

"Hold, please."

The actors freeze in place and the backstage bustle quiets. Each pair of eyes looks expectantly outward, searching for my familiar shadow in the fifth row. I lean forward, adjust my glasses on the bridge of my nose, and assess the positions of the actors onstage. Finally, I speak.

"Alex, can we go back to your entrance and fix the timing?"

I have never felt more content in any place than when I am in the midst of a rehearsal in my high school's theater. In the fall of 2013 I had my first opportunity to be involved in the direction of a main stage production, Little Shop of Horrors, my fifteenth overall theatrical credit as a high school thespian. For three hours each weekday I was blocking scenes, commenting on choreography, offering solutions to problems the actors encountered, and doing any small odd jobs asked of me. One rehearsal I remember clearly involved working with the actors playing Seymour and Audrey. The task at hand was to block them in such a way that Audrey's dead body could be realistically delivered to the mouth of the man-eating plant—not something teenage girls get to do every day. Our solution was for Seymour to carry the full weight of Audrey's body so her limp arm could dangle lifelessly, and place her legs into the plant first. That way, she could support herself while being hidden from the audience. To them, it all looked like what we call "theatre magic."

The theatre is magical in its own way. For me, it has provided the most coherent definition of "home" I have ever known. If I am feeling unwelcome in my parents' house, as is often the case, it takes a mere eleven minutes to arrive at the doorstep of my second family. I have been accepted there with two expectations attached to my presence: first, that I will be equally as accepting; second, that I will strive to make good art.

Home is also a place I associate with growing up. The maturity I have grown into during my time in the theatre has impacted my life as a whole in an entirely positive manner. This type of environment has not only taught me how to be a performer and artist of quality. It's taught me how to be a capable, responsible young woman, whether I'm holding for applause, holding tight to a friend in need, or holding my head up even in the most boring lecture. Skills learned in a theatre program extend far beyond the edge of the stage; they have taught me to speak publicly, to persevere, to collaborate, to be accountable, and ultimately, to be innovative. It is my belief that such a mix of excellent lessons is difficult to find elsewhere. I feel blessed to have caught the bug, and I remain eager to discover the new directions my life can travel in because of it.

More Final Thoughts

- Lead and teach.
- Protect the children and keep them *safe*.
- Lead by example, and ask your students to do the same.
- Plan and prepare like a professional.
- Hone your professionalism.
- Never lose your sense of humor.
- Talk to and smile at everyone.
- Learn names as fast as you can.
- Create safe places for your students to grow.
- Just because a kid is quiet doesn't mean s/he doesn't care.
- Notice and encourage every child.
- Being fair doesn't mean treating everyone the same.
- Learn to ask the right questions—over and over again.
- Secretaries and custodians rule the school.
- Attendance and finances are more important than you think.
- Secure your shared performance spaces.
- Lock up anything you can't live without.
- Whatever can be done in advance should be.
- Investigate before you plunge into unknown waters.
- Exercise transparency in all aspects of your professional work.
- Focus on the kids—especially their growth, not their goofs.
- Celebrate small victories as much as big shows.
- Delegate to those you trust.
- Trust but verify.
- Cherish the opportunity to work and make a difference.
- Create performance gifts for your community.
- Reach out for assistance *before* you begin to drown.
- Balance passion with patience.
- Remember that theatre is the collaborative art.
- Communicate and share your visions with enthusiasm.
- If it's good for the kids, pursue it.
- Teenagers are children in big bodies, swiftly evolving and changing.
- Pick your battles very carefully.
- Bravely stand up for what is right.

- Never blame a child for her/his parents.
- Express your appreciation often and loudly.
- Release your inner child as often as possible.
- Believe in yourself, the kids and the process.
- Forgive yourself when your example falls short.
- Learn and move on.
- Work like a dog (I love dogs).
- Never stop making discoveries.

Appendices

Here in the appendices, we have provided useful forms and templates that we have developed over our long careers teaching theatre in schools. We hope you will find them helpful, and these you may copy, modify and use however and as often as you like.

In addition to being here in the back of the book, these forms are also available on EducationalStages.com in Microsoft Word format (.docx), so you can easily modify them to suit your particular situation.

Also, we'd love your comments on what you like, what you need, etc. All suggestions (and *especially* compliments) are gratefully accepted. Please send us your feedback at Support@EducationalStages.com.

Appendix A

Ideal Job Worksheet

Make some choices about your priorities. You can always change them, but give these some thought now, while you can. Use this questionnaire to envision your perfect job situation. Where would it be? In what type of school and grade level? What do you have to offer a principal who might hire you? What would you want to know about them? What would clinch the deal—or be a dealbreaker—for you?

Ideal Job Worksheet

1. Geographic location?

   _____

   _____

2. Setting (urban, suburban, rural)?

   _____

   _____

   _____

3. Nearby attractions (parks, cultural, sports, woods)?

   _____

   _____

   _____

4. Housing (home, dorm, group house, apartment, condo)?

   _____

   _____

5. School type (public, private, special needs, DOD, IB)?

   _____

   _____

6. School level (elementary, middle, high)?

   _____

   _____

7. School size (small, medium, large)?

_____

_____

8. Theatre subjects you can teach (acting, tech theatre, musical theatre, film studies)?

_____

_____

_____

_____

9. Theatre specialties you can offer (stage combat, improv, choreography)?

_____

_____

_____

_____

10. Other subjects you can teach (English, chorus, speech/debate)?

_____

_____

_____

_____

11. Sports/activities you can sponsor (drama club, debate team, yearbook)?

_____

_____

_____

_____

12. Benefits that are important to you (medical, retirement, vacation days)?

_____

_____

_____

_____

13. Minimum salary?

_____

14. Deal breakers (salary, workload, safety concerns)?

_____

_____

_____

_____

15. Your vision/mission statement for your new theatre department?

_____

_____

_____

_____

_____

Appendix B

Checklist for Newbies

Chances are that you will follow the legacy of another theatre teacher in your school. If you can, try to meet the previous teacher and ask him/her a plethora of questions, such as the ones listed starting on the next page. If you don't have access to the previous theatre teacher, try interviewing an administrator or another arts educator to get as much information as possible.

Structure of Existing Theatre Program

1. How many theatre classes are there? _____

2. What levels are the different theatre classes?

   _____

   _____

   _____

   _____

3. How big are the classes usually?

   _____

   _____

   _____

   _____

4. Do any of the classes require an audition for enrollment? ☐ Yes   ☐ No
   If so, which ones?

   _____

   _____

   _____

   _____

5. Are there any combination classes?

   _____

   _____

6. Is there a technical theatre class?   ☐ Yes   ☐ No
   Are all grades allowed to enroll?   ☐ Yes   ☐ No

Equipment and Facilities Maintenance

7. What coordination should you expect from your school custodial supervisor (include contact information)?

_____

_____

_____

8. What is the contact information for the building engineer?

_____

_____

_____

9. What times outside of school hours are the facilities available for rehearsal?

_____

_____

_____

10. Is there a school system specialist for theatre equipment and facilities?

   ☐ Yes   ☐ No

   If so, what is his/her contact information and availability?

_____

_____

_____

11. Ask for a tour of any classroom, storage, technical, or performance spaces you will use.

12. Is there a lumber storage room?   □ Yes   □ No

    If so, where is it and what is the room number?

    _____

    _____

13. Is there an equipment storage room? □ Yes   □ No

    If so, where is it and what is the room number?

    _____

    _____

14. Is there a costume storage room?   □ Yes   □ No

    If so, where is it and what is the room number?

    _____

    _____

15. When is the black box and/or auditorium unavailable for classes and performances?

    _____

    _____

16. Who has access to the tech booth besides you?

    _____

    _____

17. Ask about expectations from the director of student activities, building use coordinator and/or principal concerning your responsibilities for maintaining the facilities listed above.

18. Get the following:

      ☐ Manuals and idiosyncrasies of the lighting and sound equipment

      ☐ Inventory of tools, lighting and sound equipment

      ☐ Powered personnel (Genie) lift use and policies for staff and students

      ☐ All keys, and label them!

Scheduling & Facilities Access

19. How many main stage productions and/or one-act plays each year?

_____

_____

_____

20. How many class plays each year?

_____

_____

21. How many improvisation competitions each year?

_____

_____

22. How many theatre conference field trips each year?

_____

_____

23. How many play competitions each year?

_____

_____

24. What is already scheduled for the coming year?

_____

_____

_____

_____

25. How can you access a calendar of all school events? Note which are scheduled in the performance spaces that you will use and are responsible for.

_____

_____

26. How do events in other departments impact availability of performance spaces and students that may be involved? This includes stage set-up arrangements.

_____

_____

_____

27. How much time do other performance groups (music, fashion, student services) need to rehearse in the space prior to performance?

_____

_____

_____

28. Are there any alternate facilities for rehearsal or performance?

_____

_____

_____

Money Matters

29. What is the department's current balance? _____

30. What is the current cost of tickets for school theatre department productions? _____

31. What payment methods are available? Online? At the door?

_____

_____

_____

32. Is there a class or production fee that students expect to pay?

_____

33. What do they get for that fee? (A class T-shirt, a make-up kit, rehearsal snacks?)

_____

_____

34. What is usually funded by the theatre department? The school? The drama boosters? The school district? For example, funds collected from renting the building may pay for auditorium house lights, but the school system may pay for professional installation. Another example: school textbook funds may pay for the scripts of *Our Town* that you are using for scene work in class, but if you perform the play, theatre funds will pay for scripts and royalties.

_____

_____

_____

_____

Student Strengths and Challenges

35. When casting a musical, is the casting emphasis more on those with acting ability or singing ability?

_____

_____

36. Am I expected to discuss musical production prospects with the chorus teacher?

_____

_____

37. Whom should I ask about student musicians for the pit orchestra for my musical?

_____

_____

38. What, generally speaking, is the maturity level of the students?

_____

_____

39. Are the students eager for a sophisticated acting challenge, or do they just want to have fun with lighter, shorter pieces?

_____

_____

40. Who are the student leaders?

_____

_____

41. What specific leadership opportunities exist in the department? Thespian troupe officers? Improv team captain? Lead critic?

_____

_____

42. How strict will I need to be with regard to student discipline?

_____

_____

43. Have there been any recent incidents which you should know about? Equipment theft? Illegal or inappropriate actions in school spaces? On field trips?

_____

_____

Theatre Department Traditions

44. What collaboration has taken place among staff or in the community? For example, the computer graphics teacher may use poster design for theatre department productions as an opportunity for her students to build a portfolio. Also, tech theatre students may collaborate with fashion design students to build and paint stage props for the school fashion show.

_____

_____

45. What annual events take place? An awards night? A talent show?

_____

_____

46. What have been typical warm-ups for class and performance? For example, have the warm-ups been teacher-led or student-led?

_____

_____

Feeder Schools

47. What are the middle schools and elementary schools that are in your high school pyramid?

_____

_____

_____

48. Should I include an appropriate children's theatre production in the performance season? This could be a senior directing or fundraising opportunity.

□ Yes   □ No

49. How can I find ways to collaborate with pyramid teachers? For example, how can I integrate middle school and/or elementary students from your pyramid into my production of *The Sound of Music* or *Fiddler On The Roof*?

_____

_____

50. Can I create summer programs at your school for younger students?

_____

_____

51. How can I encourage parent, community, and theatre booster support?

_____

_____

52. Can/should I employ seniors or recent graduates as camp counselors?

□ Yes   □ No

53. What policies/requirements does the school system have in place for creating these programs?

_____

_____

Theatre Boosters

54. Is there a parent theatre booster organization? ☐ Yes   ☐ No

    If so, write down their contact information:

_____

_____

_____

55. How do the theatre boosters typically support the school theatre department?

_____

_____

_____

_____

_____

Appendix C

Tech Help Request Form

Whether officially or not, you are likely to be asked to provide help to others who want to use your auditorium. You can keep these requests more under control if you establish a routine all outside users must follow. The form provided here may be customized for your particular situation. Circulate it widely, and insist that it be submitted in a timely fashion. Be sure to get feedback after the event to pass along to your wonderful techies on the fine job they did (or what needs to be better next time).

Technical Services Request Form

TODAY'S DATE		NAME OF ORGANIZATION	
NAME OF EVENT		LOCATION OF EVENT	
DATE OF EVENT	TECH HELP ARRIVAL TIME	TECH HELP RELEASE TIME	
DATE OF REHEARSAL	TECH HELP ARRIVAL TIME	TECH HELP RELEASE TIME	
DATE OF REHEARSAL	TECH HELP ARRIVAL TIME	TECH HELP RELEASE TIME	
ADULT CONTACT NAME	ADULT CONTACT PHONE	ADULT CONTACT EMAIL	
STUDENT CONTACT NAME	STUDENT CONTACT PHONE	STUDENT CONTACT EMAIL	

Help Needed

☐ HOUSE/AUDITORIUM LIGHTS

☐ STAGE LIGHTING

☐ MOVIE SCREEN

☐ LCD PROJECTOR

☐ MICROPHONE (WRITE NUMBER HERE _____)

☐ MICROPHONE STAND (WRITE NUMBER HERE _____)

☐ PODIUM

☐ ADDITIONAL EQUIPMENT REQUESTED (E.G., DVD or IPOD PLAYING) _____

☐ LIGHTING MUST CHANGE DURING THE EVENT

☐ SOUND LEVELS MUST CHANGE DURING THE EVENT

ADDITIONAL NOTES / INSTRUCTIONS

PERSON ASSUMING RESPONSIBILITY FOR EVENT	SIGNATURE
☐ By checking the box to the left, I indicate that I understand the following: 1) Student technicians are not permitted to move or change lighting equipment without the theatre director's authorization. 2) No unauthorized users may enter the tech booth. 3) Students are not permitted to have keys to the school—you are responsible for gaining access to the rooms and equipment you are requesting. 4) Nothing may be pinned or taped to curtains in the theatre.	
☐ This event has already been officially scheduled on the school calendar	

Student Techs Assigned to This Event

NAME	MOBILE PHONE NUMBER
NAME	MOBILE PHONE NUMBER
NAME	MOBILE PHONE NUMBER

Appendix D

Tech Booth Rules

Here is an easy-to-print-and-post version of rules that you may well want to display prominently. It will keep the curious and the foolish away from the expensive equipment in your lighting and sound control area, enabling your tech crew to run your shows more smoothly. And if you can also put up a "Licensed Personnel Only" sign on the door, so much the better.

TECH BOOTH RULES

1. **ONLY AUTHORIZED THEATRE TECHNICIANS ARE ALLOWED IN THE BOOTH.**
2. No food or drink near electrical equipment.
3. The booth is not a lounge or a locker.
4. Check in with the event sponsor. Find out what they need. Be helpful. Check out with them when the event is finished.
5. Take great notes—use your cue sheets.
6. Stay focused on the task at hand.
7. Avoid distracting the audience or performers.
8. Report any equipment problems as soon as possible.
9. Shut down all equipment when finished, and store microphones or other portable items.
10. Assure the booth is left secured.

Appendix E
Cultural Catch-Phrases

These are some phrases that will help shape the culture of your educational theatre program and assist with classroom management. Try some out—repeat the ones you like often and watch your words start coming out of the mouths of your students.

Cultural Catch-Phrases

IF IT'S NOT YOURS, DON'T TOUCH IT! Respect people and property.

QUIET SOMEONE NEAR YOU! This is *so* much more effective than asking those talking to be quiet.

WE ARE EACH OTHER'S SOLUTIONS. Crew chiefs meet together. You never know who will come up with a suggestion outside their own territory.

TAKE CARE OF EACH OTHER. Everything from returning a borrowed stapler, to ad-libbing to cover a dropped line, to being a good friend.

CLAIM YOUR HUMANITY! This works to keep students from getting up in the middle of instruction when the school bell rings. Precede this with, "You are not animals, conditioned to move because of a bell."

LIBERATE YOUR ARMPITS! This encourages free physical expression.

RESCUE EACH OTHER! This is useful during production work. If an actor forgets a line or misses an entrance, students should rescue the moment and each other by improvising a creative solution.

HONOR THE ART. Theatre is an ancient art that was initially considered sacred. How we conduct ourselves in the sacred space of an auditorium or black box sets a tone for the process.

THEATRE FORCES US TO BE UNSELFISH. Theatre requires commitment, self-discipline, and dedication.

TRUST THE PROCESS. Students often want the instant fix or last-minute effort—this phrase reminds them that there is a time-honored process that results in a show.

GROW YOUR GIFTS. Create and sustain a department culture centered around growth, adhering to the premise that everyone has gifts. Students need encouragement to take responsibility for growing their gifts through theatre.

Appendix F

Theatre I Identity Assignment: Who Am I?

This is a great project for Theatre I students to get to know each other and affirm their own identity and beliefs. Work this into your plans in the second semester, when kids already know each other somewhat. It encourages students to define themselves, which in turn can be applied to defining a character. Be sure to create a respectful atmosphere in the classroom, and let students know that they can share as much or as little as they are comfortable sharing with the class. Also point out that the information they present may not be held as confidential, although you can encourage the students to be respectful and not use this presentation for Facebook fodder.

Over the years, students have revealed their heartbreaking family stories, bullying experiences, sexual orientation, religious assertions, and hopes for the future. Be ready for all manner of revelations—encourage respect for all.

The intro written on the lesson sheet for the Identity Project describes the relationship between this activity and developing characters for acting.

Theatre I Identity Assignment: Who Am I?

Name _____

Presentations begin on ___ / ___ / 20___ (10 point penalty per day if late)

In order to develop your skills as an actor, it is important that you spend some time reflecting on your own identity. Identity exploration and assessment is important in developing confidence as a performer, as well as understanding character: how can you play the part of someone else if you don't know who you are in the first place?

Spending some time considering your thoughts, actions, moral code, what you care about, how you see yourself, and how you want other people to perceive you is time well spent. The analysis you use to understand yourself can be used to understand scripted characters, as well as being valuable knowledge for connecting with other performers, technicians, and the audience. Knowing yourself allows you to see how you are similar and/or different from the character you are playing.

The actor who connects with their audience uses a combination of *energy* and acting skills (projection, articulation, physicality, facial expression, vocal expression, etc.), as well as emotional connection, in creating a compelling character. This assignment gives you the opportunity to create your own script and share your story confidently with our class audience. As you construct your story, choose information that you are comfortable sharing with our group, and make sure you give the same kind of respectful listening to every member of our class ensemble that you would like to have given to you. *You will receive an audience etiquette grade during presentations.*

Grading Guidelines

To give you some structure for your identity reflection project, please include the following: (20 points each)

1. Introduction: first create an introduction in which you introduce yourself, using adjectives and giving general information about yourself. This can be in the form of a casual talk, a poem, or other verbal format. Feel free to be creative, but check with the teacher for approval. Choose a metaphor or simile that you relate to or reflects who you are; explain it.

2. Give information about your family heritage, including aspects of your family heritage (past and present) that have particularly influenced or shaped you.

3. What is your moral code? Where does it come from? This is a reflective discussion of what you consider to be right and wrong, what corresponding actions make you feel positive and proud, what corresponding choices make you feel guilty or impact you negatively. What makes you respect or not respect the moral codes of other people?

4. What do you plan on doing to make the world a better place? If this question does not interest you, why doesn't it interest you?

5. Create a visual presentation to illustrate either your family cultural heritage or the metaphor you have chosen that reflects some aspect of who you are. You can be creative with this visual presentation—it can be a costume, cultural clothing, a poster, a PowerPoint presentation, or a character box (see Glossary). Include an oral explanation of the visual aspect of your project.

Create work of which you are proud—work that you can share comfortably, but which creates a growth experience for both you and your audience.

Grades

1. Content/followed project directions   _____
2. Verbal   _____
3. Visual   _____

Preparation Grades (use of class time on task)

1. _____
2. _____

Appendix G

Organizing Labels for Mailboxes

If you can get a Classroom Keeper (that's what Staples calls it) or something that can be used for your mailbox slots, you will be able to keep track of classroom and production paperwork more easily. Here are some suggestions for labels that can be useful to identify those mailbox slots. If you download our website version of this document from EducationalStages.com, these should fit on Avery #5766 labels.

Mailbox Organizing Labels – These will print out on Avery standard #5766 labels

Class 1:_____ IN   Class 1: _____ OUT

Class 2:_____ IN   Class 2: _____ OUT

Class 3:_____ IN   Class 3: _____ OUT

Class 4:_____ IN   Class 4: _____   _____ OUT

Class 5:_____ IN   Class 5: _____ OUT

BOOSTERS   ASST DIRECTOR

STAGE MANAGER   ONE-ACT Competition

Thespian Troupe   CAPPIES

FIELD TRIP Forms   Finances: PURCHASE ORDERS

Building Use forms   Tech Help Assignments

DRAMA CLUB   _____

URGENT   PENDING

POST   FILE

Appendix H

Program Overview

The syllabus is your public roadmap of each class you teach. It identifies the content to be covered, the grading scheme to be used, classroom requirements, etc. The more detail you work out ahead of time, the better off you will be—but you are committed to doing things the way you identify them here. Your school may have a required format (and content) you must use, or you may have great latitude to determine what information to offer at the start of the year. Here is a sample that includes a brief overview.

YOUR HS THEATRE ARTS PROGRAM 2013-2014

You Are, Director   Fine Arts Elective
greatteacher@yourhs.edu(email)   xxx-xxx-xxxx (office phone)

Theatre Arts Overview for All Courses

The YOURHS Program of Studies for Theatre Arts outlines a layered approach to the study of theatre. This includes the study of increasingly sophisticated aspects of the following concepts: story, audience and actor. These concepts are connected by the development of skills of interpretation, response, and training. With this approach in mind, theatre classes in YOURHS include the following areas:

Training in the Artistic Process: Theatre Games and Warm-Up Activities

These activities require active engagement from all students in the class, leading to the discovery and development of a personal artistic process, as well as an appreciation of the class ensemble, whether in the role of actor or audience. All students are expected to engage in all class activities to the best of their ability.

Audience Etiquette

Audience etiquette is taught and required of all theatre arts students, since it is based in demonstrating respect for both the actor and the artistic process itself. This promotes an emotionally and psychologically supportive environment in which we grow. Audience etiquette includes listening, focus, and attention during any speech or presentation to the class.

Vocabulary

Vocabulary specific to theatre arts is the language of our art. Theatre vocabulary will be discussed in class, posted on Blackboard and a matching quiz will be used to assess student acquisition of these terms on a periodic basis. Vocabulary will be repeated on quizzes throughout the school year and on the final exam for Theatre I and II. Advanced Theatre III/IV students are expected to implement theatre vocabulary in written critiques and reflective essays for class.

Projects and Presentations

Projects and presentations are part of exploring and understanding the elements and history of theatre. Students will work collaboratively in groups and/or individually as we study different genres and aspects of theatre arts.

Scope and Sequence for Theatre Arts

After Theatre Arts I (or with the recommendation of the theatre director), students may choose to follow a technical theatre focus instead of, or in addition to, further theatre arts acting classes.

ACTING FOCUS	
Theatre Arts I	Introduction to the Elements of Theatre (ensemble & elements)
Theatre Arts II	Synthesis of the Elements (auditions, résumé & styles)
Theatre Arts III	Individualization (advanced production; audition required)
Theatre Arts IV	Specialization (advanced production; audition required)

TECH FOCUS	
Technical Theatre I	Acquisition of skills (safety, basic tools, sets)
Technical Theatre II	Application (safety, tools, lights, sound, sets)
Technical Theatre III/IV	Individualization & specialization (prior skills & leadership roles in productions)

All theatre students will be made aware of the many opportunities to become involved in the YOUR HS Theatre Program, including earning points for induction into the International Thespian Society, the honor society for theatre students. Also be sure to check www.yourhsdrama.org (YOURHS Drama Boosters) for info.

Appendix I

Sample Syllabi for Various Classes

Here you will find sample syllabi for syllabi for Theatre Arts I, Theatre Arts II and IB Theatre. Note the variations from the previous sample. Also notice the consistencies from class to class—for example the recurring, progressive nature of the basic standards of learning (that is, yes, students do the same types of work each year but do it better and on a more sophisticated level).

If you set out your rules of the road, so to speak, at the very beginning—and get every student and parent/guardian to sign off on them—you can avoid negotiating later in the year over items they "didn't know about." Very helpful.

Also note the use of this form to slide in some important reminders (first booster meeting, parent tech walk-through) and opt-in for publicity.

Theatre Arts I Overview

This elective class is designed to give students a deeper understanding, and appreciation for the fine art of theatre through exploration of its basic elements. Theatre I students engage in ensemble building, vocabulary, acting skills, and creative processes. These activities facilitate artistic growth through storytelling, character development, improvisation, creative movement, and original (sometimes scripted) theatrical activities and presentations.

Units of Study

First Quarter: Building the Ensemble Group

The school year begins with an emphasis on participation activities, as students play games and exercises that teach creative movement and vocal techniques for performance. Demonstration of *respect* for peers and as audience members is vital. History of Theatre: We will explore some basic history relating to the development of theatre arts, including theatre vocabulary and possible origins of theatre. Musical theatre (introductory) will be explored through choreography and group work, as well as discussion of major musical theatre composers and performers. Students are encouraged to be involved in the YOURHS plays and musical and required to attend the performance. Signing up to be an usher is a great way to see the show for free and help out!

Second Quarter: Improvisation

Through games and team challenges (TheatreSports), this quarter emphasizes improvisation. Students will engage in comical situations using audience suggestions. Students will learn and be encouraged to attend TheatreSports performances. Basic storytelling, through "Typist Narrator" improvisation and personal narrative, will include simple character building, plot development, and learning how to connect with other members of the ensemble. Students will be introduced to both short form and long form improvisation. Scene work will be introduced as students work on their acting skills in small groups, exploring selected dramatic literature. Students will have an opportunity to present a short play or scenes at the Evening of One Acts in February.

Third Quarter: Script Development for Performance

This quarter begins a more intensive approach to the creative process, including rehearsal time for a culminating workshop performance. The style of story will be focused on fairy tales, forming small casts within the class. Evaluation and critical response will be taught and applied to the work that is presented, using constructive criticism that embraces respect, and encouraging the work in progress.

Fourth Quarter: Monologues and the Solo Performance

During the fourth quarter students apply acquired knowledge and skills to create and share an identity project and a final monologue/personal narrative of their choice. We will explore theatre traditions beyond our borders through story, props and costumes.

You control your grade!

Students are encouraged to see, read or participate in plays each quarter beyond the required attendance at YOURHS performances. Filling out and turning in T.A.P. reports (Theatre Application Project) is a way to earn additional points to make up for low test or quiz grades: 10 points added to a quiz grade for each full-length play seen, performed or 10 hours of tech work. Programs, ticket stubs, and parent signatures serve as validation for director approval. If attendance or participation in a performance is not possible, reading a full-length play approved by the theatre director is an alternate option. Theatre students have the opportunity to usher for YOURHS theatre events to see them for free, as they contribute to our productions.

Rules & Classroom Expectations

- No gum chewing, candy, food, or drinks during class time. It restricts your ability to focus on vocal technique while performing, and you could choke.
- Arrive on time to class. Three unexcused tardies within a quarter equal an after-school detention. Every tardy past the first three will result in further detentions, phone calls home, and an eventual administrative referral.
- Demonstrate proper audience etiquette at all times. This includes paying full attention to your peers and teacher whenever they perform or present information.
- Please treat others with respect and courtesy. The collaborative art of theatre is a discipline that requires mutual respect.
- You must actively engage every day in this class in order to learn and grow your theatre skills. The majority of your grade in this class is assessed on your active and skillful engagement within the time that you are here.
- You will maintain an organized notebook that will be continuously created and ultimately serve as your class textbook. It will contain this syllabus at the front, all vocabulary words and definitions, general notes, and handouts.
- All other rules and guidelines that are mentioned in the student handbook for YOURHS, and YOURHS expectations in Students Rights and Responsibilities, are to be followed and obeyed at all times!

Required Materials

(Notice that cell phones, iPods, and other personal electronic devices are not listed.)

- A three-ring binder with notebook paper & writing implements
- Comfortable clothing, worn or brought daily, for creative movement
- A box of tissues at the beginning of the year

Photography

Theatre students are often involved in public performances that are photographed for publicity and archival purposes. Signing below indicates that you are aware of this and allow your child's photo to be taken for YOURHS Theatre publicity purposes.

Quarterly Grades	
Tests and Projects	50%
Active Engagements (includes audience etiquette)	50%

Grading Scale	
A	93–100
A-	90–92
B+	87–89
B	83–86
B-	80–82
C+	77–79
C	73–76
C-	70–72
D+	67–69
D	64–66
F	below 64

Final Grade	
Quarter 1	20%
Quarter 2	20%
Quarter 3	20%
Quarter 4	20%
Final Exam/Project	20%

Signatures

Students and parents, please sign below to verify that you have read the Theatre I class syllabus, rules, & expectations.

. . . . ✂ . . . .

I have read and understand the Theatre Arts I course standards and grading criteria.

Student _____ Date _____

Parent _____ Date _____

Please return this signed sheet to your theatre director ASAP.

Theatre Arts I Syllabus

(teacher's name)
(phone number)
(email address)

Welcome! Your role is to participate. This means watching, listening, doing, and thinking. You don't have to be great at everything, but you do have to try. Our game plan is to explore all the basics of theatre: from acting to stagecraft (including reading, improvising, and writing), from stage to television and theatre, to art, music, and dance. We'll try to figure out what this "theatre" thing is and what difference it makes to you and the world! It'll be fun, active and different. Please have a folder with paper and pencil in class daily. Students may leave these in a class file. Enjoy the journey!

Decorum

Remember, no T.H.E.F.T. of class time is permitted (that's: Talking out of turn; Holding up class for debate; Explaining instead of listening; Fooling around; Talk-back). Got a question about the class work? Raise your hand. Got a question *not* about the class work? Write it down and hand it to me instead of interrupting (use your Agenda if you need to leave class); I'll answer soon as I can!

Making Progress

Mistakes are good. Learn from 'em and improve! Besides, there's often *no one right answer*. In class, it's about the journey, not the destination. Just stay focused, have fun, experiment, help each other, and take time to notice why you did stuff and what you got from it. Enjoy!

Theatre Notebook

Begin keeping a journal of the road you're about to travel. How do you feel about class? What did you do? What helps or frustrates you? What are your strengths and weaknesses? Look for the milestones that suggest you're making progress. You may keep your entries in a folder in my file cabinet. Sketches and show programs can go in there, too. You'll have some assignments that are easiest to keep in this notebook, so bring in a small loose leaf binder by next class.

Web

Keep up with homework assignments by Internet. Check Blackboard (yourhs.blackboard.com) daily! *Update your email now!* (Your username and password are your student ID # until you change your password). Also see docs.google.com Username: xxxxx passwd: xxxxxx Some key info is also on the yourschool.org. *Take the survey today!* Note that you're also enrolled in the Community "organization" DRAMA CLUB. Check it out! Let me know if DRAMA CLUB doesn't show up on your Blackboard account. Also: Make *sure* we've got a *current email address* for you *both* on Blackboard & the Dramakids database on your teacher's computer (current parent email in both places, too).

Our fall SHOW. Yeah, I know it's early, but our fall show is coming up soon (auditions next week) and we need lots of people for stagecrew jobs! Sign up on the callboard outside the theatre ramp to be part of the excitement! Check out the audition info on the drama website for advice.

Drama Mama & Drama Dad

Drama Boosters are the parent support group we depend on, so please get yours to come to the once yearly big meeting on Thursday, Sept. 20th at 7:00 in the theatre. This will include the required parent walk-thru for those kids who want to do tech stuff this year.

TheatreSports

We love improv! If you like *Whose Line is it Anyway?* you'll adore TheatreSports. Save Friday, October 12th from 7:30–10:00 pm for a "freestyle" (loose rules) countywide TheatreSports night! Wanna be on the team? Club? Watch the callboard for details soon!

Theatre Arts I Standards of Learning

The YOURPS Theatre Arts Program of Studies identifies nine areas of study on which students will focus. Theatre Arts I students gain exposure to each of these areas and will participate in hands-on activities to develop appropriate skills and knowledge.

1. Scriptwriting: using improvisation to develop character and narrative; writing short scenes.
2. Acting: the language of the stage and acting; theatre games for developing body and voice; scene presentations.
3. Designing: the production team; elements of stagecraft; exposure to basic technical theatre.

4. Directing: seeing the big picture; blocking stage pictures; interpreting a script; being in charge.

5. Researching: discovering new and old ideas to apply to project work; where to find things; what becomes of actors after high school.

6. Critiquing: making sense of plays; giving and taking artistic criticism; deciding what's important to you in a play or presentation on stage, film or television.

7. Comparing art forms: discussing how theatre is like TV, dance, music, film, art, etc.; mixing 'em up.

8. Social impact of theatre and the media: discovering what difference it makes; how to be a good audience member; the conventions of different performance media; what is "good" art?

9. Artistic discipline: staying positive and creative; personalizing one's work; creative ownership; respecting oneself and the work and property of others.

Grading for Theatre Arts I

Student participation during class is the primary ingredient for success in this course. Although there will be a variety of assignments, some of which involve memorization, study, or bringing in items from home, a positive attitude, a ready imagination and a willingness to work cooperatively with others are the keys to success. Students will receive a daily grade for class work, and additional points may be earned for written, project, and performance assignments.

Notice: Homework assignments are available from our website: yourhs.blackboard.com
Address questions to YOUR THEATRE TEACHER: (school phone and email included here)

. . . . ✂ . . . .
(Please detach this section and return promptly to instructor)

☐ My child has filled out the info survey on www.yourhsdrama.org
☐ I have done the volunteer survey.
☐ I give permission for my child's image/voice to be used on drama website or publicity materials.
☐ I have read and understand the Theatre Arts I course standards and grading criteria.
☐ I will ☐ won't attend the drama parent meeting on Thurs., Sept. 20th at 7:00 pm in the theater.

Student's name _____   Period _____

Parent Signature _____

Theatre Arts II Syllabus

(teacher's name)
(phone number)
(email address)

Welcome! This should be a year of substantial growth in your knowledge and your skills as an actor. You will mostly be working in a rehearsal context on scripts which represent a broad range of theatrical styles from throughout the history of English language theatre. Girls may have to play male roles, but this helps guarantee that everyone will play a lead at some point (and in the meantime, let's hope someone will write more plays for women). Take heart: for hundreds of years, all actors were men. Your efforts represent "getting even," perhaps. Basically, each month we'll prepare 20-40 minutes of a play to present (sometimes to English classes or others) of the following types: comedy, drama, Shakespearean & musical.

Play Evaluations

Play evaluations are a major part of your individual work (other than line memorization). Once a month, you're required to hand in an evaluation according to the six-point outline I will give you, which is based on a play you've read (one you've not read before). These can be done in a single well-worded page (if you write small), but are hard to do quickly. Turn in a complete evaluation on time and you'll do well. Fail to turn these in, and you may fail entirely.

Homework

Homework includes memorizing lines (and various forms of proving it), those pesky play evaluations, some other written work, and bringing in stuff as necessary for your scenes, etc.

You'll find that the members of this class become a unit, and you will get to know everyone very well. Extra credit is earned for participation in the extra curricular plays, and it is expected that you will all contribute to the cast or crew at some point (many points). Enjoy yourself! Special privileges start to accrue in this class. We may well mount a production of a Shakespeare play (one act) which we will take into DC to perform at the Folger Student Shakespeare Festival. We have done exceptionally well at the festival in the past and, despite your relative inexperience, I am confident we will impress the judges again this year. Please note: the Shakespeare production will involve after-school rehearsal which is required class time.

Since a month's work culminates in a single class performance, often in front of an invited audience, it is not possible to make up the work even if you have an excused absence the day of the performance. "The show must go on!"...and so must you: everyone else's performance depends on yours, and vice versa. Do *not* schedule appointments on a performance day. Even if you are deathly ill, we deserve the chance to have a few minutes (hours, hopefully) to find a substitute, a new costume, run through blocking, etc. CALL! Anyone missing a performance without advance notice (school phone) will automatically, irrevocably fail the assignment.

Field Trips

We also plan on going to the theatre in Washington and meeting the cast for discussion afterward. There is a charge for this, so it is not required, but the series is fabulous, and not only of great value, but at great discount, too ($TBA for 4 plays). I hope you'll be able to attend. Details soon!

SO...rehearsals, styles, eras, plays, projects. This is a very busy class with never quite enough time, but it is a great one where all that stuff from last year starts to fit together and even makes useful sense. Be sure you have with you each day in class: something to write with, something to write on and something secure to keep it all in. There will be the occasional lecture, handout, and test.

Theatre Arts II Standards of Learning

The Theatre Arts Program of Studies identifies nine areas of study on which students will focus. Theatre Arts II students gain familiarity with each of these areas and will participate in hands-on activities to develop appropriate skills and knowledge.

1. Scriptwriting: investigate dramatic literature of other types and cultures; modify scene/ presentation elements.
2. Acting: analyze characters and motivation; perform scenes from different genres; develop dynamic range; investigate various acting/performing techniques.
3. Designing: incorporate basic technical elements into production work.
4. Directing: develop multiple interpretations for scenes; communicate directorial choices.
5. Researching: discover cultural, historical and symbolic clues in texts; employ variety of sources; analyze career issues.

6. Critiquing: apply constructive criticism to performance work; analyze conflicts within their contexts; recognize point-of-view and its impact; increase familiarity with scope of dramatic literature.

7. Comparing art forms: incorporate music, art, dance into theatre; contrast various art forms.

8. Social impact of theatre and the media: compare theatre/film/video/electronic media and their impact; discover the roots of American theatre; discuss "community standards;" compare cultures.

9. Artistic Discipline: demonstrate ownership of and enthusiasm for production work; demonstrate artistic risk taking; be attentive and responsive to constructive criticism.

Grading for Theatre Arts II

Student participation during class is a primary ingredient for success in this course. There will be a variety of assignments, some of which involve memorization, study, research and writing. Since "ensemble" collaboration is the essence of the course work, commitment to group goals and deadlines is critical not only to the student's success but that of their classmates.

The Folger Shakespeare project will involve out of class time (collaborative homework, as it were). Students will receive a daily grade for class participation, and additional points will be earned for written, project and performance assignments. No credit for show-day absence without warning.

Notice: Homework assignments are on Blackboard.

Also check our theatre website: www.yourhsdrama.org. UPDATE INFO ON WEBSITE SURVEY TODAY!

. . . . ✂ . . . .

(Please detach this section and return promptly to instructor)

☐ I have read and understand the Theatre Arts II course standards and grading criteria.

☐ I give permission for my image/voice to be used on drama website or publicity materials.

☐ I will ☐ won't attend the drama parent meeting at 7:00 pm on Thurs., Sept. 13th

☐ The website data survey has been updated.

Student's name _____ period _____

Parent Signature _____

Booster meeting Tuesday, September 13th at 7:00 in Theatre includes the required PARENT walk-thru for students who want to work tech.

IB Theatre Syllabus & Grading

Curriculum

IB Theatre involves study in these areas of theatre arts:

THEATRE IN CONTEXT Studies from an international perspective of selected texts and traditions. Research, discovery, critique.

THEATRE PROCESSES Ensemble work; performance techniques; acting techniques and characterization. Exploration.

PRESENTING THEATRE A practical study of the principles and practices of theatre production. Application, integration.

INDEPENDENT PROJECT Practical exploration and engagement in a theatre project of the student's choosing.

IB Assessment

The IB Assessment occurs during March of the final year of the course (usually two years). It involves four tasks:

1. Solo theatre piece (HL only) (External assessment) Research a theorist, identify an aspect of their theory, and prepare/present a 4-8 minute solo piece based on that aspect.
2. Director's notebook (External assessment) Select a published play and develop ideas for how it could be staged.
3. Research presentation (External assessment) Plan/deliver a 15 min. presentation to peers that demonstrates research into a convention from a theatre tradition not previously studied.
4. Collaborative project (Internal assessment) Create/present a 13-15 min. original piece for a specified target audience, from a starting point of their choice.

Grading for IB Theatre

Students will receive course credit for daily class participation, responses to reading assignments, collection of materials for possible portfolio inclusion, participation in outside theatre activities, performances and other special projects undertaken.

Notice: Homework assignments are on Blackboard. Also check www.yourhsdrama.org for relevant theatre information, including link to the official IB Theatre Guide (new).

READ THIS! PLEASE NOTE: Parents' Booster Meeting, Thursday, Sept. 13th at 7:00 pm in the YOURHS Theatre. Includes required parent walkthrough for students interested in tech work.

. . . . ✂ . . . .

(Please detach this section and return promptly to instructor)

☐ I have read and understand the IB Theatre course standards and grading criteria.
☐ I give ☐ do not give permission for my child's image/voice to be used for website/publicity purposes.
☐ I give ☐ do not give permission for participation in occasional events out of class or off site without direct faculty supervision. I understand that non-required events suggested to IB students are not XXPS responsibility.
☐ I will ☐ won't attend the Booster meeting/tech walkthrough on Sept.13th
My child has provided the data requested in the survey on www.yourhsdrama.org

Student's name _____ period _____

Signature _____

Parent Signature _____

Appendix J
Suggested Materials

Here is a small list of developmentally appropriate books for creative dramatics presentations for elementary school, and some valuable resources for middle school and high school as well.

Kindergarten

- *Draw Me A Star* by Eric Carle (Penguin Putnam Books for Young Readers ©1992)
- *The Very Hungry Caterpillar* by Eric Carle (Penguin Putnam Books for Young Readers ©1994)

1st Grade

- *Where The Wild Things Are* by Maurice Sendak (Harper Collins ©1963)

2nd Grade

- *Bringing The Rain To Kapiti Plain* by Verna Aardema (Puffin Books ©1992)

3rd Grade

- *The Great Kapok Tree* by Lynn Cherry (Voyager Books ©1990)

4th Grade

- *Things Can Always Be Worse!* by Lois Kipnis (Dramatic Publishing Company),

5th Grade

- *The Warrior and the Wiseman* by David Wiesniewski (Harper Collins ©1989)

6th Grade

- Oral interpretation of poetry in groups, with creative movement and a theme
- Check out *Plays* Magazine for scripts identified by appropriate age group, cast size, theme, etc.

Middle School

- Junior Musicals, handled mostly by MTI (Music Theatre International) or School Editions
- *The Wizard of Oz*
- *Peter Pan*
- *The Diary of Anne Frank*
- *Willy Wonka and the Chocolate Factory*

High School

- Check out the most popular plays and musicals of the past year on SchoolTheatre.org.
- Check out the plays presented for Cappies consideration at Cappies.com.
- *Let's Put on a Musical* by Peter Filichia (Back Stage Books,©2007) is an oversimplified title for a must-have book; it profiles dozens and dozens of musicals, from plot to characters to assets and liabilities of each show.
- *500 Plays* edited by Theodore Shank (Macmillan Publishing ©1989) profiles tons of straight plays, plot plus production notes. Dated but very valuable.
- *The Backstage Handbook* by Paul Carter and George Chiang (Broadway Press ©1994. A very visual compendium of all things technical, from the size of a screw to types of lights to angles of ramps. A must-have for tech work!

- *Backstage Forms* by Paul Carter (Broadway Press ©1995). Forms/checklists for copying to organize every area of technical production.
- *Stage Production Handbook* by Kathryn Michelle Busti (Theatre Things ©1992). Forms/checklists for copying for each stage crew of what to do when, plus forms to assist.

Appendix K

Publishers of Musicals and Plays

Here is a list of websites for finding playscripts and whom to contact for the rights to perform the plays. There are many other smaller publishers out there, but we've included the "big guys" to get you started.

ORGANIZATIONS, SERVICES AND COLLECTIONS

FINDAPLAY.COM (findaplay.com) Who publishes what? Although not perfect or totally complete, you submit a title or author and this website tell you the publishing house.

THE GUIDE TO MUSICAL THEATRE (guidetomusicaltheatre.com) On this site you can find an alphabetical listing of musicals, matched to their U.S. and U.K. publishers.

THE OXFORDSHIRE DRAMA NETWORK (oxfordshiredramanetwork.org) A directory of British play publishers large and small.

STAGEPLAYS.COM (stageplays.com) A wide variety of American and British plays, musicals and books. Includes "scriptfinder" of gender and cast size filters.

PUBLISHERS OF PLAYS AND MUSICALS

BROADWAY PLAY PUBLISHING, INC. (broadwayplaypubl.com) Specializes in full-length, contemporary, American plays, dramas and comedies set mostly in the 19th century, dramatic adaptations of classic plays and literature, and one-acts. Digital archive available.

BROOKLYN PUBLISHERS (brookpub.com) Provides high school play scripts, middle school and youth theatre plays.

DRAMATIC PUBLISHING CO. (dramaticpublishing.com) A top resource for school friendly plays. Not the most complex or difficult material, but easy to produce.

DRAMATISTS PLAY SERVICE (dramatists.com) If Samuel French doesn't have it, these guys do.

HEARTLAND PLAYS (heartlandplays.com) Online service providing plays for professional, community, university, high school, children's theatre or other educational or producing organizations.

ELDRIDGE PLAYS (histage.com) Offers hundreds of full-length plays, one-acts, melodramas, holiday and religious plays, children's theatre plays and musicals of all kinds.

HEUER PLAYS (hitplays.com) Serves the educational and community theatre markets with plays which are "entertaining and yet thought provoking, family appropriate and yet edgy, and which provide a standardized formula for technical production with flexibility for directors desiring a greater challenge."

MUSIC THEATRE INTERNATIONAL (mtishows.com) One of the big guys for musicals. Easy to work with. RehearScore and other support materials. MTI Junior musicals are simplified, packaged materials for middle schoolers for many shows.

MYSTERIES BY MOUSHEY (mysteriesbymoushey.com) Audience participation mysteries, varied settings and durations. Easy to produce. Good for fund raisers.

PLAYS MAGAZINE (playsmagazine.com) *Plays* magazine, inexpensive source for ready-to-roll scripts plus permission. Great for elementary level, classic tales dramatized, etc.

PIONEER DRAMA (pioneerdrama.com) Pioneer is a leading play publisher for schools and community and children's theatres.

PLAYSCRIPTS (playscripts.com) Lots of good high school material in this catalogue. You can read 90% online before you buy.

PREMIERE MUSICALS GUILD (tebreitenbach.com/musicals/) Premiere publishes new musicals to school and community theatre groups at reasonable prices.

RODGERS AND HAMMERSTEIN MUSIC THEATRE LIBRARY (rnh.com) All the Rodgers and Hammerstein classic musicals and many many more.

SAMUEL FRENCH, INC. (samuelfrench.com) This company owns more professional straight plays than anyone on the planet (and a few musicals, too).

STAGESCRIPTS, LTD. (shop.stagescripts.com) This British company's works vary from family-friendly comedy and pantos to some distinctly edgy contemporary drama, and top quality, but mostly unknown musicals.

TAMS-WITMARK (tamswitmark.com) Publisher of many many classic musicals. Only sends "sides."

THEATRICAL RIGHTS WORLDWIDE (trw.com) New kids on the block, with a limited number of top musicals. Fast service and lots of cutting edge support materials.

Appendix L

Auditioning Using the ADDIE System

A.D.D.I.E. is a system that helps you organize your work and accomplishments. It can be applied to almost any task, but it's especially useful for auditions and technical theater work.

Analyze — Analyze what you already have at hand and what you need to get done.

Design — Design/decide what you envision. The more detail, the better.

Develop — Develop your plan of action to reach that vision, and keep experimenting until you think you're there (or out of time).

Implement — Implement your plan. Get it up and running.

Evaluate — Evaluate what you've accomplished and what you've learned (positive and negative) from the process and the product you created.

Auditioning Using the ADDIE System

A = Analyze

What do you need?
- Know the rules of the venue/show: e.g., what time; location; room #; how long: how many; what type; resume/headshot required; appointment required; contact info.
- Find out the requirements of the show: e.g., accent; style; special skills; vocal range.
- Know what is the show about! What characters are a good match with what you have to offer?

What do you have?
- Know thyself: type; age-range; energy; vocal range; dance training; etc.

D = Design
- Select a monologue (or two) of the same type as the show being auditioned.
- Select one which shows *you* off to best advantage, with the fewest obstacles.
- Stay within your own age range, with no special accents unless required in the play.
- Determine its purpose in the play, and to whom it will be addressed.
- What is *your* interpretation of this audition piece? What is your character's objective during this piece?

D = Develop
- Divide the piece into beats; articulate the objective or tactic for each beat.
- Experiment with different beats/tactics. Be sure to delineate a distinct physical (and perhaps vocal) change to mark the change of each beat.
- Try different levels (lying down, sitting, standing, standing on something).
- Don't settle for your first choice, but don't reject it either.
- Clarify when the piece builds, rises and falls, especially its climax.
- Get so totally off-book that you don't even have to think about the words.
- Pay attention to where your eyes will be focused throughout the piece.
- Presume you may use a chair and perhaps one prop. Use them well.
- Play with intensity, a driving need to reach your objective.
- Also rehearse your ride-in/slate and your ride-out.
- Respect the time limits lest you lose your best moments.

I = Implement

- Dress for success (just shy of a costume).
- Arrive so early that even the unexpected can't make you late.
- Recognize that every moment from your arrival is part of your audition.
- Be polite; be supportive of others; be generous.
- Be prepared with your headshot/resume. What other skills can you offer?
- Do warm up before your audition, but don't distract others.
- Briskly and brightly go to your place to slate. Say your name slowly and clearly!
- Never apologize! Don't complain; don't explain. Just do your best!
- Show them how much you love performing, especially a featured scene like this!
- Go full tilt!
- If asked to make changes, this is good. Do so promptly and definitively.
- Ride-out should include a shift of mood and a heart-felt *thank you* to them.
- Avoid a post-audition "scene" as you depart.

E = Evaluate

- Be objective about how it went. A good impression lasts a long time.
- Take suggestions to heart, but use your own judgment.
- If an audition piece continues to be unsuccessful at landing you a role, replace it.

Appendix M
Audition Card

You can duplicate and distribute this audition card (or download it as a Microsoft Word document from our website, EducationalStages.com) to collect information about your auditioners, as well as their self-assessment and conflicts.

AUDITION CARD

Fill out this card now, and hand it to the stage manager as soon as possible. Write neatly.

NAME	GRADE	STUDENT ID #	HEIGHT	WEIGHT
EMAIL		PHONE		
PREVIOUS EXPERIENCE				
SPECIAL SKILLS (MUSICAL INSTRUMENTS, JUGGLING, ETC.)				

CHECK ALL THAT APPLY:

- ☐ I WANT A CERTAIN ROLE _____
- ☐ I CLOSELY MATCH A CERTAIN ROLE _____
- ☐ I DON'T REALLY KNOW THIS PLAY YET
- ☐ I WILL ☐ WILL NOT UNDERSTUDY
- ☐ I WILL ☐ WILL NOT BE IN THE ENSEMBLE

SKILL LEVEL SELF-EVALUATION

	Can solo	Good in a group	Not my strength
ACTING	☐	☐	☐
DANCING	☐	☐	☐
SINGING	☐	☐	☐

CONFLICTS

On the back of this card, list any time day or night you're unavailable for rehearsal. Include what the conflict is, when it is, how long it lasts, and whether or not it is flexible.

AUDITION CARD

Fill out this card now, and hand it to the stage manager as soon as possible. Write neatly.

NAME	GRADE	STUDENT ID #	HEIGHT	WEIGHT
EMAIL		PHONE		
PREVIOUS EXPERIENCE				
SPECIAL SKILLS (MUSICAL INSTRUMENTS, JUGGLING, ETC.)				

CHECK ALL THAT APPLY:

- ☐ I WANT A CERTAIN ROLE _____
- ☐ I CLOSELY MATCH A CERTAIN ROLE _____
- ☐ I DON'T REALLY KNOW THIS PLAY YET
- ☐ I WILL ☐ WILL NOT UNDERSTUDY
- ☐ I WILL ☐ WILL NOT BE IN THE ENSEMBLE

SKILL LEVEL SELF-EVALUATION

	Can solo	Good in a group	Not my strength
ACTING	☐	☐	☐
DANCING	☐	☐	☐
SINGING	☐	☐	☐

CONFLICTS

On the back of this card, list any time day or night you're unavailable for rehearsal. Include what the conflict is, when it is, how long it lasts, and whether or not it is flexible.

Appendix N

Production Contract

The production contract prevents misunderstandings and sets a professional tone from the very start by spelling out to both students and parents the expectations and obligations involved with a production.

While it may be true that parents will sign anything (as their kid rushes out the door), it will nonetheless give you a leg to stand on when conflicts arise or cast members decide to drop out after your casting is finished.

PRODUCTION CONTRACT

I, _____, agree to participate in the YOUR HS production of
_____ and with the following understandings.

1. This production will take a lot of time, including rehearsals occurring after school, occasional evenings, and occasional weekends; several performances; and set strike following the final performance.

   - If my grades drop, my parents may pull me from the production. After Tech Day, parents agree to a conference with the director(s) prior to doing so.

   - I agree to attend all rehearsals/work sessions for which I am scheduled. There is a rehearsal calendar on YOURHSWEBSITE. If unsure, I will show up and find out. Updates may be posted on the callboard outside the drama room, and/or outside the chorus room.

   - Rehearsals are never canceled by rumor. Unless a cancellation is officially posted, I will attend all rehearsals as scheduled..

2. Prompt attendance at every scheduled rehearsal is crucial to a successful production.

   - If I must be tardy, absent or leave early, I will email DRAMADEPTemail and/or call (classroom phone) ahead of time and update my situation.

   - I understand that even pre-planned, inevitable or excused absences never improve the production and that my role may be reassigned for the benefit of the production, regardless of the reason(s) I missed rehearsal, at the discretion of the director(s), at any time.

3. I am serious about my commitment to the success of this production.

   - I will honor my prior commitments: if I have rehearsal, I will NOT accept "a better offer" that would keep me from rehearsal. If a conflict arises, I will request release from that day's rehearsal from the Director(s)—not the stage management—and abide by their decision.

   - My current commitments are listed on page 2. Anything else comes second, as indicated above.

   - I agree to sell or purchase at least five tickets (or reservations by season pass holders) to this production during the first two weeks of rehearsal. Tickets are on sale through WEBSITE and from order forms made available to the company.

- • I may also forfeit my role for failing to display sufficient artistic discipline (learning lines, cooperating with cast/crew, etc.).

4. I will abide by all Student Rights and Responsibilities as outlined by YOUR SCHOOL DISTRICT/YOUR SCHOOL.

5. I understand that my behavior reflects on the drama/music departments as a whole.

6. I will assure that a current emergency care card is on file in the drama room.

7. I give permission for my likeness to be used in publicity materials connected to this show.

8. I have submitted my Dramakid Survey for the current school year on YOURHSWEBSITE.org.

Parents:

1. I have submitted our volunteer questionnaire (for parents) for the current school year on YOURHSWEBSITE.org.

2. I understand there is is a parent meeting scheduled on TBD in room 522 to learn more about responsibilities and expectations for cast, crew, and parents.

3. I understand that Tech Day rehearsals (Election weekend) are mandatory: Nov 1-3

I HAVE READ AND AGREE TO THE CONTRACT ABOVE:

Parent name: _____

Parent signature: _____

Email address: _____

Phone # _____

Student name: _____

Student signature: _____

Email address: _____

Phone # _____

Conflicts

Please list all conflicts here: piano lessons, weddings, whatever routine or special events already committed to, now till set strike. Be sure to include any chorus events!

Conflict	Date	Start/End Time	Flexible?	Comments

Appendix O

Production Packet

A full production packet will provide your students and their parents with a thorough overview plus details about your show. From show concept to rehearsal dates to special days— add in whatever you need (e.g., costume requirements, prop needs list, etc.), and track who has and has not received all this information. Banish "I didn't know" forever!

20XX-20XY: A Season of Transformation

YOURHS THEATRE in association with YOURHS Drama Boosters presents:

PRIDE AND PREJUDICE

by Jane Kendall, from Jane Austen's novel

Stage Manager: Joe Schmo
Technical Director: Jane Schmo

MANY THANKS TO ALL WHO AUDITIONED AND WEATHERED THE LONG HOURS OF CALL BACKS!

Cast

ROLE	ACTOR	UNDERSTUDY
Mr. Bennet		
Mrs. Bennet		
Jane Bennet		
Elizabeth Bennet		
Mary Bennet		
Catherine Bennet		
Lydia Bennet		
Mr. Collins		
Mr. Bingley		
Miss Bingley		
Mr. Darcy		
Lady Catherine		
Lady Lucas		
Charlotte Lucas		
Mr. Wickham		
Hill		

Ladies & Gentlemen at the Netherfield Dance

YOUR HS THEATRE PRIDE & PREJUDICE
by Jane Kendall, from Jane Austen's novel

AUDITION AGREEMENT

AUDITIONS: TUES. 2/21 2:30-5 p.m. WED. 2/22 2:30-3:30 p.m. ROOM 175
CALLBACKS: THURS. 2/23 2:30 p.m. UNTIL...
PERFORMANCES: April 19, 20 & 21, 2012 7:30 p.m. Tickets: $10

Produced by special arrangement with THE DRAMATIC PUBLISHING COMPANY of Woodstock, Illinois.

Parental Permission

Pride & Prejudice is the YOURHS Theatre spring mainstage production that will be critiqued for Cappies consideration for nominations and awards that are presented at the John F. Kennedy Center in June. While it is always our goal to offer our very best efforts in creating exceptional educational theatre productions, Cappies inspire us to think in detail on every level of production. Our Cappies show, in turn, motivates us to raise the bar on historical period research, acting methods, costume design, set design, lighting design and properties and publicity management. We intend to collaborate with the YOURHS art department, as well as offer an opportunity for students in the YOURHS music department, to join us in the world of 1800 Regency/Empire England, in order to create the elegant world of Jane Austen.

Our expectations for all students involved with this production are very high. Dedication and commitment to excellence and preparation are at the forefront of our usual production process, and Cappies add another aspect to YOURHS Theatre: to display preparation and student leadership. Students who are cast in the show, and those who are not cast but wish to be part of this creative process are needed to dedicate the time and effort necessary to create displays of our process, to draw the Cappies' attention to our work. While student leaders for stage management, set construction and technical design will come from tech theatre and advanced theatre classes, contributing artists for every aspect of this show are vitally important. Theatre is "the collaborative art," and we hope that many students and parents are ready to collaborate in order to deliver a truly exceptional production to our community, including the Cappies critics. After the success of *Beauty and the Beast* last December, expectations are very high. We invite you to be part of this student-designed process, in which we bring forward our best selves to work together and create the beauty that is theatre.

Please read the attached code of ethics for YOURHS Theatre. If you have already filed one of these for a previous production or theatre class, please review it with your student. The same applies to the school system notice specifying that students must be in school in order to attend rehearsals or performances, and keep academic standards a priority while balancing the work of theatre. Communication is a wonderful thing, and early notice to the stage manager concerning absences is a necessary consideration to others. ***Absence without excuse or communication will result in removal from the cast and/or crew, at the director's discretion.*** Cast or crew leadership positions are expected to also notify an understudy or stand-in for the rehearsal they will miss, so that blocking can move forward. It is also the responsibility of the absent student to gather missed blocking/information prior to arrival at the next rehearsal, so that valuable time is not wasted.

All YOURHS parents and committed students are invited to assist our student designers in building the set, costumes, props and painting. Cappies consideration requires as many aspects as possible to be student led and designed if we are to be eligible in every performance and technical category. Adult assistance is still allowed, but under the direction of the student designers, and students must build and create as much as possible. Direction of this production still falls to our theatre director, whose artistic vision will be conveyed in a collaborative manner to the students throughout the process. Days that are marked as "tech days" are open for parents to join us in set, costume and props construction. Transportation for all rehearsals and tech days is the responsibility of each student and parents/guardians.

If you understand and agree to your student auditioning for *Pride and Prejudice*, please sign below:

Parent/Guardian Signature _____ Date _____

Student Signature _____ Date _____

YOURHS THEATRE PRIDE & PREJUDICE
by Jane Kendall, from Jane Austen's novel

REHEARSAL SCHEDULE

WEEK 1: 2:30-5 p.m. except Wed. 2:30-3:30 p.m.

Mon. 2/27/2012	FULL CAST; FULL READ THROUGH, SCRIPT DISTRIBUTION
Tues. 2/28	pp. 11-18; Bennet Family + Hill
Wed. 2/29	pp. 18-25; Bennet Family + Hill + Charlotte & Lady Lucas
Thurs. 3/1	RUN pp. 11-25
FRIDAY 3/2	NO REHEARSAL—THEATRE DEPT. TRIP TO NYC!

WEEK 2: 2:30-5 p.m. except Wed. 2:30-3:30 p.m.

Mon. 3/5	pp. 25-32; Bennet Family, Bingley, Miss Bingley, Darcy, Hill
Tues. 3/6	pp. 32-37; Bennet Family, Wickham, Hill,+ Bingleys, Darcy at start
Wed. 3/7	pp. 37-42; Mr. & Mrs. Bennet, Elizabeth & Jane, Mr. Collins, Hill
Thurs. 3/8	RUN ACT I, pp. 11-42 Off-book
Fri. 3/9-Mon. 3/12	NO REHEARSAL; Mrs. Dillard in California

WEEK 3: 2:30-5:30 p.m. except Wed. 2:30-3:30 p.m.

Tues. 3/13	DANCE ENSEMBLE FOR THE BALL AT NETHERFIELD
Wed. 3/14	DANCE ENSEMBLE FOR THE BALL AT NETHERFIELD
Thurs. 3/15	pp.43-56; Full Cast, minus Lady Catherine
Fri. 3/16	pp. 56-61; Mrs. Bennet, Lizzy, Mr. Collins, Jane 2:30-4 p.m. RUN THRU Act II, Scene 1 (pp. 42-61) 4-5:30 p.m. Off-Book
Sat. 3/17	TECH: 9 a.m.–2 p.m.

WEEK 4: 2:30-5:30 p.m. except Wed.-NO REHEARSAL

Mon. 3/19	pp.62-71; Bennet Family, Charlotte, Mr. Collins, Hill
Tues. 3/20	pp. 72-75; Lizzy, Darcy, Hill (proposal; come memorized) 2:30-4 p.m. RUN THRU Act II, Scene 2 (pp. 62-75) 4-5:30 p.m. Off-Book
Wed. 3/21	NO REHEARSAL—CHILDREN'S THEATRE TECH/DRESS
Thurs. 3/22	pp.76-84; Bennet Family, except Lydia, Lady Lucas, Hill
Fri. 3/23	pp. 84-87; Bennet Family, except Lydia, Hill, Darcy CHILDREN'S THEATRE! 7:30 p.m. Come and support!
Sat. 3/24	CHILDREN'S THEATRE! 10 a.m. Come and support! TECH: 12-6 p.m.

WEEK 5: 2:30-5:30 p.m. except Wed.; TECH AS POSSIBLE

Mon. 3/26	pp. 88-97; Bennet Family, Wickham, Hill
Tues. 3/27	pp. 97-107; FULL CAST
Wed. 3/28	RUN THRU ACT III; FULL CAST Off-Book
Thurs. 3/29	FULL RUN THRU WITH FULL CAST Off-Book
Fri. 3/30	FULL RUN THRU WITH FULL CAST Off-Book
Sat. 3/31	TECH: 9 a.m.-2 p.m.—HAPPY SPRING BREAK!

WEEK 6: 2:30-6 p.m. except Wed.; TECH AS POSSIBLE

Tues. 4/10	FULL RUN THRU with preliminary costumes & props onstage
Wed. 4/11	NO REHEARSAL
Thurs. 4/12	MUSIC TRIP; Rehearse scenes and do Tech as possible
Fri. 4/13	MUSIC TRIP; Rehearse scenes and do Tech as possible
Sat. 4/14	TECH: 1-6 p.m. (ACTs in the morning)

WEEK 7: PRODUCTION WEEK!

Mon. 4/16	DRESS REHEARSAL #1 2:30-6 p.m.(Prep+Run); 6-8 p.m. Dinner+Notes TECH finishing if necessary after notes.
Tues. 4/17	DRESS REHEARSAL #2 2:30-6 p.m.(Prep+Run); 6-8 p.m. Dinner+Notes TECH finishing if necessary after notes.
Wed. 4/18	NO REHEARSAL IF ALL IS WELL; SAVE THE DATE, JUST IN CASE TECH FINISHING TOUCHES!
Thurs. 4/19	OPENING NIGHT! ACTOR CALL: 5 p.m. TECH CALL: 6 p.m.
Fri. 4/20	PERFORMANCE! ACTOR CALL: 5 p.m. TECH CALL: 6 p.m.
Sat. 4/21	Cappies PERFORMANCE! ACTOR CALL: 5 p.m. TECH CALL: 6 p.m. Cappies SET-UP IN CAFETERIA: 4 p.m. (YOURHS Critics expected to help.)

MONDAY, APRIL 23RD: STRIKE THE SET! ALL CAST & CREW REQUIRED TO HELP IN ORDER TO GET THESPIAN POINTS + IT'S THE RIGHT THING TO DO!!!

Appendix P

Crew Chief Explanations and Expectations

This is great introductory information for middle school, class, or any newbie coming into your theatre program. It's a chart that lists each crew, the skills each crew will need, the responsibilities of each crew, and an overview of what each crew's time commitment/schedule will look like. It should prove very useful to post when soliciting new crew chiefs for a show.

Crew Chief Explanations and Expectations

Tech Weekend is 2/1–2/2
Pre-tech Workdays are 1/25–1/28
Show Dates: 2/14–2/16
Strike: 2/16

CREW	SKILLS NEEDED	RESPONSIBILITIES	SCHEDULE
Stage Management	Hyper responsible, patience, leadership, commitment, Must be in HS	Everything! Planning/ administrative. Company management.	Before auditions until cast party
Run Crew	Self-control, fast, responsible, quiet, physically strong. Total commitment to final 2 weeks of rehearsals and shows	Moving set/scenery. Wear all black. Move quickly/quietly.	2/1 until strike. Same rehearsals as cast. Tech Weekend
Props	Creativity, "do-er," resourceful, artistic/organized, imaginative, follows directions	Making, painting, buying, organizing, borrowing, maintaining, fixing all objects handled by actors	Meetings January—end of show. Tech Weekend
Costumes	Follows directions, sewing, reliable & patient, creative eye, ironing/fabric work	Making, finding, borrowing, fixing, maintaining all costumes. Helping with quick changes & fixes.	Meetings in Dec & Jan. Tech Weekend until strike. BIG commitment
Set Construction and Deco	Experience with power tools, responsible, calm, physically strong, follows directions, quiet, creative, works quickly	Building the set/scenery and some props—decorating the stage	Pre-Tech & Tech Weekends until show Strike

Paint Crew	Follows directions, can paint, works well with others	Painting all set, props, road signs, stage, and CLEANING up paint	Meetings Jan. Tech Weekend and other meetings as needed
Publicity	Great at selling, outgoing, creative, responsible, passionate	Getting the word out, setting up posters, road signs, emails, press releases, clips for school TV show	Meetings begin in Jan
Programs	Organized, good at editing & formatting, expert at MS Publisher	Collecting ads, bios, and information for program, editing, and making all programs	Meetings begin in Jan
Lighting	Follows directions, safe, quiet, interested in stage lighting	Helping hang/aim and fix all lighting instruments, working the light board & spot	Meetings Jan, Pre-Tech Weekend until strike
Sound	Follows directions, safe, quiet, resourceful with computer sound or iPod/iPad/other device	Sound effects, microphones, fixes to equipment, running sound cues	Meetings Jan, Pre-Tech Weekend until strike
Make-up	Artistic/creative, can take direction well, attentive to details	Design and do the hair/make-up/wigs/face painting for the actors	Tech Weekend until strike—all rehearsals, some meetings beforehand
House	Reliable, leader, outgoing, helpful	Hand out programs, take tickets, sell concessions, clean up	Meetings Feb, All shows & strike

**Opportunities to help out without having to commit—just check the VOLUNTEER BOARD outside D106.

**Crew members selected based on application, experience, conflicts, and other criteria.

APPLICATIONS DUE FRIDAY, DECEMBER 13th to D106.

Appendix Q

Exercise in Leadership

Here is a handout to use during an early crew chief meeting. Develop more materials from the dossier in chapter four, and make leadership a consciously developed skill.

Exercise in Leadership

Name: _____   Job: _____

This exercise is about priorities. Observe the priorities listed below. In the first empty column, rank them in the order that you exhibit them in your own life. In the second empty column, rank them in the order in which you would hope to see them in an ideal leader.

Personality Trait	You	Leader
Being encouraging		
Being punctual		
Being organized		
Being patient		
Being safety-conscious		
Being popular		
Being talented		
Being capable		
Being clear		
Being experienced		
Being industrious		
Being a "big picture" person		
Being thrifty		
Being detail-oriented		
Having high standards		
Relaxed, fun to work with		
Being _____		
Being _____		

Appendix R

Crew Chief Sign-Up Instructions and List

Here is a list of likely crew chief positions you may want to fill with student leaders. Note that there are two options—either just sign up, or submit an interest statement. So, be sure to select the option that suits your preference, and minimize the instructions you post with your list. As always, the easiest way to save time and modify is by downloading the version on EducationalStages.com

Crew Chief Sign-Up List

Students interested in tech leadership positions: Please sign up here if you would like to be a crew chief on this production. Crew members should sign up during the week of auditions. This list is NOT "first come, first served." At the first staff meeting on (date) we will determine what staffing would make for the best production. Or...

Write a "passion statement"—a paragraph briefly outlining why you are interested in the position and what you bring to contribute to the success of this production. Cite resume items, such as previous show experience, research, creative insight and ability. Attach a resume if possible.

Turn in your passion statement to the theatre director by (date). All theatre students may apply, but tech theatre students will have preference. (This opportunity will be posted on the callboard, on BlackBoard, and discussed in theatre classes.)

AD	TD
PM	DRAMATURGE
SM	ASM
LIGHTING	SOUND
SET DESIGN	CONSTRUCTION
DECORATION	PAINTING
PROPS	COSTUMES
HAIR	MAKEUP
SPECIAL EFFECTS	PUBLICITY
VIDEO	PROGRAM
TICKETS	HOUSE MANAGEMENT

Appendix S
Crew Chief Task Calendar

This template will take a lot of modifying to match your own needs, but look how helpful it will be to clarify just when each job has to have progressed, and by how much! And once you've modified it for your own school, only the dates need changing for future productions. Give and post a copy of these targets to your crews and parent helpers, and everyone will know what it means to stay on track.

Glossary of Abbreviations/Local Terms

AGC Artistic Concepts Group, a local theatre supply house

CC crew chief

FCPS Fairfax County Public schools

GOOD SHOW GRAMS notes written by audience at intermission, delivered to cast/crew later

GMR *Good Morning Robinson*, a high school daily news television show

MIM *Mondays in the Middle*, a middle school weekly news television show

MS middle school

PO purchase order

ROPROCO nickname of local group producing the show prior to this one

RUN CREW BOX cube filled with supplies (spike tape, glo-tape, scissors, flashlights, etc.)

RUSSELL name of theatre to be used for this show

SS7 seventh grade "sub-school" location of 7th grade lockers in this large secondary school

MS CREW CHIEFS Task Calendar—*THE WIZ*

Stage Manager: Hannah email@whatever.com
Production Manager: Cody email@whatever.com
Design Assistant: Jamie email@whatever.com
Choreographer: Jessica email@whatever.com
Directors: Ms. Teacher email@whatever.edu
Ms. OtherTeacher email@whatever.edu

1. Get a script from the stage manager today—READ: Take notes! Ask questions! Highlight pertinent information!

2. Update your email info on Blackboard. Make sure Hannah has your ID to add to Blackboard WIZ TECH if you aren't connected yet.

3. CREW SELECTION: The spreadsheet "Crew Kids" will be shared with you via Google Docs, available on Blackboard. Highlight the box with your crew for each member (so we know if some students are on more than one crew). If you want to see the application, see Ms. Teach.

4. EMAIL YOUR CREW **ALL EMAILS MUST BE SENT TO MS Teacher/MS OtherTeacher BEFORE SENDING OUT TO YOUR CREW!** Basically, draft your email and send to email@whatever.edu and otherteacher@whatever.edu. We will send you a confirmation—forward this to your crew as is. Thanks! – Introduction and welcome. – First meeting date, time, location (as found on the Crew Calendar in Wiz Tech Blackboard) – EmergencyCareCard (ECC) attachment- must be turned in first meeting. Can't hold kids past buses without ECC. – Contract attachment – must be turned in first meeting. – Let them know payment ($15 cash or check to SchoolName) for T-shirts must be put into the stage manager's box in D106 with their NAME, CREW, and SIZE. These are due by 1/27. That way, it won't be your responsibility!

5. If you want a MEETING or WORK SESSION, you must email Ms. Teacher & Hannah the request. Ms. Teacher will confirm. Hannah will add to the Crew Calendar and send email to CCs. Other CCs need to work around this or piggy-back on the time.

6. If you want something POSTED on BLACKBOARD, email Ms. Teacher & Ms. OtherTeacher- we will forward to Hannah after approving it. Let her know if it goes to CAST Blackboard or TECH Blackboard.

7. Learn how to do a purchase order (PO). Learn where to get one. Our account # is 33801 00 00. Ms. Teacher must sign it before it goes to the finance office. NEVER PAY TAX. If you do, you will not be reimbursed.

8. Bios (CCs only) and complete, correctly-spelled crew list by Tech Day or not included in program or T-shirt.

9. We have 2 weeks and 3 weekends off for winter break. We have to use the time to schedule work sessions. Please get your conflicts to Hannah ASAP—let her know when you are NOT available. The directors want to work with specific CCs and Crews during the break. Additionally, we will be holding open rehearsals, which is a great time for a work session.

10. Parent Volunteers: the list is available on Tech Blackboard

Set Design/Construction

BY 12/20	• Map out the set dimensions with Ms. Teacher during RAISE • Inventory the types of platforms (lumber & choral) available
BY 1/17	• List of supplies, materials, lumber, to Ms. T for approval • PO to Finance • Arrange for parents (see Ms. Teacher for list) to help buy/deliver the lumber
1/27 or 1/28	• Secure parents (maybe 3–5 – see Ms. T for list) for pre-tech building (week of Jan 28)
BY 1/28	• Tape out plan onstage • Draw out (have Ms. Teacher) arches & decorative pieces
1/27 or 1/28	• Pick up all supplies/lumber/etc. and load in to ramp • Label ALL SUPPLIES RMS DRAMA very clearly & permanently! They are to be put back in D106 at strike. • Build set with parents Teacher Workdays & after-school
2/2–2/3	• Tech Days
2/15	• Opening Night
2/17	• Strike

Publicity

BY 12/20	• Map out the set dimensions with Ms. Teacher during Tutor Period • Inventory the types of platforms (lumber & choral) available
BY 1/6	• Make flyer/poster w info from publisher • Get approval • PO (where to get printed from?) and estimate due • Get info on how to send out to newspapers, MIM, GMR, LCD screens, lunches, schools • Order posters
BY 1/20	• Send flyer to Mrs. FinanceLady (FinanceLady@whatever.edu) • Get flyer approved by Student Activities • Post flyers (SS7, SS8, Main Office, D106, outside D106, Russell display cases, cafeteria, Blackbox, Drama Board) • PO for paint & rollers/bins/brushes—signed by Ms. Teacher and turned in to the Finance office • Confirm with Mr. HSGuy that RoProCo signs will be returned and white-washed by 1/25 (so we can paint evening 1/26 during show strike) • Email crew painting dates • T-Shirt design front & back to Ms. Teacher for approval. Email crew chiefs reminder
BY 1/24	• Pick up Home Depot road sign painting supplies • Make flyer into transparencies for road signs
1/27	• Collect T-shirt numbers/sizes from Ms. Teacher • Call/email Colin Chapman chapmancf@gmail.com or Stan Darke darke-graphics@aol.com for estimate (give him numbers & sizes). We will need t-shirts ready no later than Monday, Feb 5. Make PO- take to Finance. Send artwork.Road signs traced & painted • List of locations confirmed by Mr. HSGuy • Email or call parents for delivery by Tech Day (2/1). Ms. Teacher has list • Elementary school flyers made and distributed
BY 1/31	• Press release to Ms. Teacher for approval • Press releases to area papers • Preview email to Ms. Teacher for approval • Display case MS • Pick up t-shirts & distribute by end of rehearsal when ready
2/1-2/2	• Tech Days
BY 2/2	• Banner signs for MS overhang & Russell Theatre overhang

2/16	• Strike
	• Road sign retrieval/whitewash signs, clean up supplies, label in box, store in D106

Set Painting

BY 1/17	• Floor paint design
	• Set design paint over
	• Supplies list to Ms. Teacher for approval (don't forget whitewash and black floor paint)
	• PO Home Depot (and wherever else)
	• Work with Publicity for road sign paint sessions
BY 1/21	• Pick up supplies & paint
	• Label all supplies RMS Drama
	• Organize a crew afternoon/evening Jan 28 floor painting
2/1-2/2	• Tech Days
	• Try to get all painting done BEFORE tech days
	• usually EVENINGS, after rehearsal
2/14	• Opening Night
2/16	• Strike (road signs and painting floor back to black)

Props

BY 1/6	• Preliminary prop list to Ms. Teacher & Ms. OtherTeacher
	• Identify location for storage
	• Collect/build/borrow/buy
1/20-1/24	• Come to rehearsal to get updates on lists
	• Focus on electric component this week
1/27	• Prop tables set up
2/1-2/2	• Tech days
	• All props ready to use for Sunday Tech Run
2/14	• Opening night
2/16	• Strike

Costumes

BY 12/20	• Basic look through/inventory MS & HS Costume closet • Find/inventory/set aside garment bags & racks in D106 and/or HS Drama • Read script, character breakdown by scene • Character/cast list with measurement chart (check with Ms. Teacher & Ms. OT)—Get measurements • Contact PARENTS for first meeting (need machines) over Winter Break • General supplies list to Ms. Teacher for approval • PO wherever for supplies to Ms. Teacher, then the Finance office • Designs & inspiration board
BY 1/10	• Check for working machines D106 • Buy/label/set aside all supplies • Fabric, patterns, rentals selections/approval; PO; pick-up- "Have" everything by this time • Patterns/approval; PO; pick-up • Label garment bags • Call and arrange for parents to help
BY 1/27	• Assign dressing rooms • Pull all costumes and arrange in dressing rooms • Major pieces rented or built by now • Teacher Workdays are main building days—we'll call cast in groups
2/1-2/2	• Tech days—fixes and changes only
2/14	• Opening night
2/16	• Strike

Lighting

TBA	We will learn with FCPS! We will plot during this time
Jan	Hang & aim/focus /work with PreviousShow—inventory what's up already
1/27–2/1	• Program subs • Plot ready to go • Cues/spot cues • Orchestra lights • Exit lights covered
2/2	• Cue to cue
2/1-2/2	• Tech days

2/14	• Opening night
2/16	• Strike

Sound

BY 1/17	• PO for Guitar Center/ACG for miscellaneous • Extra clips? Extra cable? Gaff? Batteries? Shopping list & PO • How many working mics? Do we need to borrow? If so, get them • Pick up items • Sound effects collecting
1/8-1/28	• Set up board/label mics • Check all mics/speakers • Get general levels • Cues into script • Sound effects collected/approved by Ms. Teacher
1/29-2/1	• With actors
2/1-2/2	• Tech days
2/14	• Opening night
2/16	• Strike

Set Deco

BY 1/10	List of needs from directors
BY 1/17	• Sketches due in color to Ms. Teacher • Supplies/materials list for approval • PO to Finance
BY 1/24	• Purchases made, labeled
2/1-2/2	• Tech days
2/14	• Opening night
2/16	• Strike

Make up

BY 1/10	• Sketches due in color to Ms. Teacher • Inventory • Supplies/materials list for approval (do an INVENTORY first) • PO to Finance
BY 1/22	• Purchases made, labeled, inventoried • Crew assembled and trained
1/27-1/28	• Teacher workdays—actors in for design completion and crew training
2/1-2/2	• Tech days
2/10-2/11	• Previews
2/1-2/13	• Dress rehearsals
2/14-2/16	• Shows/strike

ASMs

BY 1/10	• Cast checklists—soda, t-shirt (and size), tech lunch, bio, Ziploc bags of makeup, ads • Check monitors • Copy good show grams
BY 1/25	• Set up ASM stations
BY 2/3	• Run off preview passes • Preview scene selection, intros, Run Crew (Stage Management)
BY 1/10	• Glow tape & spike tape—call for prices or online (Barbizon) • PO signed by Ms. Teacher and turned in to Finance Office
BY 1/24	• Tape picked up or delivered • Locate/label run crew box • Chart transitions (see Ms. Teacher for template)
1/27–2/1	• Wrap doors • Strike everything backstage • Flashlights • Sweep stage • Spike areas • Run cues
2/1-2/2	• Tech Days
2/14	• Opening Night

2/16	• Strike

House Management

2/1-2/4	• Decorate lobby • Clean house • Organize/plan concessions sales • Contact concession parents (Ms. Teacher has list) • Make concession posters • PO for flowers & ribbon (good show grams)
BY 2/10	• Fold programs • Get cash boxes • Make PO petty cash & PO Costco • Get change, concessions, money bags • Make "good show grams" • Purchase flowers & ribbon
2/14-2/16	• Ushers, programs, concessions, good show grams • Money counted and given to Administrator, change kept

Appendix T

Online Resources

Here are some of our favorite places to find things. It is obviously not an exhaustive list, but we'd love your suggestions to add to it. Email them to Support@EducationalStages.com

Backdrops

Rentable. Expensive. Consider painting your own—a huge, satisfying project.

CHARLES H STEWART (charleshstewart.com)

GROSH BACKDROPS AND DRAPERIES (grosh.com)

Boosters

NATIONAL BOOSTER CLUB TRAINING COUNCIL Help for setting up and insuring booster clubs and activities. (boosterclubs.org)

PARENTBOOSTERUSA Help for seing up and running a booster organization. (parentbooster.org)

PAY4SCHOOLSTUFF Guidance and forms for managing things that kids and parents must pay for. (Pay4SchoolStuff.com)

SIGNUPGENIUS Software to clearly, easily get/post volunteers for events, etc. (SignupGenius.com)

Cheap Stuff and Lots of It

ORIENTAL TRADING COMPANY The king of plastic "tchochkes" from aardvarks to zippers. (orientaltrading.com)

Copyright

CORNELL UNIVERSITY A clear and concise checklist from Cornell University to help assess whether you can use copyrighted material or not. (copyright.cornell.edu/policies/docs/Fair_Use_Checklist.pdf)

LIBRARY OF CONGRESS Information from the Library of Congress about what can and cannot be used without prior permission. (loc.gov/teachers/usingprimarysources/copyright.html)

Costumes

THE COSTUMER One of many costume rental vendors, they offer a free costume plot for most shows; a great place to start even if you plan to design and make your own. Fabric. (thecostumer.com)

THE COSTUMER'S MANIFESTO The Costumer's Manifesto is a treatise and a treasure trove of information about costumes, from history to how to. Check this out! (costumes.org)

ROSE BRAND Drapes, cycs, backdrops or costumes. (rosebrand.com)

Flying

FLYING BY FOY The industry leaders. They install the rigging and provide the training, then you run the show and either take the rigging down or pay for them to do so. (flybyfoy.com)

ZFX FLYING EFFECTS The other guys. (zfxflying.com)

Improvisation

IMPROV ENCYCLOPEDIA A compendium of theatre games and improvisation starters and formats and more. Tons of information. (improvencyclopedia.org)

UNEXPECTED PRODUCTIONS An exhaustive list of possible formats for improv games. (unexpectedproductions.org/living_playbook.htm)

Lighting

BARBIZON LIGHTING COMPANY Stage lighting supplies and equipment vendor. Sales and rentals. (barbizon.com)

WEST SIDE SYSTEMS Virtual Light Lab is a cyber black box with a figure to be lit by various instruments with any color gel from a variety of lighting positions. A terrific way to experiment online with angle, intensity, color, etc. (westsidesystems.com/f-vll/vll.html)

Masks

PARTY CITY Halloween masks on the inexpensive side (partycity.com)

THEATRE-MASKS.COM A wide variety of quality masks for many theatre uses, from neutral masks to Commedia character masks (theatre-masks.com)

Miscellany

THEATREFOLK Scripts; blog; discussion and online resources on useful topics (theatrefolk.com)

THEATRE HOUSE Costumes, props, makeup, lighting gel, fabric, special effects (theatrehouse.com)

Musical Accompaniment

THE MT PIT No orchestra available? MTPit sells professional audio files to use in performance as accompaniment for your musicals. (TheMTPit.com)

Organizations

AMERICAN ALLIANCE FOR THEATRE AND EDUCATION Journal articles, conferences, advocacy, research and more. (aate.com)

EDUCATIONAL THEATRE ASSOCIATION EdTA runs the International Thespian Society, the honor society for excellence in high school theatre arts. These guys also have a wonderful, interactive forum for chatting with peers about related issues that arrives as a daily email. (SchoolTheatre.org)

Playwriting

CELTX Free software for properly formatting scripts, screenplays, video projects, etc. Very clever and easy to use. The paid version permits multiple simultaneous writers on a project. (Celtx.com)

FINAL DRAFT The industry standard for formatting film and play scripts. Relatively pricey, but check out the iPad and Educational pricing. (finaldraft.com)

Scripts

FINDAPLAY Put in a title or author and find the publisher of the acting edition. (findaplay.com)

STAGEPLAYS.COM ScriptFinder lets you enter genre and cast size per gender, and finds titles that fit your parameters. (stageplays.com)

Set Design

SCENOGRAPHICS Rentals of blueprints and basic instructions for building sets for both straight plays and musicals. Very thorough and user friendly. (scenographics.com)

SKETCHUP Trimble Sketchup—formerly Google Sketchup—is a robust but extremely user friendly CAD drawing program. Great tutorials, too. (sketchup.com)

Sound

AUDACITY Audacity is a free program for recording sound effects or music, with some editing capacity included. Very useful. (audacity.sourceforge.net)

MIXERE Mixere is an old program, but permits PC users to order, control and run sound effects and files for a show. Very easy to use, but can be glitchy. (mixere.sourceforge. net)

QLAB QLab is a very user friendly Macintosh computer program for modifying and controlling sound effects and music in a show. (figure53.com/qlab)

Stage Combat

THE SOCIETY OF AMERICAN FIGHT DIRECTORS Contact these folks to lead you to trained fight choreographers and workshop leaders in your area. (safd.org)

Weapons for Stage Use

PREFERRED ARMS THEATRICAL WEAPONS Rental of stage weapons: swords, guns, etc. (preferredarms.com)

Appendix U

Field Trip Prep Checklist

Field trips call for a lot of organization and planning. This checklist should help you keep things from falling through the cracks.

- ☐ Identify field trip goal and destination
- ☐ Establish who can participate
- ☐ Select available dates

Determine basic cost (registration, tickets, transportation, food, housing, whatever)
- ☐ Get estimates for bus costs from approved carriers, travel agents
- ☐ Get quotes from hotels/motels for room costs (including taxes!!!)
- ☐ Float idea of trip to get rough estimate of number of participants

Seek administrative approval
- ☐ Identify academic purpose of trip/connection to Learning Standards
- ☐ Provide itinerary
- ☐ Provide cost/pricing plan
- ☐ Provide parent permission form
- ☐ Provide request or plan for transportation
- ☐ Provide request for substitute teacher/plan for class coverage
- ☐ Provide purchase orders for sub/hotel/registration/whatever else

☐ Receive administrative approval

☐ Schedule bus and hotel rooms. Record confirmation #s and contact/date/time

Publicize trip to appropriate students
- ☐ Clarify purpose, activities, destination, dates, times involved
- ☐ Clarify costs included and any need for additional cash/food/etc.
- ☐ Solicit parent chaperones to assist with transportation/supervision
- ☐ Provide field trip/event permission forms to be signed and returned
- ☐ Provide behavior contract to be signed by student and parent
- ☐ Provide Emergency Care information form to be filled out
- ☐ Emphasize deadline for forms/money to lock in participation

☐ Set up classroom location/record for collection of forms
☐ Set up classroom location/record for collection of money (deposit daily!)
☐ Distribute attendance roster to school for teacher and clinic notification
☐ Collect up final forms (check for omissions) and payments
☐ Nag the slackers!
☐ Send field trip roster to faculty at least two weeks prior to your trip.
☐ Make a duplicate of all forms received
☐ Send on registration forms/money as needed to destination
☐ Prepare driver packets w roster/cell #s/Emergency Care info per traveling group
☐ Meet with participants/chaperones to go over rules, game plan as needed
☐ Get school credit card in case of emergency expenses, to pay for hotel, etc.
☐ Distribute group packets to chaperones; share their/your cell #s
☐ Collect EpiPen or other required medications from clinic
☐ Check out with Office and update if any attendance changes
☐ Establish standard rendez-vous point on site and time of first meet-up
☐ Figure out what/who has been left inadvertently behind...
☐ Off you go!

Appendix V

Field Trip Letter to Parents

Modify this to your particulars and print out on official letterhead stationery. Give plenty of details and plenty of advance notice. Be *really* specific—someone is certain to misread your instructions. Format for clarity.

(print on school or theatre department letterhead)

Date

Dear Theatre Parents:

Your student will have the opportunity to go to the Folger Theatre in Washington, D.C. for the Secondary School Short Play Festival on (Date). This is a unique experience in which students can view performances on a stage modeled after Shakespeare's Globe Theater. The atmosphere at the Folger Festival is infused with high energy and enthusiasm for the Bard; this visit is sure to enhance and expand your student's knowledge of Shakespeare and his works. Attached, you will find the necessary field trip permission form, which must be signed and delivered to me no later than (date two weeks prior to field trip). Please include a check for (amount), made out to YOUR High School, with Theatre Dept. written in the memo. This will pay for bus transportation and lunch. All students are expected to dress nicely— "business casual," since we will be representing our school and wish to make a positive impression. No T-Shirts or torn jeans, please; tennis shoes are fine.

As noted in the Field Trip Permission form, we will be leaving from the Theatre Room XXX/ Door #X at 7:30 a.m., so it is vital that your student is on time. We will return to YOUR HIGH SCHOOL at approximately 5 p.m.; parent pick-up or other similar transportation arrangements are required. Students will be encouraged to call parents for pick-up when we are close to the school, for more specific arrival times. Thank you for supporting your student's commitment to YOUR High School Theatre. Our program offers a variety of educational theatre opportunities aimed at assisting students with their artistic development; this trip is sure to be meaningful and memorable. Please feel free to contact me with any concerns or questions. This letter and other information pertinent to the trip will be posted on Blackboard.

Looking forward,
Your Name, Theatre Director
Your High School
Your email / Your Office Phone Number
Your cell Phone (especially for a field trip)

Appendix W

Response to Patron Complaint About Show Content

For that priceless moment when your choice of show (or something said or done within it) offends an audience member, it may be helpful to refer to some of the information here. Do try to avoid being defensive, and support the notion of making good choices for your students and audience while recognizing that different folks have their buttons pushed, so to speak, by different things. You can reduce the chances of offending audience members by warning your community–through initial publicity–of productions that are for mature audiences.

(print on school or theatre department letterhead)

Dear Patron:

Thank you for your letter of concern about our recent production of _____.
The feedback we receive from our audience assists us in continuing to improve our shows.

Most of the plays produced here at _____ have been done professionally on a Broadway stage, and thus were written for primarily adult audiences. While this guarantees that the artistic rough edges have been ironed out after so many performances, it also means that the language and behavior used by the characters reflects the personality and circumstances of their time. Please keep in mind that play publishers license scripts to be used as written, and prohibit any changes to be added, made—or deleted—from the text. Any changes without prior permission is a violation of copyright laws. Scripts are intellectual property; changing dialogue even to conform to community standards means risking a lawsuit, so we can't, even if that creates a few uncomfortable moments onstage.

Playwrights have very little time to establish, for an audience, the personalities and intentions of their characters. Harsh or even offensive language is one of the most efficient red flags that a character is up to no good…and will probably pay for it before the play is done. To soften the language would be to soften the character, and make them less deserving of their fate. That could change the point of the whole show.

Each member of an audience enters the theater from their individual experience, to join in the communal experience of watching a play. As such, different people are sensitive to different issues, and that can cover a lot of ground. Some are offended by cursing, but not by abusive behavior. Some are offended by smoking but not by sexism. Some are offended by sexual innuendo but not by violence. And so on. Please remember that the theater is a safe place to investigate the consequences of conflict. Without conflict, you haven't got much of a play. With conflict, we can learn to lead better lives than we saw among the characters on that stage, and to emulate those who triumphed over the adversity they faced.

We hope you will agree that on balance, the sweep of our storyline and the efforts of our actors and stage crews outweighed the moments that may have made you wince and wish that that wasn't part of this play. As they say, "you've got to take the bitter with the better." Thank you again for sharing your thoughts and concerns. We hope you will continue to support our theatre program here at _____.

Sincerely,
Your Name, Theatre Director
Your High School
your email / your office phone number

Appendix X

Use of Weapons on Stage

Prior to incorporating prop weapons in a show, be sure to check with your principal and your school district's policies concerning the use of prop weapons. Many educational theatre settings (festivals, competitions, field trip performances) have very strict rules about prop weapons, and may even require a permission form from your principal. Do your prop weapon research prior to choosing a play that requires them.

Many plays require the use of weapons, and many schools have strict regulations about weapons and look-alike weapons. Here are some suggestions for walking that tightrope:

Have your ducks in a row (chain of custody for starter's pistols or other dangerous items; very strict rules about who may handle such items; clarity about the consequences of taking a prop weapon outside of the safety zone of classroom/stage, even by accident).

If you use prop weapons in a production, you can advise your audience by displaying a written notice in your printed program and/or in the lobby. Here's a sample notice you can use:

> This production uses stage properties as weapons. No actual weapons are used. All stage combat and the use of such related props are carefully planned, tracked, and rehearsed.

If you need to reassure your audience even more, you could add this to the notice, as well:

Please enjoy the show with confidence that the violence and its effects you agree to believe in tonight are strictly those of the play's characters, as portrayed by well-rehearsed actors who remain quite safe indeed, as do those who watch them. It is also worth noting that you are likely to see any character who is violent come to a bad end. As such, our play does not encourage violence but shows us all its terrible consequences to both the victim. . . and the perpetrator.

If you happen to be sitting in the Principal's office with some worried parent who is concerned about whether your drama program is portraying and encouraging violence, or even violating the school's weapons policy, here is what you could tell him/her:

"I know that you see what you think are real guns (or other weapons), so you ask why we are allowed to use them. It's because these stage weapons are very different, for many reasons that I'll discuss with you.

"Our school system prohibits real weapons because—quite simply—they are dangerous, and having them around puts anyone and everyone in the school at risk. However, stage prop weapons are safe and entirely predictable. We know precisely who will use which prop—and in the course of the play, we know why—and we know exactly where (within inches)—and when (on cue)—and with what scripted results. The staged "violence" must be so well-rehearsed that both the student wielding the weapon and the supposed "victim" can safely repeat the event at each rehearsal and performance.

"We never use real guns—not even with blanks. If knives are needed in the play, they are all blunted. And even when we use starter's pistols, we track them extremely carefully. Only those who are in charge of the props and the actors that use them are allowed to handle them. We emphasize that we never allow stage prop weapons to be removed from our rehearsal or performance spaces, and we secure them immediately after we finish the rehearsal or performance."

Appendix Y

Recommendation Request Form

As noted in Chapter 6, one of your responsibilities as a theatre teacher is to write college recommendations for your students. And while you hope that your students will all get their requests to you in plenty of time for you to complete and send their recommendations to their chosen institutions, there will inevitably be some who wait until the last minute (and beyond). You should, therefore, establish a routine for all your students to follow in making their requests.

In addition, you need to place some responsibility on your students to provide you with enough information to enable you to craft their recommendations simply and directly. This Appendix provides you with a form that you can give to your students and require them to use when requesting a recommendation from you.

Make sure that they read it and provide you with the information you need about them, their qualifications, and the program that they are applying for. If you can get your students into a routine for this process, it will simplify your life and theirs.

Recommendation Request Form

From: _____   Date: _____

Check all that apply:

- ☐ General letter to be used for more than one place. Please save for future use.
- ☐ Situation-specific letter to _____
- ☐ You will receive an email from the place I'm applying to, giving you the link to their recommendation site, to submit online.
- ☐ When finished, please forward to guidance counselor at _____
- ☐ When finished, please place in the attached stamped, addressed envelope(s), and let me know via my email address: _____
- ☐ Recommendation is due to **me** by the following deadline
   _____
- ☐ Recommendation is due to _____ by the following deadline _____

Brief description of program you want a recommendation for:

_____

You can find out more about this program at the following website:

_____

Please see attached page(s) where I remind you about moments/situations where the qualities I want the college/program to know about, that distinguished ME from other qualified applicants, really shine through. I understand that I should not only include a resume of my theatre activities, but what's most useful are anecdotes from during class (I am, after all, applying to be a student) that reveal my good qualities (initiative; leadership; industry; persistence; inquisitiveness; generosity; honesty; research skills; creativity; collaboration; communication; etc.). The more I write, the more you will have in mind when you write on my behalf.

- ☐ I understand this recommendation will be available for me and family only.
- ☐ I understand that I have waived my right to see this recommendation.
- ☐ I promise to send you gentle/creative/positive reminders, since I know this is above and beyond what you are required to do, and that you're very busy with lots of other obligations. I don't mean to be annoying, just to keep this on your radar screen since it's very important to me.

Thank you!

Appendix Z

Playwriting Lesson Plan Templates

Some kids love to write; by contrast, other kids find writing intimidating. Yet all these kids may have great ideas that they should find a means to express. You can make the most of every student's creative gifts by using the playwriting assignment that is outlined in the templates in Appendix Z.

This assignment can serve as an introduction to playwriting for Theatre I students. The improvisation game, *Fairy Tale in a Minute* (then 30 seconds, 15 seconds, 5 seconds) establishes a non-threatening springboard to enable students to learn to write short scripts. Students prepare preliminary presentations throughout the process, which allows teachers the opportunity to evaluate their students at various checkpoints.

Playwriting Format: Theatre Arts I

By applying acting/improvisation skills and working together, students will create a formalized, original script in small groups. In the form of a Fairy Tale, each group will be asked to develop through improvisation, and subsequently write down, a one-act script suitable for children's theatre. Preliminary improv presentations will provide opportunities for peer/teacher feedback and supportive ideas for further development. Written assignments will be handed in for grading, so please make sure all work is neat and legible; final scripts must be on Word/spell-checked.

WEEK 1 (DUE XX/XX) Meet in groups, write down outline of plot, character and cast list.

WEEKS 2 & 3 Work on developing and writing down dialogue. Preliminary presentations (can be part improv, part scripted): be sure to use playwriting format, as presented in class. There are two ways to format play dialogue. Here's an example of one way to format dialogue:

> SALLY
> Hello, Jane. I can't believe I haven't been asked to prom yet! Have you?
>
> JANE
> Uh, kind of…
>
> SALLY
> What do you mean, "Kind of?"

And here's another way to format dialogue:

> JANE: Paul and I are going out, and he's a senior, so I sort of assumed…
> SALLY: Assumed? Well, I hate to tell you, but I wouldn't assume anything. Paul is so unreliable anyway.

Make sure second lines do not begin under the character name, but are lined up evenly with dialogue. Character names should be in all caps and may be bolded.

WEEK 4 Completed, typed in format scripts are due on (date here), by end of class. Students may use the computers in class and email in a Microsoft Word document as an attachment to ThisEmail@myschool.edu for printing.

WEEK 5 Work-in-progress preliminary presentations will be graded on (date here).

WEEK 6 Polish, implement feedback, finalize all costumes, props, scenery for **Final Presentations on (date here); a poster/flyer design and program are due at the time of the final presentation.**

Additional notes:

- Students will be periodically asked to present works-in-progress as evaluated preliminary presentations, to promote student accountability for productive use of class time.
- Students will be expected to work in their own groups only.
- All students within the group are expected to participate equally and to the best of their ability.
- A list of who is responsible for what, within the group, will be turned in with the group outline at the end of the first week and approved by the teacher.
- These performances will be considered for placement in the theatre department Evening of One-Acts on (put date here), if all members of the group are available and committed.
- **GRADES for the quarter**: Prelim (Group); Script (Group); Process (Ind.); Final (1 Group, 1 Ind); Program (Group); Poster (Group)

Playwright Project Outline

Group members:

_____

_____

Title of your original 10 minute fairy tale:

_____

_____

Outline should include:

- Cast list with characters assigned
- Setting (time/place)
- Each act and scene being presented
- Brief synopsis of what's going on in the scene to be performed
- Which scenes contain your audience participation, chase and/or planned, carefully choreographed and practiced stage combat.

Cast:

_____

_____

ACT I, Scene 1 (I,i)

- Setting:

    _____

    _____

    _____

- Characters:

    _____

    _____

    _____

⊛ Action:

_____
_____
_____
_____
_____
_____
_____
_____

The following rubric can be used to assess student participation for the Theatre I playwriting unit, but can be adjusted to create a general assessment rubric for theatre class acting scenes. Students are evaluated on both process and performance goals, according to teacher observation and professional judgment. You can also experiment with asking students to anonymously use this rubric to assess other group members or their own work. Expectations for preliminary presentations should be clear:

PRELIM #1 Scripts in hand are allowed, but characters should already be clearly defined, plot action clear, and basic blocking assigned. Students are taking the leap from their initial improv of the fairy tale into a more formalized script. Be generous and encouraging.

PRELIM #2 Students have lines memorized, and have improved from the previous preliminary presentation, but all costumes and props may not be implemented at this time.

Since it will take time for each group to present their graded preliminary presentation, you probably need only two or three prelims prior to final presentations. Follow each preliminary with a class discussion of things that worked and things that needed improvement. Guide student feedback toward specific acting skills and theatre vocabulary studied in class.

Playwriting: Graded Assessment for Preliminary Presentations

Theatre I

Name and date: _____

Process

PERCENTAGE OF TIME ON TASK Working toward the performance goal; following directions; not socializing with others in person or on electronic device (25)

RESPECTFUL COLLABORATION Contributing helpful ideas to the process; actively engaged in creating blocking and action; listening to others and their ideas, in order to create/interpret a script (25)

RESPECTFUL COOPERATION Working courteously with others; focus on the project (25)

TIMELY WORK ETHIC Respectfully following the directions given by the teacher, including due dates (25)

100 points possible. **TOTAL:** _____

Performance: Acting Skills

PROJECTION Speaking loudly, without shouting (10)

ARTICULATION Using tongue, teeth and lips to enunciate and speak clearly (10)

ENERGY Commitment to an energetic effort to create a character (20)

ENSEMBLE Listening and speaking to other characters; connecting/reacting to them (20)

STAYING IN CHARACTER Consistently verbally and physically conveying character; actively listening and reacting. (20)

VERBAL EXPRESSION Character voice; emotional connection in speaking; verbs, adjectives emphasized in acting choices (10)

PHYSICALITY Physical expression of character via character walk, posture, gestures, facial expression (10)

100 points possible. **TOTAL:** _____

Glossary

504 PLAN Mandated classroom accommodations for a student with special needs

AATE American Alliance of Theatre and Education. Publications, annual conference for educators and academics

BEAT The duration of a single idea or intention, whether expressed in words or actions

BLACKBOARD Software for posting and receiving assignments, plus many other teacher/student features

BLOCKING Basic stage movement, including entrances/exits, crosses, sitting/standing, etc.

CAPPIES Critics and Awards Program. Chapters in the USA and Canada train HS students to be theatre critics, see and review each others' shows, and vote and hold an awards gala along the lines of the Tony Awards

CHARACTER BOX A student fills then explains items in a decorated box which represent their character, literally or figuratively.

CYC A cyclorama is a seamless upstage backdrop, often sky blue, lit to create different moods.

DEVISED THEATRE A performance technique in which themed material is developed through research, improvisation and experimentation.

DMX A 5-pin connection/cable for transmitting digital information to/from a lighting control system

DE The Department of Education (Federal)

EDTA The Educational Theatre Association. Sponsors ITS. Publications and outreach for theatre arts educators. www.SchoolTheatre.org

ESOL English Speakers of Other Languages

EVOLUTION MOVEMENT GAME Player mimics a music-inspired gesture/movement from previous player in the circle, then evolves it into a new gesture/movement, and offers that to another player to mimic/evolve. Repeat endlessly.

FORMATIVE ASSESSMENT Any tool (e.g., discussion, quiz) for a teacher to determine student corrections/changes/improvements along the way toward completion of an assignment or unit of study

GOING UP (ON LINES) Forgetting one's dialogue

IB International Baccalaureate program. Specialized global standards and curriculum for juniors and seniors that may lead to an IB Diploma.

IEP Individualized Education Program. School mandated accommodations for special needs students

ISTA International Schools Theatre Association. Workshops, conferences, and training for the IB Theatre program

ITS International Thespian Society. Honor society for high school (and MS) theatre students. Sponsors statewide conferences and annual late June conference in Lincoln, NE

MELODRAMA "CUE STORY" As teacher narrates a brief melodrama, student groups assigned to each character respond to the mention of their character's name with the agreed-upon phrase and gesture (e.g., "Woe is Me!" for Pitiful Polly)

MYP Middle Years Program of the IB Program (grades 6-10)

PCC Phase coherent cardioid. A floor microphone that catches sound from one direction

PZM Pressure zone microphone. A floor microphone that catches sound from all sides

SETC Southeastern Theatre Conference

SIDE A script containing only that character's lines and cues (cf. Tams-Witmark musicals)

SLATE Audition introduction of one's name and the piece/character

SOL Standards of Learning. State mandated areas of study for each discipline

SPIKE To mark the stage floor with the location of a set piece using spike tape or glo-tape

STRIKE To remove set pieces (or an entire set) after a scene or production. Final clean-up.

SUMMATIVE ASSESSMENT Any tool (e.g., presentation, test) evaluating a student's work at the conclusion of an assignment or unit of study

THEATRESPORTS A brand of competitive team improvisations based on audience suggestions

TYPIST NARRATOR An improvisation game wherein students act out a story as it is narrated

XLR A 3-pin connector/cable used primarily to connect microphones to a sound system

Index

ABOUT THE AUTHORS

DOUGLAS CHIP ROME is a theatre educator and director who has worked in Los Angeles, New York, London, and the Washington, D.C. area for over thirty-five years. He is past president of the Theatre Arts Directors Association; serves on the Governing Board of Cappies International; and introduced TheatreSports improvisation to theatre education communities throughout the Commonwealth of Virginia. He has also toured musical, dramatic, comedic and improvisational productions to Off-Broadway and the Edinburgh Fringe Festival in Scotland. He has extensive experience in curriculum development, and co-authored manuals on theatre safety; created a pilot training program for new theatre teachers in Fairfax, VA; created and curated the FCPSDrama website and the FCPS Blackboard site, and helped develop *Bringing Drama to the Core*, a collection of lesson plans in core subject areas using theatre tactics to deliver the content. He has presented at numerous conferences including the American Alliance for Theatre and Education; the International Thespian Society; the Virginia Theatre Association, and the Southeastern Theatre Conference. He has two wonderful children, and lives with his wonderful wife in Burke, Virginia and Cape May, New Jersey.

ZOË WAGES DILLARD began her teaching career in Fairfax County Public Schools in 1983 at Falls Church High School and collaborated with Chip Rome on a variety of professional activities. Her life journey took her to North Carolina where she wrote and implemented a Bryan Family Foundation Grant to host a Folger Shakespeare Library Festival for Catawba County Schools. In Greensboro, North Carolina, Zoë served as Theatre teacher/director at Morehead Elementary Cultural Arts Magnet School, as well as an adjunct instructor in Theatre Education Methods at the University of North Carolina at Greensboro. She wrote and produced a children's play, *Go Forth, Grasshopper!* and has edited Shakespeare scripts for student use and production. Returning to the Washington D.C. suburbs in 2002, Zoë resumed secondary teaching and, in collaboration with Westfield HS Summer Stage Director Lori Knickerbocker and the Herndon High School Drama Boosters, established a summer musical theatre program, as well as an elementary age theatre camp at Herndon HS. Her work with composer/worship director Don Halterman at Centreville Presbyterian Church resulted in community theatre outreach productions and an original, faith-based musical theatre piece, *Weaver*, including musical contributions by actor/choreographer/composer Colby Dezelick. Zoë has presented at the North Carolina Theatre Conference, American Alliance for Theatre and Education and the Southeastern Theatre Conference. She lives with her supportive husband and Ruth the rescue dog. Both of their daughters are educators.

CPSIA information can be obtained
at www.ICGtesting.com
Printed in the USA
FFOW01n0931310517
36131FF

9 780986 358708